if

wishes

were

horses

if wishes were horses

a memoir of
equine obsession

susanna forrest

Atlantic Books

LONDON

First published in Great Britain in 2012 by Atlantic Books,
an imprint of Atlantic Books Ltd.

1 3 5 7 9 8 6 4 2

A CIP catalogue record for this book is available from the British Library.

Hardback ISBN: 978 085789 127 3
Export and Airside Trade Paperback ISBN: 978 085789 128 0

Designed by Nicky Barneby @ Barneby Ltd
Set in 11.75 / 14pt Joanna MT
Printed in Great Britain by the MPG Books Group

Atlantic Books
An Imprint of Atlantic Books Ltd
Ormond House
26–27 Boswell Street
London
WC1N 3JZ

www.atlantic-books.co.uk

For Mum, Dad and Matthew, with love.

Contents

Contents

List of Illustrations

She was not an easy child and, later yet, she conducted a
vigorous, though unsuccessful campaign to be given a pony.

Maude Boleskine, daughter of the Antichrist in
Satan Wants Me (1999) by Robert Irwin

Parents who allow their child to ride give them something
which is of incalculable value. A child who is happy on
his pony's back has something which will be to him a glorious
memory that the years cannot dim.

The Young Rider (1928) by 'Golden Gorse'

The Trail

A pony is one of the most wondrous things that can
happen to anyone.

The Princess Pony Book (1962)

East Berlin's surfaces are pied with graffiti: spray-painted 'tags'; paper cut-outs gummed in peeling layers of palimpsest; stencils of hand grenades, bananas, political slogans and dachshunds; giant murals by professional street artists that cover five-storey fire walls. Walking through the same district every day, you notice fresh ones as you might clock a new species of flower emerging from the ground, or tune into a different birdsong – a kind of urban nature trail that changes with the seasons. Because I never saw any artist at work, the images seemed to sprout from nowhere, a little bit of subconscious bubbling up to the surface like a rash or a dream.

The hooves were new.

I first saw them on Kastanienallee – Horse Chestnut Avenue. A trail of white hoof prints the width of my spread hands appeared next to the pavement and walked across the pedestrian crossing. Someone had meticulously cut out the stencils and made their way across the road, spraying one, then another, in a pattern I recognized as a walk: the two left hooves struck the ground close together, the two right hoof prints were spaced wide. One, two, three, four. An invisible pony. When it reached the kerb, it vanished.

A little while later I found a second set, which sauntered across the

3

road at Veteranenstrasse and marched up to a mysterious 'Equine Institute', where a bridle hung in the window. There the invisible horse planted its front hooves squarely on the doorstep, as though peering in. A third horse walked clean across the middle of a busy junction outside a police station. Up by the Mauerpark there was a fourth set, which approached the metal railings by the road. A section of the railings had been painted in red-and-white stripes like showjumping poles, and chipboard 'wings' had been strapped to the sides. As a finishing touch, two evergreen plants in pots had been placed on either side and fixed to the rails with bicycle locks. The invisible pony cleared the showjump and clattered off across two lanes of traffic and a tramline into the park, where it appeared and disappeared, walking the length of an old stretch of the Wall.

After that it was as though the pony were everywhere, or he had a herd of friends trotting around Berlin at night, always just round the corner, always after I was asleep. I began to look out for the pony every day, to see what he'd been up to the night before. He'd make skittish circles outside a coffee shop, or hobble across Stargarderstrasse like a deer with all four legs roped together.

I couldn't predict where he would appear next, so I just had to go out and walk, covering miles of Berlin's broad, grey pavements in the pursuit of the invisible ponies. My friends reported sightings, which I mapped. One horse crossed through the dingy, red-brick cloisters of the Oberbaum bridge, which linked Friedrichshain in the east to Kreuzberg in the west, while another pranced down the red carpet before the stars at the Berlinale. A third pegged across Alexanderplatz and a fourth propped up the counter at a sausage stand, resting one hind hoof.

It was as though a herd of those elusive, magical horses from the pony books I'd read in my childhood had somehow slipped through into my grown-up, urban life. Now they flickered in and out of view, for ever on the next page, like the mysterious Water Horse in Patricia Leitch's *The Black Loch*, which surges out of a dark lake at midnight, or golden Flicka, always disappearing over the hills, escaping the whirl of a lasso. The spray-painted spoor was the only clue that they had been there.

One night, on the trail of a set of hoof prints on Christinenstrasse, I passed an empty office filled with blue light. There, behind dirty windows and under a bare wire that dangled from the ceiling, was a life-size model of a black horse, who looked out into the street with ears pricked. Behind the rain-streaked glass he seemed absolutely real. I thought he might flare his nostrils and sigh, his sides rising and falling, then turn back to pace the room.

Of course, I had a horse once, a towering Arabian the colour of fire. I used to sit on the back seat of the family car and gallop him through the fields that flashed past the window. We blazed over farmland, motorway verges and moors, and one summer we crossed America from Montana to Las Vegas. He could Only Be Ridden By Me. I think we won the Grand National twice and the Derby to boot. He was all about speed; that was what I thought of when I rode him, running and running at 100 mph, with the grass flashing beneath us, before he checked himself at a ditch and rose over it like a supersonic stag.

He was beautiful from the tip of his curved ears to the last strands of his tail. He was mine, because no matter whether I was coming out worst in little-girl politics at school, or my parents had told me off, or my brother wouldn't let me into his den in the woods, Ground a Fire was devoted to me. Sometimes he was me.

To summon him up I'd hold my hands up in front of me, wrists crooked to make front hooves. I could feel the swivelling horse ears on top of my head, and I'd paw the ground with my foot and scuff my shoes. Leaping sideways with my head down, tossing my mane when something scared me, off I'd gallop on my hind legs, right hoof down, left hoof always striking out a step in front, curling my knees, launching myself clear of the ground like the horse in Figure 3 of 'The Canter', flying for a split second. Then I'd whinny and my clarion call would echo round the valley (or cul-de-sac) like thunder!

He was visible only to a few. I think my mother probably knew what he looked like even without seeing the drawings I laboured over and Blu-Tacked to my bedroom walls. My brother couldn't see him, nor could my father, but my best friend Cheryl could, and we galloped alongside each other round the school playground, dodging the boys playing football and the girls hopping over skipping ropes.

Once, on a deserted beach, I truly heard him neighing, just as Charlotte Brontë heard the Duke of Zamorna call her name in a dreary schoolroom. I had thought he had evaporated when I hit my mid-teens. He was too big to be the invisible pony; perhaps the hoof prints belonged to another woman's imaginary horse, careering around on the loose once more.

How do you get back to Narnia? It's easy, just a matter of finding the right wardrobe. And how will you know which one that is? Well, that's harder. It may not be in the same room, or even in the same house, any more. I suppose it should be familiar somehow – something in the grain of the wood, the smell of it, the panelling of the doors. There might be superficial changes that could throw you off the scent, like new doorknobs, perhaps, or a different lining. The wardrobe will be fundamentally changed too because you have to allow for shrinkage. You are no longer the same size, perhaps not even the same person, as you were when you last opened the door and blundered into a new world, rather than the back of the wardrobe.

If you're very lucky, you find yourself at the lamppost in the woods before you even realize you've gone through the wardrobe, and from there you only have to follow the path.

I pulled out my German dictionary and began to compose an email to a stable in suburban Berlin to arrange my first ride in eleven years.

I don't even remember the first ride of my life, or why horses got to be so important to me. By the time I was conscious of where I ended and the saddle began, it was too late: I was imprinted like a goose when I was only a few months old. What did I fix on? A photographic reconstruction is required. It's a creature with blunt, metal-tipped feet that could have killed me with a single blow; a head longer than my body, set with eyes the size of my fists; an enormous torso poised on legs that held me five feet clear of the ground, balanced on my wodge of terrycloth nappy on a smooth leather pad.

My mother's hands hover near by: one behind me and one ready to clap my fat little leg to the saddle, in case the beast shifts on its feet. We're at the bottom of my grandmother's garden just outside Grantham, and she's the one who takes the photograph, a Polaroid, long since lost – probably lying in the bottom of a cigar box or one of those vast, flat, 1950s chocolate boxes with flowers on the lid that filled the drawers of that house. Our friend Denise stands before her horse, holding the reins under its chin with a light grip. She doesn't need to do much more.

Dusky seems to have an understanding of what human babies are and how gently they should be treated; she's had a foal of her own and she stands calmly while this uncertain, wriggly and probably squealy bundle is perched on her back. She's a 'hunter' – part Irish Draught and part something else: a marmalade chestnut with a hogged mane and a tail streaked with burgundy. Once a year on Boxing Day Denise takes her to hounds, and she forgets she's meant to be a reliable matron and prances like a two-year-old on her first start at Newbury. This must have been spring, judging by my age, and she's forgotten all about that till she next hears the sound of the huntsman's horn.

When my mother presses me firmly to the dished seat of the saddle and they lead Dusky forward, every step that the mare takes must feel like the corner of a mountain moving. The great plates of her shoulder blades shift in front of me, her quarters rise in peaks behind, and her hooves skirr and clop on the crumbling tarmac driveway. I'm not scared, though. There's a smile on my face.

Note the maternal conspiracy. This thing was transmitted down the distaff line, no question. Denise kept Dusky in a field at the bottom of my grandmother's garden where my mother had kept her own horses in the 1950s and 1960s. The last of them was an old point-to-pointer called Merino, who had never mentally quit the racecourse and who expired on a grass verge a few weeks before my parents' wedding, following an exuberant and ill-judged pursuit of a string of ponies from the local riding school. My mother was heartbroken. As they passed the spot in the white-ribboned car on the way to the church, my grandfather told her that the cheque from the knacker's yard had arrived in the post that morning.

It was my grandmother, a saddler's daughter, who made an heirloom out of a pony ride, hiring a rotund and insouciant brown Dartmoor from a local riding school to carry me up and down the garden on a later visit. For my first Christmas she and my grandfather bought me Dobbin, the rocking horse, with fawn-corduroy skin, brown-leather hooves and white-plastic bridle. He was stuffed with hay, which squeaked as you rode him, and had a tufted mane the texture of tough cotton wool. From the expression on my face as Grandpa legs me onto Dobbin in another photograph, you can tell that I know very well that this is the indoor version of Dusky. I'm ten months old. I can't speak, but I know a horse when I see one.

The rest is mania. My poor mother can't have realized what she had just unleashed, even if she'd been afflicted with the same malady as a girl. I pored over black-and-white photos of her three horses – Merino, Suzy, the New Forest pony, and the liver-chestnut hunter, Beau Brummel – and I badgered her for stories about them and about Nonny (short for Anonymous), my grandmother's dapple grey. I was proud that my mother had once worked as a secretary for one of the big Newmarket vets and met the Prix de l'Arc de Triomphe winner Vaguely Noble himself. I drilled my friends over garden showjumps made of bamboo canes and upturned flower pots, and I commandeered half the dining room to construct a stableyard made of cornflake boxes for my Sindy horses – King's Ransom, Dallas and Arabian Knight (sic) – who subsisted on dry lentils and barley poured into miniature nosebags.

I just loved horses. Horses mattered tremendously. I was brimful of adoration, which came slopping out of me at home, in the playground at school, at my non-pony-mad friend's house and at Brownies.

'Did you know that Arab people keep horses in their tents?'

'The smallest horse is a Falabella and the biggest was a Shire horse twenty hands high.'

'I have three Sindy horses.'

'Mum says I might be able to go on a trekking holiday when I'm ten.'

'They sell horses for meat! French people eat them! Cheval burgers!'

My dog-eared collection of Horse and Pony magazines was full of girls similarly touched. One girl was allergic to horses but wore a mask for grooming, while another smiled after having her front teeth kicked in by a riding-school pony. A third wrote in to enquire about jockeys' diets as she was worried she might outgrow her chances of winning the Derby. There were letters with photographs of horsy tea towels that had been fixed to bedroom walls, or of pony poster collections (Sharon Spiers had 247 and counting; you got a new one in the magazine centrefold each fortnight). I wept when I saw pictures of beaten and starving ponies in the magazine. I was inconsolable when I saw a top sprinter fracture a leg and crumple to the track in a big American championship race.

I didn't understand that my parents would never buy me a pony for Christmas. I wanted that pony so much that it became real enough to feel its breath on the short hairs on the back of my neck. Now, I realize it didn't matter that there was no special horse, because after Dusky came the cavalcade: ponies from riding schools, from trekking centres in Galway and Devon, Appaloosas in Montana, ponies lent, ponies hired, ponies loved. Real, unforgettable ponies, even if they never quite matched up to Ground a Fire. I can still name them all.

Red, Honey, Tino, Dandy, Petita, Gypsy, White Heather, Pickles, War Bonnet . . . There was Joe, a small strawberry roan who moked along nicely enough in the indoor school but really came to life on the gymkhana field, scooting around the bending poles. Dapple-grey Cricket, who hated the colour blue and goggled nervously at the Norfolk Line lorries with their royal-blue tarps that rumbled respectfully past our riding-school troop on hacks. Thin, nervy Kylie, who would jump only if you held her just right, so you had to clear your brain and think down the reins to her mouth, feeling her tongue testing the bit and watching her ears bat back and forth before finally conveying her decision – to leap or to stop dead and pitch you into the fence. Mikalo, the skewbald who bucked so high I thought his hind legs were over my head, a split second before all his hooves *were* over my head and I was rolling through spiky wheat stubble.

I remember the enormous cobby bay Jasper, with his mane that stood up on end and his ears that wobbled hopelessly as he did his own version of a trot, which was as peculiar and as comfortable as riding an armchair that lurched and swayed along on each of its four castors in turn. And Pegasus, tall, grey and beautiful if you overlooked his parrot mouth and the blue and pink spots on his skin, which came courtesy of an Appaloosa ancestor. His mane was always crinkled from being plaited and he had a habit of breaking from a canter to a trot with a little skip of his hind legs. Then there was Derwen, the pretty Welsh mountain with a snow-white coat, black eyes, dished face and the tic that probably ruined his show career: of suddenly, violently jerking his head to the floor and upending the child on his back like a duck in a pond.

Later, when I gave up on riding schools, there was Mactavish or Tav, a friend's wily cob whom I rode on long, mazy rides as a teenager.

He was henna-orange like a Highland cow and notorious throughout Norfolk. Wearing Mum's forty-year-old green-tweed hacking jacket with my own mismatching, navy-blue breeches and a black, silk-covered crash cap, I steered Tav into the centre of the show ring to complete our Handy Pony performance. The grim-faced judge told me, 'I remember that pony. He threw me. I suggest you get another show pony.' Tav straddled his legs and prepared to pee on her feet.

It was impossible to tell her that Tav was my only chance of a show pony. My riding career was tapering out – no more lessons, no new horses to ride, just A-levels and university to come, followed by a job, not at the British Racing School or a showjumping yard. I'd lost my nerve and let the reins slip from my hands so easily that it was a decade before I picked up the trail again on Kastanienallee.

By my first Christmas in 1977, when I was climbing on and off Dobbin and twisting up his cotton-wool mane in my gummy fingers, there was a whole pony world out there waiting for my attention. There were shops full of toys marketed for my soft little brain – Sindy horses, Barbie horses, rocking horses, hobby horses, plush-stuffed Shetlands, fine-carved Breyer resin models, and coy My Little Ponies fluttering just off stage on their sparkly pink wings, ready to swoop on my generation of girls as soon as we hit the double whammy of peer pressure and pocket money. There were books on pony care written for seven-year-olds; a host of competing magazines with 'I ♥ my pony' sticker sets and free hoof picks; a canon of literature with its own classics and pulps; anthologies that juxtaposed Saki and the Koran; a folklore of ponies bought for £5 who won red rosettes; and a hotchpotch world mythology of unicorns, pegasuses, eight-legged horses and mares that dragged the sun across the sky.

If you took to the lanes in the green-belt suburb of Norwich where we lived, you would pass fields that were never ploughed or sown but which delivered a cash crop to the farmers every month – rent shelled out by pony owners who kept their heart's desire behind wood-and-wire fences, surrounded by dock, nettles and a bric-a-brac of rusting oil drums and worn tyres collected for showjumps. I pushed handfuls of grass through those fences for the ponies and rushed to my bedroom window when I heard the horses trotting by, ridden by girls and women. Riding schools everywhere waited for my custom, offering real native ponies, now bred to carry children like me on official bridle paths, not to haul coal in mines or lug dead deer down mountainsides. Most of those children would be girls and their teachers would be women. In ten years of riding lessons I never shared the ring with a boy. Membership of the Pony Club would peak in 1982 at 43,817 members and only a fraction of them were male.

Horses were all about heroines, not heroes. I got glossy annuals for TV series starring women – *Follyfoot*, *The New Adventures of Black Beauty*, *White Horses* – and reissues of my mother's favourite pony books from the 1950s with cover photos of slack-haired 1970s girls, posing incongruously as Ruby Ferguson's Jill or the Pullein-Thompson sisters' numberless, chipper young equestriennes.

Across Europe, North America and Australasia, millions of other little girls galloped, snorted and pawed the ground as their mothers had done before them, dreaming that one birthday morning they'd wake up and there would be a pony picking at the lawn under their window. And nobody questioned this. Why? Where does it all begin?

Hunters and Amazons

In the war between the Greeks and the Amazons, the Greeks,
after their victory at the river Thermodon, sailed off in three
ships with as many Amazons aboard as they had succeeded
in taking alive ... Once at sea, the women murdered their
captors, but, as they had no knowledge of boats and were unable
to handle either rudder or sail or oar, they soon found
themselves ... at the mercy of wind and wave, and were blown
to Cremni ... on Lake Maeotis, a place within the territory of
the free Scythians. Here they got ashore and made their way
inland to an inhabited part of the country. The first thing they fell
in with was a herd of horses grazing; these they seized, and,
mounting on their backs, rode off in search of loot.

The Histories by Herodotus, translated by
Aubrey de Sélincourt (2003)

The first little girl who loved a pony ate it.
We ate horses for 90,000 years before we thought, 5,500 years
ago, to ride them. The first appetite they satisfied was hunger. 'Horse
meat is characterized by extreme tenderness ... red in colour with a
specific aroma and a mild flavour ... so tender that there's practically
no cut which requires lengthy cooking,' advises the French *Centre
d'Informations des Viandes*. 'The herbs and spices which combine with
much subtlety with this meat are, in particular, tarragon, basil,
rosemary, thyme, oregano, chervil, parsley, mustard, ground pepper,

not forgetting garlic.' There's little fat in horse meat and an unusually high amino acid content. It makes excellent sashimi.

The finer points of prehistoric cuisine have not been passed down to us, but our ancestors were accomplished butchers and hunters. Anthropologist Marvin Harris calculates that in the Stone Age more horses were eaten per caveperson than in any other period, and men loved to paint them. The cave walls of Palaeolithic Spain, France, Italy, Mongolia and Siberia were alive with dinner: spotted steak tartare, golden-dun entrecôte with sooty legs and crested manes, herds of silverside pursued by flying spears. The femurs were broken open for marrow and the tendons scraped so keenly that the bones were notched. The succulent, cherry-dark meat was swiftly charred over open fires and gobbled down by hunters and their families.

At Solutré in the Bourgogne, discarded horse bones from the period are packed nine metres deep in a single hectare potter's field. Over a period of 20,000 years, 100,000 animals were ambushed as they raced through a chicane of limestone rocks, then felled, stripped and consumed. In Robin Hood Cave in Neolithic Derbyshire, someone dreaming of lunch etched a horse's head on a rib bone, its mane bristling and upright, its jaw delineated, the chin groove perfect.

The fat times came to an end in Europe a few thousand years later, when the number of equine skeletons in the pits dwindles as the traffic of migrating horses tails off. Caught between the encroaching hunters and the slow-spreading great forests that overran their grazing grounds, only a few small concentrations of horses remained. By the end of the Ice Age, horses had fetched up east in the Iberian peninsula and west on the 5,000-mile sweep of grasslands that lay beyond the Carpathians. They thrived, at home on the vast steppe that resembled North America, where they had once evolved from the runty leaf-eater, Hyracotherium, to the rangy, swift grazer, Equus caballus. Here horses began a new phase of development, which stemmed from a leap of thought and imagination, and not the slow grind of evolution.

*

'Ukok' means 'the end of everything'. The Pazyryk herdsmen of the Bronze Age returned their dead to this Siberian plateau, a nub of Russia 7,500 feet above sea level, surrounded by the peaks of the Altay, Terektinskiy and Kuray mountains. Although the meadows in this corner of the steppes are not lush turf, horses can graze knee-deep in the fibrous grasses, picking at feather grass and wormwood in the autumn. It is slashed with rivers that reflect back the uncanny, intense blue of the sky; in spring there are wild flowers, purple iris, white campion and anemones.

In 1993, Russian archaeologists excavated one of the great round barrows or kurgan tombs that rise out of the plateau. They removed the cairn above, stone by stone, and then diggers carved a square hole into the mound. They found two intact burial chambers that had flooded with meltwater and then frozen.

One held six old geldings, their forelegs tucked under their chests, their blackened skulls poleaxed and tufted with scraps of chestnut fur, their stomachs still full of June meadowgrasses, their heads laid east to greet the Sky God. They had saddles: pads of leather that sat on either side of their spines, joined by a bridge of wood at each end and held in place by a breastplate, their cruppers and girths fastened with horn buckles. Over these lay felt pads stuffed with stag fur, topped by blankets trimmed with tassels and appliquéd with images of lions and griffons with curled beaks whose paws were raised in a heraldic gesture. The horses' manes were hogged under a leather guard, their tails shorn at the tailbone and plaited below, their eyelashes clipped. Their ears had been perforated and nicked into curvilinear motifs that echoed the swirl of the animal appliqués and served as a brand of ownership. They wore bridles with cedarwood cheekpieces of rams' heads tacked with gold leaf.

In a second chamber lined with logs, the archaeologists found a coffin carved from a single larch tree, filled with ice. They thawed it with warm water, poured in a cupful at a time for three days. Finally the horses' mistress swam up to them through the ice, part bone and part bare flesh, stippled with scraps of gold foil. The woman who had the pick of these horses for her final ride lay alone; she was not a concubine nor a headman's wife, but perhaps a priestess, certainly a rider, 2,400 years old. Wrapped in marten fur, she wore a raw-silk tunic over a bright-red and maroon wool skirt topped with a band of yellow silk, under which her white felt riding boots came up to her thighs. She still wore an imposing headdress more than half her height, adorned with snow leopards, and a stag with a full rack sprang from her forehead. Her arms were tattooed with more stags whose antlers ended in flowers. Someone had tucked a mirror in a pouch behind her knees and left her a dish of horse meat skewered with a bronze knife. The woman's eye sockets were packed with deer fur.

Over on the other side of the steppes, at Pokrovka on the southern tip of the Urals, east of the Caspian Sea, the kurgans are humbler. The Sarmatians burrowed into old burial mounds to rest with their ancestors. They feasted on horse meat at funerals and left the bones ringing the tombs. In a catacomb barely two and a half feet tall, with a packed-earth ceiling, lies a thirteen- or fourteen-year-old girl, her head to the south, her legs arranged as though hugging the sides of the horse that will carry her into the next world. A bronze arrowhead is tucked in a leather purse hanging from her neck; a great boar tusk dangles on a thong from her waist; a dagger lies by her right leg; and to her left is a quiver of arrows with bronze, three-flight tips. A warrior-priestess.

The Sarmatian girl and the Pazyryk priestess's people were part of a Eurasian steppes culture that emerged from the Ice Age on the backs of horses. It perhaps lives on in today's Mongolian herdsmen, whose sons and daughters race one another for miles across the grassland, and whose women wear tall headdresses decorated with gold. Some of these peoples were semi-settled but generally they were nomadic in varying degrees, moving their herds of livestock back and forth between summer and winter pastures. They spread out from the Caspian Sea area: west as far as China; south to the Aral Sea, the Pamir Mountains and the Karakum Desert, in the pursuit of trade: bronze, copper, gold and eventually iron.

There is no way of identifying the first rider of the steppes cultures. The shift in the use of the horse from meat source to mount came about slowly; perhaps the skill of riding was gained and lost many times before it 'took', but the earliest evidence found by archaeologists comes from the settlements at Botai in north Kazakhstan in 3,500 BC or thereabouts.

As the Botai were already husbanding horses for meat and milk, it was an easy continuation to breed them for riding too, once they had learned how to control them with rudimentary bits. Horses coped better than cows or sheep on the steppes. They could dig down through the snow to find coarse grass, and thrive on this low-nutrient fibre in quantity. They smashed ice with their hooves to get at the water underneath. Cattle and sheep followed them and drank and ate. Archaeologists foraged in the middens and the burial sites of the settlement for specimens of horse teeth. When they compared them to casts of the molar P_2 of domesticated horses, they saw that both the ancient and the contemporary teeth were abraded in the same way, whether by bits made of rope, metal or horn. It was easier to herd cattle on horseback than on foot. In a society where you are only as rich as your cattle's pasture and the trading routes you negotiate, mobility was king.

Traces of fat from koumiss, or fermented mares' milk, was found in Botai pottery. Botai children would have been raised around horses, drinking their raw milk, which is easier on a child's stomach than that of cows as it is closer in composition to human breast milk. A thick layer of dung on one patch of ground indicated that horses were kept in a yard or even a stable. The cannon bones found by archaeologists were longer than those of the local wild horses, suggesting that the Botai had begun to improve their stock.

The acquisition of horses and the generation of them became

integrated into human settlements and lives as horses became a blessing beyond a full stomach. Horses made the steppes contract. They were the transformational object that gave the interlinked cultures of the grasslands, such as the Scythians, the Sarmatians, the Pazyryk and the Botai, their paradigm shift. On their backs, the steppes people travelled greater distances, either as traders or as herdsmen, buying their raw silks from India and silver from the Near East, swapping precious metals for skins, trading horses for cows in Transcaucasia, acquiring carpets and damask from Persia, and lacquerwork, embroidered cloth and mirrors from China for their kurgans.

Warriors made smaller bows so that they could raid other settlements on horseback, coming out of nowhere to seize goods and people. Much later they used crude chariots. In many of these societies, women like the Sarmatian teenager fought alongside men. Their bones show combat wounds where they raised their left arms in defence, while arrowheads have been found buried in their ribcages. In another kurgan on the Ukok plateau a tall Pazyryk girl of sixteen was unearthed with her battleaxe, bow and knife. Herodotus believed that Sarmatian women, like the teenage warrior-princess at Pokrovka, rode out to fight because their ancestors were Amazons who joined forces with Scythians. They were certainly descendants of the Massagetae from east of the Caspian, whom Queen Tomyris led to defend her lands against King Cyrus. She brought home the Persian's head in a bag of human blood, so that the warmongering king could drink his fill. Lesser women were often buried without horses but in their riding gear.

The mounted warriors and herdsmen-traders poured down the land bridge between the Black and Caspian Seas, into Mesopotamia and the Levant, passing on their language, the lost root of the Indo-European tongues. They went east to China and south to India, bringing with them burial rituals that would be recorded in the Rig Veda. They also pressed west into Europe, first as scattered bands and eventually settling, taking with them their horses and their bronze-working skills. They became the Germans, the Slavs, the Balts and the Scandinavians. At the time that the priestess and the warrior girl were buried, some of them had become the Celts: racers of horses, and hunters who fought alongside their women, buried their important dead in the same way as the steppes people and were accompanied to the other side by little horses. When the Celts came to Britain, they may have found horses already there, waiting for them, cut off from the European continent since 20,000 BC; perhaps they also brought their own with them.

In 300 BC, a woman was buried on a hilltop in east Yorkshire, curled under the body of a chariot with bits and trappings for her horses and an iron mirror tucked behind her knees. When Caesar launched the first of his invasions of Britain in 55 BC, there were Celtic charioteers and cavalry waiting for him, perhaps with women warriors among them.

Back to School

Already one can seem to see him, poor, innocent beast, miserable in the memories of an army of beginners, his mouth so accustomed to being jerked in every direction, without anything in particular being meant by it, that neither Arabia nor Mexico can furnish a bit which would surprise him, or startle his four legs from their propriety. No cow is more placid, no lamb more gentle; he would not harm a tsetse fly or kick a snapping terrier. His sole object in life is to keep himself and his rider out of danger, and to betake himself to that part of the ring in which the least labor should be expected of him. The tiny girls who ride him call him 'dear old Billy Buttons', or 'darling Gypsy', or 'nice Sir Archer'. Heaven knows what he calls them in his heart! Were he human, it would be something to be expressed by dashes and 'd's'; but, being a horse, he is silent, and shows his feelings principally by heading for the mounting-stand whenever he thinks that a pupil's hour is at an end.

In the Riding School: Chats with Esmeralda (1890) by
Theo. Stephenson Browne

Following an exchange of emails, stilted on one side (mine) and forbearing on the other (the riding club), I booked myself a private lesson, then purchased a cheap pair of rubber riding boots and some black polyester jodhpurs for forty euros, all in. Early one morning I took the U-bahn out to the suburbs of Berlin. As the train ticked past the stations, I scanned a notebook in which I'd scribbled a few useful German words – *Steigbügel, galop, sattelgurt, halt* – and tried to waggle my ankles inside the inflexible boots, which had been moulded into right angles.

We rose evenly out of the tunnel and into a cutting; it began to drizzle. At my station I disembarked, fell up the exit stairs when the *verdammt* boots hooked on them, and emerged into steady rain on the road to the riding club. Finding the entrance, I turned and padded on my thin, rigid soles up the drive, which twisted briefly through oak and pine trees, and emerged by a large riding hall or *reithalle*. I tried the door of the riding club office but it was locked, so I wandered tentatively down a passageway with rubber-tread flooring, self-consciously browsing a noticeboard sparsely papered with adverts for competitions, horses for sale and back issues of a pony magazine called *Wendy*. At the end of the corridor I found a windowless changing room lined with dented lockers etched with the names of horses and decorated with hearts: 'I ♥ Gräfin' and 'Freddie ♥ ♥ ♥'. It was deserted, despite the rain.

I found human and equine life – the clank of fork on wheelbarrow and the scrape of impatient hoof on concrete – in the large modern barn at the back of the yard, where thirty-odd loose boxes, like pens at an agricultural show, had been constructed. Each had a name plate for its inmate, a headcollar on a peg, a rug hanging on a bowed chain and a grooming kit in a little white cotton sack. The horses were all headless, with only their backs visible above the door as they fossicked in piles of breakfast hay. I peered through the bars into a few boxes and clucked to the horses before being taken in hand by a girl who dug out for me from an old dresser a white plastic polo helmet of discomfiting thinness. After checking a computer printout, she told me I was on Zofe and that the instructor would be waiting for me in the *reithalle*. She took me to the door of Zofe's box and I looked in.

A chestnut mare, she stood saddled, bridled and martingaled, ears pointing east and west, indicating martyrdom. These ears were half an inch too long for beauty, though her head was well shaped and her eyes large. She had a sheepskin rag tucked under the bony grooves of her chin to protect it from being rubbed by her noseband. A brushstroke of white ran down her face from her forehead to her nostrils and round the curve of her upper lip, as if about to drip off onto the straw. Like Dusky, she was one of those bright winter chestnuts who mellow in the summer to a milder shade of tan orange. The stripe gave her an honest, open expression despite her weary air, which I forgave her as it was so early. From every box around her rose the sound of horse molars grinding hay, while she alone stood unfed, waiting for whatever fresh boredom we were about to inflict.

Outside the rain was falling steadily. It gathered on the door jamb of the barn and dripped in sequence. I slipped the bolt on the door, slid it back and went up to the mare, putting out a hand to stroke her neck and shoulder. She ignored me, presumably hoping I'd go away. 'Hello, Zofe,' I offered. Not a flicker back. I bunched the reins in one hand under her chin, feeling that both they and I were insubstantial next to Zofe, and clicked my tongue. With a sigh, Zofe shifted her weight and accompanied me out into the open air with a willingness that surprised me.

The instructor was waiting at a mounting block in the porch of the reithalle, a great hangar with brown dirt underfoot and mirrors fixed along the far wall at the rider's height. At our end were two viewing galleries, one above the other. The top was enclosed in glass; the bottom was open and dusty like a pavilion at a tournament, with spare whips resting on the ledge. The instructor and I each took a side of Zofe and adjusted the stirrup leathers, and then he gave her girth a final tug and told me to climb on. I put my foot in the iron and mounted without the block. With that, eleven horseless years ended like a five-minute intermission and I shifted into place as I'd done years before on Joe or Red or Jasper.

I laced the reins through my fingers, in at the pinkies, out at the top of the fist and pressed under my bent thumbs, and gave myself a once-over. My knees were light against the saddle flaps as they always had been – appalling my mother, who'd been taught to leave no daylight between leg and saddle; heels down, toes up, legs like a frog kicking upwards to the top of a pond, elbows at waist, hands sprung, firm but not clenched.

The teacher stepped back. When I pressed my right calf to Zofe's side and squeezed my right hand, the mare turned right and walked into the hangar. As we ambled round a furrow at the perimeter of the *reithalle*, tiny brown birds exploded up out of the dirt under her nose like caps in an action film. The rain had stopped and a yellowy light strained through the corrugated-plastic windows.

The instructor circled the centre of the arena after us, laconically dishing out advice to me while chatting with a teenage girl who was watching from the lower gallery. He issued commands in a ringing, enunciated fashion as if he were a cavalry riding master in a theatrical production.

'Im *Arbeitstempo, Trrrrrab!*' My hopeless little list of German vocabulary failed. 'Fleißig, fleißig,' he kept saying, fleißig at the walk, fleißig at the trot. I intuited that this meant I should be riding with more impulsion and squeezed Zofe's sides harder.

While my brain struggled to translate the instructions trilled from the centre of the ring, my body adjusted constantly to Zofe's movements and changes of gear. My left thumb would stopper the reins while my right hand slipped down to shorten one side, then my right hold for the left. I could still rise to a trot, bobbing up and down as neatly as I'd done for endless hours round the sand school at the age of six. When we changed rein down the centre of the school, I slipped my whip from one hand to the other without a conscious thought even though it was years since I'd even considered the action.

'Bodily memory' is the name that psychiatrist Thomas Fuchs gives the phenomenon of being able to forget that we are consciously doing something we have long ago learned by heart. We 'forget what we have done or learned explicitly, and . . . let it sink into implicit, unconscious knowing', he wrote in a paper titled 'The Memory of the Body'. 'It unburdens us from the necessity to constantly find our bearings again.' Even the dualist Descartes, Fuchs pointed out, conceded that a musician did not deliberately recall each position of his fingers on the neck of his lute note by note but relied on a quicker, 'implicit' memory that seemed to come from the fingers themselves. Five hundred hours of stored-up riding lessons and laconic riding instructors – 'Heels down!' 'Shoulders back!' 'Stop hanging on to her mouth!' – guided each gesture I made. I might have rediscovered an ability to fly by stepping off a building and fluttering away, as natural as you please.

Zofe was like any good schoolmistress, mild but not guileless, good-natured, but lazy now that she was working without other horses. She pointed her toe when she was at the same end of the school as the instructor, but idled when his voice was coming from the opposite end of the hall. She made me laugh out loud as I watched her ears signalling her mood, and I felt lighter. 'Oh come on, old mare,' I teased her when the instructor had his back turned, 'you funny thing.'

After fifteen minutes, though, my 'bodily memory' was shot and I was riding like someone who had not been in a saddle for over a decade. I'd misremembered it all, thinking it must be easy to mould a horse's spine into a perfect curve with subtle prompts. I'd imagined pressing my right calf against the horse's side and applying the left just behind the girth, making a pivot around which the horse flexed muscle and bulk like a great, thick fish, its head dipped intelligently, the corner of the right eye watching me, an ear rotating to catch a clicked cue. In practice, I squeezed and squeezed until it began to feel as though I were carrying Zofe around the ring with my inner thighs.

First came the command to canter, 'Handgalopp!' as we trotted into a corner, and then the trigger, 'MMMMMARSCH!' I squeezed with legs that were beginning to feel chewed and tender, and, when that failed, flapped them, jouncing about in the saddle, my inside foot rattling in the stirrup. When, with one eye on my whip, Zofe flicked her tail, humped her back with annoyance and finally rolled into a grudging canter, I was out of balance. The effort of sitting her canter caused a prick of pain to bore into my hip joint and the muscle of my inner thighs to burn as if scalded.

By 9 a.m. Zofe had worked up a light sweat and I was beginning to doubt that I'd be able to walk back to the U-bahn station. Perhaps I'd have to stay on horseback for ever. We were pootling around at a trot when the instructor said something I didn't understand. At once the mare hit the brakes and dropped her head like a seaside donkey. I felt like a seaside donkey too. 'Gut!' said the Herr in the middle of the ring, who, I now realized, had been telling me to slacken off the reins and cool Zofe down. It struck me that each time the teacher had given us an instruction that involved slowing down, Zofe had understood it and carried it out before even my magical, unthinking, bodily memory could react. Her German was rather better than mine.

I slid off onto limp legs and pressed a hand flat to Zofe's warm neck, a rider's thank-you after she'd been so forgiving of me. Why does any horse put up with us? I poked a finger under her headstall into the sweaty, sweet spot that a horse can never scratch to satisfaction and I rubbed as she half closed her eyes and leaned against me.

I waddled home, the perspiration on my face blotted by the fine dust of the reithalle floor, my hair silky with sweat, my jodhpurs reeking up the U-bahn carriage and a vague smile on my face.

I spent the next three days rubbing Deep Heat into my thighs.

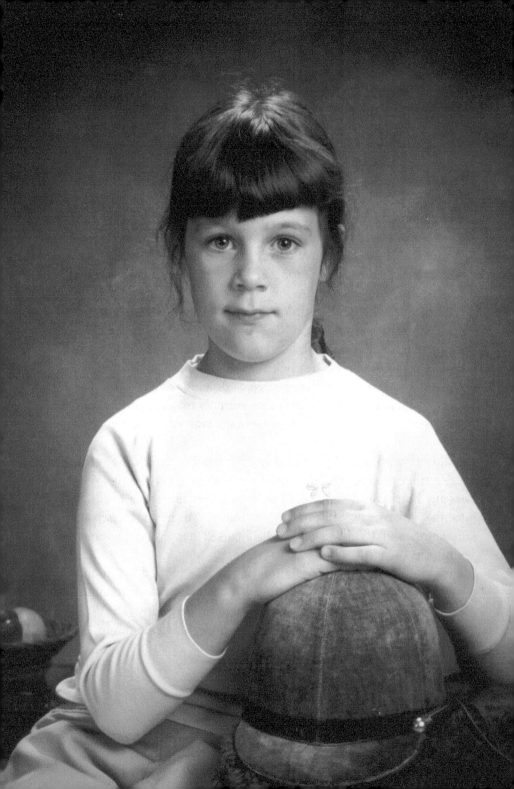

Gymkhana

One day I saw a notice that there was going to be a children's
pony gymkhana the following Saturday, and I decided to go.
I came away from the gymkhana sadder but not much wiser,
after seeing quite small children doing the most marvellous
things on ponies and riding them with a technique which
left me gasping. But I'm going too far ahead.

Jill Crewe in *Jill's Gymkhana* (1949) by Ruby Ferguson

M y circlings and bouncings with Zofe in the *reithalle* were a start,
and they'd made me curious. It would be good, I thought, to
dip into the rest of the horse world I remembered and see whether I
recognized it. It would fill in the humdrum lessons in the *reithalle* and
maybe throw up something more exciting to do. My German wasn't
good enough for me to get to grips with the equestrian scene in
Berlin and, in any case, I didn't want to discover a foreign Narnia; I
wanted to sound out my old Narnia and see how it had changed. The
next time I was home to see my parents, I rooted out a Pony Club
gymkhana and on a summer's day set off for an Essex village in my
mother's car.

Someone in a pub pointed me to the farm that was doubling as a
showground and I drove on, distracted because the lanes seemed to
be full of women riding horses and ponies that were wrapped in
sophisticated brushing bandages and rubber overreach boots. The
only signs that I could see lashed to lampposts advertised a donkey

derby. I stopped to ask directions from a lady mounted on a big cob and wearing a fluorescent-pink hi-vis tabard, and she sent me back a few turnings to a gate and long drive. I rolled down the drive and ended up at the back of a large brick house alongside a collection of sports cars and jeeps. A pack of Labradors ran out, followed by their owner who told me affably that I was looking for 'Mill Lane, not Mill Road', then waved me off as I crunched back out.

Mill Lane, once found, twisted past some 1970s houses and a windmill, its sails stilled, before outrunning the neat gardens and becoming a country road between fields. I parked the car under some trees and climbed out. Over the distant pop-pop of bird scarers, I could hear the sound of a Tannoy – 'Ring three, please' – and an excited squeal. I headed towards them.

The first field had about a dozen horseboxes in it – not trailers, but lorries that could take four or five ponies at a time, interspersed with shiny Range Rovers and four-wheel drives. The horses were tethered to the sides of the boxes, bopping at hay nets or drowsing in the sun: small fat ponies, 'blood horses', and a flea-bitten grey that looked like a miniature Arab. A blonde, tanned mum in shorts was ripping padded leg bandages off a smart skewbald.

A little roan the colour of ginger beer, with a grass belly behind his girth and a strip of white sheepskin bridging his nose, whinnied excitedly – he must have been the pony I'd heard from the lane. As I headed for the next field, I was overtaken by a girl of about nine in white breeches, nonchalantly carrying a trophy the size of an espresso cup. She joined her friends at the gate to watch the ring, which was scattered with Lilliputian show jumps, none of them more than a foot off the ground. The girls all wore putty-coloured jodphurs and white shirts with a purple-and-silver Pony Club tie, like the one I'd once bought at a jumble sale and never dared to wear. Scraps of their conversation reached me as I passed them, looking for the main ring:

'How many classes have you done?'

'Yeah, I came first in the working hunter.'

'Good luck in your class.'

'Are you doing novice, George?'

The third field, behind a tall screen of oak trees, seemed to be the most promising, with a course of larger, brightly coloured fences set up and a caravan for the commentators. An ambulance was parked to one side, its doors open as the paramedics lolled in the front seats. It was almost midday and the sky was cloudless; a plane from Stansted flew overhead, already too high to be heard. I found a shady corner next to the ring where dew was still sitting on the cobwebs in the grass and settled down to watch a few yards from a gaggle of mums parked in the sunlight on deckchairs. There didn't seem to be anyone else there who wasn't connected to the ponies and the children.

Several of the jumps had large wings to funnel nappy ponies into the poles, but the one nearest to me was very narrow. I had a feeling that I'd see at least one little sod swerve round it and drop some poor jockey on the ground at my feet. Half a dozen girls were walking the course, measuring the distances between the fences by taking big strides, smacking their whips on their rubber riding boots and biting their lips in concentration.

'I'd want to go diagonally into this.'

'Yeah, as tight as you can, really.'

'And cut corners.'

'And go fast when you can't cut corners.'

The caravan loudspeaker started up: 'One, two, one, two, hello! Hello! Hello!'

The girls walked back to the collecting ring, where their mothers were waiting with the ponies, and mounted, the ponies pushing their noses out and taking advantage of the girls' being in midair over the saddle to set off in choppy, excited walks.

'Start warming up!' someone yelled, and they began to mill about. A girl on a pretty, busy grey with a dished face walked him up and down, dangerously near a roan who swished his tail peevishly in warning. Two bays were pushed into canter in single file round the collecting ring, one eagerly tagging behind the other, the big knobbly plaits on their necks unravelling a little at every stride.

'Can I go second?'

'Jenny, you're first to start,' said someone to the girl on the grey with the dished face.

'Jenny on Winkle!'

Winkle scurried into the ring in a state of high excitement, Jenny drawing up and looping the reins to point him at the first jump. He scrambled over it and went on to the next, which he got a little too close to but popped over neatly. As he bounced into my corner and Jenny circled him towards the narrow fence, his pretty, neat little head bobbed from side to side, while his wicked, mobile ears signalled his intention to dodge left or right and reach his friends by the most direct route. Jenny dug her heels in and redoubled her grip; thwarted, Winkle nipped over the jump with a snort and scampered for the last. They were clear.

I could hear Jenny's voice, full of relief, '*Good* boy!' as they passed 'Lizzie Walker on Lucky', an unhappy-looking combination, who cantered in a slow, hard-fought circle, waiting for the whistle.

Lucky had a white face and a neck like a bull; his eye rolled with conflicting desires to go at these piffling fences at a clip, yet also to be back among the clannish mass of ponies in the collecting ring. He whacked the first, which stood, then all but crawled under the second before leaping over it at a perpendicular and heading off like the clappers towards the fourth. The Tannoy clicked on. 'You're eliminated for missing a fence.' Pause. 'Stupid girl.'

The mums worked as ring assistants, replacing poles that had been kicked out and offering advice from the sidelines in chorus with the other girls.

'Legs!' they called.

'Hit him behind the girth.'

'Make him jump it from there.'

A plump girl called Lucy with a red face entered the ring on a cob, which flung out its forefeet at a trot and farted impressively. He held his head high, thick mane bristling with mischief, and everyone began to call out encouragement. Lucy pointed him at the first and he took it explosively.

'Good boy,' she called, but didn't pat him because she daren't risk taking her hands off the reins. At each fence Lucy and the mums called 'Hup!' and then 'Good boy' when he was clear. Then he put in a mean-spirited stop at the narrow fence close by me, at which the girl went over his shoulder and hit the poles heavily. The cob dashed off with his reins trailing, feinted when a mother ran out to grab him and then, conceding that the game was over, allowed himself to be caught.

'You're eliminated, but carry on,' declared the caravan. Lucy's cheeks were wet.

The mums sprang into action and knocked up a little cross-pole. Lucy was comforted and legged back into the saddle. Then she rode the cob away, circled him and cantered for the small jump, emitting a 'Get your bum over there!' at the crucial moment and sending the cob over in a bound to a burst of applause and a chorus of 'Well done!'

The group of mums on deckchairs chatted as they watched the riders come through, calling out to daughters to ask whether they'd got the studs on their horses, or to tell them there was a spare hairnet in the lorry. The girls brought resting ponies over to graze near by. Winkle drowsed with his saddle off, the sweat on his coat dried to flat points, Jenny holding his reins. Comments were made *sotto voce* about some of the riders, like the girl on the thoroughbred who was left behind every time her horse jumped, flopping heavily back into the saddle as he landed.

'I suppose there's no marks for technical,' one mum muttered out of the corner of her mouth. 'If it goes all right, it goes all right, but her stirrups are too long for jumping.'

I was thankful for the cool dew, even though it was evaporating fast, and I moved back towards the trees, out of earshot of the mums, as the sun shifted and invaded the shadows. As the afternoon went on, a little breeze got up. A friendly lady with short hair and glasses, who turned out to be the organizer, came striding across the field to check that I wasn't a paedophile. When she heard why I was there, she enthused that 'All these children keep their ponies at the same DIY livery stable. There's camp coming up soon as well. Lots of stories there!' We chatted a bit before she was called to the stewards' tent, but I decided not to enquire about going to the Pony Club camp.

The sober struggles of little girls conquering cocksure, wilful ponies were all familiar to me. I had ridden every fence with them and 'hupped' just as they had, and thought dark thoughts about the girl with the thoroughbred who couldn't ride, but this wasn't quite the door to my Narnia. I'd never joined the Pony Club, sticking instead to the chop-and-change realm of the riding school, where you dipped in and out of the horse world, never fully immersed; it was a weekend treat, not a daily duty; an escape, not a commonplace. My mother loved horses but she was not a Pony Mother who chased me round the working-hunter course, and I'd won more rosettes at virtual 'shows' with the Breyer model horses that decorated my shelves than I had with solid Tav. Whatever it was I'd had in mind when I thought of my Narnia, it was something both more nebulous and more vivid than a collecting ring on an Indian summer's day in Essex.

I wished the girls and the mothers and the ponies a fist of red rosettes and more trophies the size of espresso cups; I wished them a good camp and full marks in their B tests, but after the Handy Pony class I went home to find a more familiar wardrobe that led to Narnia.

Ladies

Upon an amblere esily she sat,
Y-wympled wel, and on hir heed an hat
As brood as is a bokeler or a targe;
A foot mantel aboute hir hipes large,
And on hir feet a paire of spores sharpe.

The Canterbury Tales (14th century)
by Geoffrey Chaucer

The Chronicles of Ely say that sometime in the late tenth century AD the Abbot Byrhnoth was on his way to see King Edgar when he happened to pass through the New Forest. He left his train of attendants and the path in order to answer the call of nature, strolling a little way into the woods and then a little way further. He came to a clearing where he was astonished to behold Edgar's queen, Aelfthryth, surrounded by ponies. Luckily he froze before she could catch sight of him, because she appeared to be brewing a potion. As he watched in horror, she downed the concoction and was transformed into equine form (or perhaps donned a horse's skull). She began to dance and caper with the ponies in a shamelessly pagan fashion, even lewdly exposing herself like a mare in season. Midway through her corroboree she spotted the abbot watching her, and the good man fled and did not stop running till he was back in his wagon. He urged his men on and away.

Shaken, Byrhnoth arrived at court and, after gathering himself together, was ushered in to see the king. He did not breathe a word about the rites he'd seen and thankfully their business proceeded smoothly. Afterwards, he was in such an amicable frame of mind that he decided to drop in and see the queen in her apartment. He found her alone and bursting to get the burden of her sins off her chest. Drawing him aside, she began to confess to a titillating and exhaustive list of sexual adventures. As he struggled to keep up with this rolling inventory of misdemeanours, she finally launched herself on him, bent on seduction.

The abbot pushed her away and begged God to forgive her. Furious, the queen gave a signal to her hidden ladies-in-waiting who sprang out, brandishing daggers they had been heating in the fire, and stabbed Byrhnoth in the armpits. As he expired on the flagstones, they let up a great wail at his sudden and mysterious death.

Aelfthryth was not unmasked as a priestess of the horse cult nor as a murderess until she made a full confession years later, in which she had to admit to killing not just the abbot but also her stepson, King Edward, so that her son Ethelred the Unready might rule instead. Renouncing her pagan ways and her days of frolicking with the ponies in the forest, she retired to a nunnery she had founded at Wherwell.

It was not a good time to be a heathen: the old ways were being subsumed into the new Christian religion from the East. It was a faith that expected purity, not power, of its women, and it did not, as a rule, approve of warrior-queens and priestesses – nor of dancing with ponies.

Some four centuries later, in 1383, Anne of Bohemia rode into Norwich sitting sideways on her horse, looking as curious to some of the natives as if she had sat down to dine with her back to the table. The saddle was a kind of cutaway howdah, like the frame used to pack goods on a horse's back. It had been upholstered to cushion her behind and given a 'planchette' on which she rested her slippered feet. While she was not the first woman in England to ride side-saddle, she gave the practice a fresh gloss of respectability and symbolism: Anne had travelled from her home to marry Richard II with as much self-reliance as a sack of grain, but with many times the virtue, purity and piety of mere cereal. With this example, England was introduced to the notion that the quick of a woman was something so delicate that it must not have contact with leather and animal, even through layer after layer of cloth and padding.

Once you have put women in long skirts to cover their forked legs and taken away their thigh-length felt riding boots, you begin to create an exoskeleton of convention that obscures common sense. No matter that an earlier queen, Eleanor of Aquitaine, was reputed to have ridden into a crowd of crusaders, dressed as a knight with scarlet boots and wielding a sword, to exhort them to fight. No matter that all six of Charlemagne's daughters had ridden out to hunt with him on cross-saddles nearly six hundred years earlier. No matter that women had been depicted hunting astride in a prayer book, the Taymouth Hours, and certainly no matter that mobs of lewd women had, according to one chronicle of 1348, turned up in men's dress at tournaments 'on excellent chargers or other horses splendidly adorned'. Now womankind was divided, as on the red and black Greek pots, into Amazons – bow-wielding hoydens in striped trousers who rode astride – and goddesses who preserved the line of their chitons and their virtue by sitting on their horses as though they were sofas.

Englishwomen did not abandon the cross-saddle, though. They continued to be depicted riding in what was increasingly seen as a manly fashion, although over the course of the centuries this practice fell from the everyday into outré exception. There are fifteenth-century images of the Wife of Bath straddling her ambler while the Prioress and her nuns proceed to Canterbury sitting sideways on their palfreys, although that's the illustrator having a dig at the respective virtues of those ladies.

After this setback, it took the innovations of Mary of Burgundy and Catherine de Medici in the sixteenth century to bring the side-saddle and women back to the hunt proper. Mary slung her knee over the high pommel of a man's saddle for security. Catherine had a second pommel added so that her right leg was held in a notch between the two horns, though people whispered that she did it in order to showcase her calves. She might actually have invented this modified saddle because she had broken her leg out hunting, as Balzac describes it as having a 'velvet sling' for her two feet.

The planchette was replaced by a metal, point-toed slipper for the left foot. This arrangement was not particularly safe, as even the daintiest of feet could be trapped in one, nor was it hugely practical for jumping, but then, there was little to jump and it wasn't a skill with which many bothered, either male or female. These new innovations did mean that a lady could gallop and remain a lady, though, and that, increasingly, was what mattered.

Costessey

It is impossible to lay down a hard-and-fast rule as to the age
at which a girl may be allowed to mount a pony or donkey, as it
is to control the spirits and daring of a foxhound puppy.

The Horsewoman (1892) by Alice Hayes

. . . it is not uncommon to see a very tiny child starting on his
riding career full of confidence, and this must be maintained at
all costs. A tiny niece used to say, 'Nothing can hurt me when I
am on Comma's back.'

The Young Rider (1928) by 'Golden Gorse'

When my mother finally gave in and let me, at the age of five,
have proper riding lessons, we were living in the Bay Area city
of Palo Alto in California. My father hadn't taken up my suggestion
that he leave his job as a computing science professor and become a
bus driver so that we could afford a Shetland pony, but he had
applied for a seven-month sabbatical, working for Xerox at the Palo
Alto Research Center. Mum took me, not to a stable but to the cam-
pus at Stanford near the research park, where there was an enormous
red barn with a weathervane and white beams on the gables like the
barn where Wilbur watched as Charlotte spun her web (we were
reading E. B. White in my first-grade class). It had been built over a
hundred years earlier for racehorses on the stock farm belonging to

the governor of California, Leland Stanford, and it remained an antique in a city that consisted of buildings barely more than thirty years old. In 1877, Eadward Muybridge had photographed a mare of Stanford's called Sallie Gardner at the farm as she galloped across a series of tripwires that triggered cameras. The sequence of images revealed for the first time the pattern of a horse's hoof fall and that for a fraction of a second the horse left the ground altogether.

I never left the ground with Socks, a black pony with a thick silky coat, four white legs and a blaze, but at least I didn't plummet to earth. With a leading rein clipped to a headcollar under his bridle, we circled an outdoor school surrounded by muddy 'turnouts' where other horses pressed up against high, rickety fences to converse with their neighbours. On a plinth between the real horses stood a statue of an Arabian with a fall of bronze stalactites for a mane, his head turned towards the parkland. Socks's saddle pad was faded from scarlet to pink and worn to holes in places; I clutched the lip of the pommel to steady myself. I learned to walk and to rise to trot a little, straining and wobbling upwards on puny legs before falling back with a thump that bounced me straight out of my seat again. I was taught to groom a horse's tail by taking the whole of it in one hand and then letting a few strands at a time fall down to brush, until you had the whole thick hank untangled. When we returned to Norfolk, my mother found a local riding school and lessons fell into a weekly Saturday slot.

Our village, Old Costessey, was a triangle of roads between the shallow, sandy-bottomed River Tud and a tributary of the Yare called the Wensum. Its name, pronounced to the bafflement of outsiders as 'Cossy', meant Cost's Island, perhaps because the rivers had often flooded the water-meadows lying on either side of the raised land and wooded hill where Cost's settlement had stood. It would have risen as a St Michael's Mount of sorts over the low, Norfolk countryside, but by the time my parents moved there in the late 1970s, Costessey was no longer an island. Our modern detached house, which stood on top of the hill in a cul-de-sac, had been built on what one of my teachers told me ruefully had been the best brambling field in the village. It was still surrounded by woods that were excellent for the re-creation of cross-country courses, though, and below the woods at the bottom of the hill, parallel with the Wensum, ran The Street, where there was an old-fashioned butcher's, a square brick Baptist chapel, an old flint Anglican church and, at the easternmost end of the village, the old mill by the Drayton road.

In 1910 the painter Alfred Munnings had watched his friends race a Norfolk trotter on foot down The Street for a bet struck in The Bush public house, which in his memoirs he slyly called 'an establishment of lesser fame — a haunt of harpies of the lower world, connected with the trotting fraternity of Norwich'. It was still a closeted and clubby place when I was a child, but always did better than the large pub near the post office, which was forever reopening with beer-and-carvery deals that failed to tempt the locals.

Opposite this hapless pub stood a red-brick Catholic church, which had served the local 'family', the Jerninghams, until they died out early in the twentieth century. At school we took part in a BBC project to update the Domesday Book 900 years on and were told that Costessey had had the only hunting park in Norfolk to be listed in the original tome. Elizabeth I herself had hunted deer in the Jerninghams' 'wild beast' park in 1602 while touring the county. The family's last home was a mock-Tudor hall built in the 1830s west of Costessey on the road to the neighbouring village of Ringland; the house had passed out of the family less than a century later when they turned it over to the War Office. Its grounds had been used during the First World War for training infantry, cavalry and artillery troops, before the whole construction was dynamited. A single gothic brick tower remained as a centrepiece to a new golf club that we passed on the way to my riding school, heading along West End. The estate and long-lost game park were carved up into parcels of land and sold to workers from Norwich, who parked old railway cars on their plots or knocked up jury-rigged houses and prefabs. These in turn were eventually replaced by bungalows and the tracks between them metalled over, the whole being rechristened New Costessey.

After the Second World War, Norwich had grown west towards the village until it was subsumed as an outlying suburb, and you could drive from the city to the mill at the far east of the village without being surrounded by fields at any point. A strip of the water-meadows, which remained prone to flooding and inimical to housing developments, prevented the village from being joined to Drayton and Taverham. This green belt was scored with a stretch of the old Norwich to Reepham railway line, dismantled and made over as a footpath called Marriott's Way, which ran from the centre of Norwich to Reepham. We reached the Railway Line via Windmill Lane, a tarmacked road lined with bungalows that gave way to a leafy sunken path between fields, at the end of which was a junction of bridle paths and a view down the shallow Wensum valley to the Railway Line itself. You could see and hear traffic heading into Norwich in the mornings along the Drayton High Road and out again in the evenings.

At various points I'd worn rabbit runs through the verges of this network of tracks to reach a fence and push through handfuls of grass for horses on the other side. Most of them were owned by Mr Peruzzi, a local scrap-metal merchant who kept trotters for racing, showjumpers for his granddaughters and an ever-changing population of shaggy coloured cobs who pulled the family's collection of restored carriages and tradesmen's carts at local shows. Mr Peruzzi himself drove a Mercedes at the speed of a horse-drawn carriage, processing in stately fashion through the village.

My new riding school was the stableyard of one of the Jerninghams' old farms, which had been stripped for gravel quarrying, leaving behind a blasted, open expanse of sand and persistent weeds in which sat a three-sided yard as strange as an oasis. Already introduced to *Black Beauty*, I recognized the row of old-fashioned loose boxes with raked floors and wooden walls topped with bars. A barn attached the stables to the building that housed the offices, and between rides the dozen ponies would be tethered in their tack in the yard where they picked at hay. Like the red barn at Stanford, it was slightly tumbledown, a place where wisps of straw could agglomerate in corners and spiders flourish without too much disturbance from humans.

A school was marked out on the sea of yellow sand, which was not the dry, quartzy type found on north Norfolk beaches, but damp, turmeric-coloured stuff that dropped in soft clumps through your fingers. On a wintery day we perished in the winds that swept across the old quarry. My teacher told me that my new thick string gloves made my hands too clumsy, so I buried my bare fingers into Gipsy's scurfy brown mane and didn't cry till I got back to the car after my lesson.

Most of my riding clothes were from jumble sales because I grew so fast, but my mother bought me my first pair of thick, beige, second-hand jodhpurs from the riding-school office, as well as a battered, dun velvet cap that had to be attached to my head with a laced-on harness and a black rubber cup under my chin. I wore wellies, as I continued to do until I was a teenager – each time the lady in Russell and Bromley's measured my feet with the tickly plastic slide, she would exclaim that I'd gone up another half-size – but I yearned for some proper jodhpur boots. I managed to retrieve from my grandparents' house my mother's old pair – stiff leather with a bloom of fine copper-green mould – and kept them in my bedroom cupboard, occasionally checking to see whether my feet had grown enough to fill them.

One of my favourite tropes in pony books was the moment when the heroine, like the beggar-maid princess at the end of the fairy story, is suddenly rewarded with an outfit befitting her virtues. Jill Crewe finds fawn jodhpurs and a checked riding jacket for 12 and 6 in Ruby Ferguson's Jill's Gymkhana, and Ken takes Jinny to the expensive saddlery in Patricia Leitch's Chestnut Gold and, with a flourish of cosmic generosity, conjures 'a brown tweed hacking jacket, yellow polo-necked sweater, a crash cap with an orange silk tied over it, cream-coloured jodhpurs, string gloves and black rubber riding boots'.

There was another, more sheltered ring protected by a huge bank of grassed-over sand, knit in place by rosebay willowherb, where I finally, momentously, got out of a trot when Tino and I jogged solo away from the ride. The teacher gave the instruction to canter and, in a magical moment, I booted and Tino's gait turned from a choppy trot into a bowling canter. Overcome with the realization that I would never be on a leading rein again, I leaned further and further forward, forgetting my heels until my legs were bent like hairpins and my feet just below the cantle, and slipped gently off Tino's shoulder.

With cantering came the chance to ride away from the school, down the long exposed driveway to the road and out to the Ringland Hills where we would hack through the woods. The girls who taught and supervised us were as nonchalant and sophisticated as older sisters, living in a uniform of jodhs, blouson jackets, straw and perms. They rode one in front and one behind to signal to passing cars when to stop and when to overtake the crocodile of children and horses as we followed the winding road from Costessey to Ringland. After ten minutes we reached a gap in the hedgerow that opened onto a seven-furlong field that was cropped down to stubble each summer. One girl led us off the road and into the field, the other backing her mount, the pretty Arab Petita, out in the road and waving cars on as we filed up off the tarmac.

'Ready? Hold on to Mikalo, sometimes he bucks.'

The nose-to-tail line of plodding ponies broke into a trot and racked faster through the stubble, tossing their noses and jockeying alongside one another. Finally you felt them gather and burst into a canter and we were transformed into an unruly band, charging through the hollow wheat stalks – one bucking, one bolting, two little ones at the back snorting to keep up with the bigger ponies – rioting the length of the field. It was my first introduction to that shared exhilaration between horse and rider, between small pony and seven-year-old girl, a pure pip of euphoria, when you knew you'd never stop him till he pulled himself up, but you didn't care.

Greenacres

Come to the stable. Come to where the horses are, and
the sweet, grainy, pungent smells.

Talking of Horses . . . (1973) by Monica Dickens

I knew the roads leading to Greenacres, Dusky and Grandma off by
heart, and I wished they would go by faster. Grantham was only
two hours from Costessey but in child time, cooped up in a car and
impatient to be at your destination, that is equivalent to a day at least.
When we'd negotiated the huge roundabout at Swaffham that
marked the end of Norfolk, there were still miles to go across the
Fens and the air that reached us through the vents was mephitic with
cabbage. I galloped Ground a Fire across the fields, dodging the
polytunnels of tulips and the dark Leylandii hedges around isolated
old council houses, and leaping him over the smaller dykes. At Long
Sutton, he trotted with us on the metalled road over the Crosskeys
bridge, unfazed by the flashing lights warning that the bridge was
about to swing open.

Just before Grantham, the flat horizon flexed and the landscape
changed to one of gentle, rolling hills before Lincolnshire plunged
into the Vale of Belvoir. Our springer spaniel's pink and brown nose
began to quiver as we turned the final corner near Belton House.
She'd sit up on the sticky leather back seat of the Maxi between my
brother and me, swaying on her wide-apart front legs, snuffling, her
ears hinged forward like an elephant's. Then she'd be on her feet and

45

standing on our laps, claws digging into our legs, to press her nose to the open window. When we pulled up outside the house, she'd launch herself out of the car, race to my grandmother for a quick greeting and then rush out to the back of the house, which opened onto a huge lawn spreading down to the river. We drank tea or squash in the dining room while she lay on the lawn like a tense sphinx, pointing at the red rubber ball that she'd left at the top of the slope by the patio. Eventually my father would go out with my Uncle John's old cricket bat to belt the ball. Away she would go like a hare with flying strides, barely touching the ground more than the ball itself, catching it with a triumphant snork and wheeling in a wide circle to come cantering back, her tail high.

I waited for the sound of Denise's car crunching and bumping down the drive at the side of the house, and the sight of it framed in the end window of the living room. That was my cue to go to the tea tray and fish out a handful of crumbling white cubes of sugar, root for my wellies in the coat room and pull the warped back door shut behind me, then, suddenly shy, cross the garden to the river. The bridge that led to the fields and stables was a bare concrete arc with a white-painted wooden fence bolted to the sides. As I crossed it I glanced down at the river, just deep enough for my grandmother to float the canoe she'd built in an evening class over ribbons of rich green weed and sandy shallows with drifts of pebbles. At the far end of the bridge, I ducked under the wooden pole latched with baling twine that served as a gate, and followed the pour of concrete down into the yard past the familiar whitewashed walls of the old granary where Dusky had her stable, making for the garage with the muted-khaki door in which Denise kept the tack and stacked hay and straw bales on pallets.

Denise's car began to bark and rock. I called out to her German shepherd, Taurus, who was bottled up inside it, leaping from the boot to the front seat and back again. Denise emerged from the garage in her jeans and green wellies, her shaggy brown curls with a little straw in them, to let Taurus out. He raced up to me and let me sink my hands into his thick black-and tan ruff.

'Do you want to come and see the horses?' Denise asked, knowing that the sugar lumps were burning holes in my pockets. 'Come on.'

In the shade of the garage there was a gate framework of metal pipes filled with chicken wire and held to with a loop of chain. We slipped through it and across a muddy, hoof-pocked patch of the back field to where the horses were waiting in the sun. Denise had bred two foals from Dusky and both were the same bright chestnut as their dam. They came pressing up to us for sugar. Tango the gelding was stockier, like his mother, with a broad white blaze and socks. Denise had broken him in but he never took to traffic, so now he led an idle, bachelor existence, enlivened when his mother or sister left for a ride and he stood at the side gate and screamed till he heard them on the lane again. He crunched his sugar and poked me with his nose when I tried to rub his forehead. Zoe was finer in build, with a narrow stripe on her nose. She bit, and had once chased me until I took refuge behind the old mare, who snapped at her daughter and drove her away. I offered her her tidbit carefully, with my thumb tucked as far under my hand as I could make it go. Then Dusky nosed through between her children, ears back and then pricked when she reached me, to brush the last of the sugar gently from my palm. I patted her neck and felt all was right with the world.

After this ritual, Denise and I moved on to the steady labour of horsekeeping, in which I, kitted out with a special small garden fork, was of little help. There was sodden bedding to change and drains clogged with dark-brown straw, pungent with horse pee, to unblock. Once we found a rat mashed to pulp in Tango's bed. In the fields there was slippery, ribbed ragwort to haul out, so acrid it burned your hands as you tried to grasp it, its roots grappling the ground, and dung to be collected in the wheelbarrow and pushed up the narrow, wobbling plank to the top of the muck heap. I groomed Tango with the plastic currycomb when he was moulting, turning the air into a snowstorm of gingery tufts of hair, like being caught in a vacuum bag. Water buckets had to be filled at the ferocious tap and carried, slopping, to the stables. Occasionally Denise would embark on a project like repainting Dusky's stable, clipping out Zoe, or building little cross-country jumps – she swinging the mallet, me holding the posts. Once a week she brought a bottle of milk, which she poured into a plastic trifle bowl. Dusky was fetched from the field and I watched, amazed, each time as she dropped her muzzle into the bowl and, with a thin, sucking squeak, made a pint of milk disappear.

On Saturdays, we would tack up Dusky and I would be legged onto her to graze my fingers on the bristle of her hogged mane, holding the reins as Denise threaded the lead rope through the bit to take us over the bridge and up the drive. We walked under the horse chestnuts on the strip of tarmac by Belton Lane where cars came peeling round the corner but slowed for me, Denise and the steady old mare. Then we would stop the cars to cross the road into the Queensway council estate where Denise had grown up, with its long, gradual hill lined by post-war, red-brick semis set in gardens divided into tidy lawns and straight-edged rose beds. Princess Drive branched away into cul-de-sacs, crescents and 'groves' until we reached one house, where Denise's mother came to the door to give Dusky a carrot and to smooth her flat palm down the mare's nose, and tell me I was getting tall.

Horsemanship

I wonder how Men are so Presumptuous to think they can ride as
Horse-men, because they can ride forward from Barnet to London,
which every Body can do; and I have seen Women ride astride as
well as they.

A New Method and Extraordinary Invention to dress Horses, And work them
according to Nature; As also, to perfect NATURE by the Subtilty of ART; Which
was never found out, but by the Thrice Noble, High and puissant PRINCE
William Cavendishe (1657)

Long before the side-saddle came to put a crimp on things, girls
who rode had vanished from the foreground and into the
scenery. We know that young European princesses, when grown,
were capable of following the hunt, but there is little written spe-
cifically on the subject of children riding until the latter half of the
nineteenth century. Still less is recorded about the way that girls or,
indeed, anyone learned to ride. We have to wait for the Renaissance
and the rediscovery of Xenophon's *Art of Horsemanship* to find a new
approach to equestrianism surfacing in the literature. With a classical
blessing, equitation became a science as much as a sport or a standard mode of transport, something to be taught and perfected, not a
discomfort borne for the sake of travel or warfare.

One of the first schools for riding was founded in Naples in the
1530s by the Italian riding master Federico Grisone, who issued *Gli
Ordini di Cavalcare* – just one of a growing library of vade mecums

written by competing teachers and experts who often borrowed freely and without credit from the Greek cavalryman, for, once the market for riding education opened, everyone had an opinion. The academies in Italy, France and Spain taught what came to be known as the *haute école*, a military drill of regulated paces and 'airs above ground', which had scant direct practical use in the battlefield but that looked impressive on the parade ground and did much for the general obedience of a horse. These manoeuvres were adapted into an equestrian ballet that would become modern dressage.

Boys could earn their chops early. The six-year-old Spanish prince, Balthasar Carlos, was painted on horseback by Velázquez in 1636, his face impassive under a black velvet hat, a pink sash across his chest and a capelet billowing behind him as he wields a baton like a sceptre, his feet snug in golden stirrups. Beneath him, mastered, is a red-roan pony with a mane as long, kinked and abundant as those on the Andalusians ridden by kings and queens in their portraits, his plump belly bared as he rears and holds a levade. A year earlier Velázquez had painted Balthasar's father Philip IV in the same attitude with the same pink sash.

These new establishments were finishing schools where continental princelings were educated in *hippike*, the art of the horseman, for 'The highest one can say of a Prince is this, that he rides well, a phrase which embraces his virtue and his bravery,' as Bernardo de Vargas Machuca wrote in *Teorin y Exercicios de la Gineta* in 1619. Bravery was not required of princesses, unless in childbed, and their virtue was of an altogether different kind. Nobody sent an infanta or a princess to Antoine de Pluvinel's Parisian school to learn to sit a levade for her portrait; girls raised at court presumably learned from grooms, or perhaps from ladies-in-waiting. They might be depicted having a lively canter, but as William Cavendish, the 1st Duke of Newcastle, sniffed: 'I have seen Wenches Ride Astride, and Gallop, and Run their Horses, that could, I think hardly Ride a Horse Well in the Mannage.'

For a few hundred years to come, these books would not contain any advice on riding side-saddle that was actually written by ladies, nor even any mention of how a gentleman should leg a lady rider onto her horse. In this silence, girls still learned how to sit a canter and to duck under branches when galloping through a forest in pursuit of a stag. Elizabeth I carried silver-tipped arrows with clipped peacock-feather flights and her own knife for gutting stags; she designed for herself a skirt just long enough to cover her stirrup. She hunted till her late seventies, on a side-saddle upholstered in black velvet and embroidered with pearls and gold thread, swagged with embroidered silk trappings. At her request Claudio Corte of Pavia came to England as riding master for her own stables in 1565. Later she brought Prospero d'Osma to London to assess her studs and the horses she bred to race and for the army. When d'Osma established his own riding academy in Mile End for aspirational Englishmen who wished to understand the new continental fad for teaching a horse to caper and curvet, Elizabeth did not attend. Her most famous mount, the grey she borrowed from the Cecil family to ride at Tilbury, was a palfrey of state – a lady's ride – not a courser of state, as her father would have ridden to the battlefield, and when she is pictured riding him he has three feet safely on the ground.

A band of princesses, eccentrics and courtesans persisted in riding astride for sport, although their numbers were dwindling in England. (On the continent it was another matter; Marie Antoinette and Catherine the Great were both painted riding cross-saddle.) Sir Nicholas L'Estrange of Hunstanton, Norfolk, rolled out one notorious East Anglian case as a racy anecdote: 'The Bury Ladyes that usd Hawking and Hunting, were once in a great vaine of wearing Breeches; and some of them being at dinner one day at Sir Edward Lewkenors, there was one Mr Zephory, a very precise and silenc't Minister.' The clergyman was appalled to learn of this practice and 'declaimd much against it', whereupon another guest, Robert Heighem 'undertooke to vindicate the Ladyes, and their fashion, as decent to such as might cover their shame'. After all, he pointed out, 'if an Horse throwes them, or by any mischance they gett a fall, had you not better see them in their Breeches than Naked?'

'O no, by no meanes,' spluttered Mr Zephory, still horrified at the thought of women in trousers.

'By my Troth, Parson,' rejoined Heighem, 'and I commend thee for't, for I am of thy mind too.'

With the exception of a few enthusiasts like Cavendish, however, the *haute école* did not really 'stick' in Britain, where the male natives preferred to race and to hunt their horses as they had since Celtic times. Hunting was gradually changing from the formality of pursuit in the old enclosed parks such as Costessey to a harum-scarum chase across the open countryside. Queen Anne must have learned to ride as a girl and she expected the same of her ladies-in-waiting, like the dashing Miss Forester, who appeared at Ascot opening day dressed in a man's riding coat and a periwig. When the queen herself grew too fat to ride, she hunted 'furiously, like Jehu' in a spindly *calèche*, which she drove for forty miles in a day, according to Jonathan Swift in his *Journal to Stella*. On 22 September 1702 at Bramham Moor, she gave a cup valued at £100 to the victor in a series of heats of races for children aged six or under, each horse carrying a maximum of twelve stones, which seems mighty generous. Perhaps there were girls among them. Perhaps.

It was not until the Enlightenment brought in a fuller appreciation of the notion of childhood, that children and child riders began to emerge in the literature in their own right and not as miniature adults. 'Nature wishes children to pass through childhood before they become men,' wrote Rousseau in *Emile*, his treatise on education. 'We know nothing of childhood; and with our mistaken notions the further we advance the further we go astray. The wisest writers devote themselves to what a man ought to know, without asking what a child is capable of learning. They are always looking for the man in the child, without considering what he is before he becomes a man.' Parents ruined their children as they might ruin a horse with training, as they 'will have nothing as nature made it, not even man himself, who must learn his paces like a saddle-horse'.

Rousseau himself was not an advocate of riding tuition, asserting that 'without passing through the riding school, the traveller learns to mount his horse, to stick on it, and to ride well enough for practical purposes'. His educated and wealthy readers knew better. Any child left to find his own way on a horse would not ride well enough for social purposes, as de Vargas Machuca's advice still held: a boy could not become a leader of men if he could not manage his own horse. In response to demand, a new crop of riding establishments were opening in London that would cater for both adults and children, to educate riders in basic techniques, as well as princely *haute école*.

The Foubert family, whose Huguenot ancestor first established a London riding school in 1679 when he fled France, taught riding in Soho Fields and in 1696 built an indoor riding school on the site of Kingly Street near what is now Oxford Circus. When the founding father of the circus, Philip Astley, opened his amphitheatre on the Lambeth end of Westminster bridge, he offered riding lessons in the mornings for both ladies and gentlemen. Tattersall's, the horse dealers par excellence, built a riding hall in London in 1766 so popular that, in honour of it, indoor manèges in Germany are still sometimes known as 'Tattersalls'. One Captain Carter, billed in *The Times* in 1796 as 'Equerry to his late Royal Highness William Duke of Cumberland', offered 'Small, gentle, and pleasant Horses' for 'teaching young Ladies and Gentlemen from School'.

The new, playfully didactic style of pedagogy championed by Rousseau's enthusiastic followers required nursery-level reading. With the flood of educational chapbooks and the first true literature for children came the earliest pony book for juveniles in 1799. Dick's *Memoirs of a Little Poney* are 'Supposed to be Written by Himself' although they were in truth composed by an anonymous author under the pseudonym of Arabella Argus.

'I trust the following memoirs of my chequered life will prove that I am not wholly uncultivated, nor have been an inattentive observer of human manners. And if my strictures tend to produce more uniform favour to my kind, or to soften one obdurate heart among the lords of creation, I shall not regret that I have written, nor will my history be read without improvement,' began Dick, before embarking on a tale designed to place the child reader firmly in the pony's hooves.

The philosopher Jeremy Bentham had asked of animals ten years earlier, 'The question is not, Can they reason? nor Can they talk? but, Can they suffer? Why should the law refuse its protection to any sensitive being?' Gentlemen's sporting magazines recommended that 'tenderness' be shown to horses and began to run reports of exceptional cases of animal cruelty, such as the horrible tale of a pony twelve hands high who was forced to gallop sixty miles in six hours with a man on his back beating him with a spiked stick until the fat 'melted' off his kidneys and they were 'worked raw against one another'. Dick brought to the nursery the new morality of the nascent animal rights movement: 'The most stupid animal is not insensitive to kindness, but revolts from oppression,' he notes, after managing to unship an ignorant little boy who jabbed his sides with spurs and tugged his mouth. Later, he darkly warns that 'the reign of Tyranny cannot last forever.'

The little dapple-grey protagonist is a somewhat pompous, philosophical creature, whose antecedents are Houyhnhnms and the talking horses of folk tales. He lives, however, in the real world of grooms, farmers and 'young Masters and Mistresses' who will read his memoirs. Of his time with his most benevolent owners, he says, 'I now felt myself a servant, not a slave.' He witnesses a highway robbery and learns about man's mysterious preoccupation with 'the purse' and its contents, which cannot be eaten nor worn. He must suffer the 'exquisite torture' of being gelded at the hands of gypsies who steal him, when 'Nature produced me a male, but my tyrants were not satisfied with her decrees.' They also crop his ears. 'Ye tasteless sons of men!' he abrades them, before shrugging it off with 'I submit, however, to destiny.'

A few adventures on, our hero is given to a little girl with consumption and falls into a *tendresse*, exclaiming, 'Did she pat me, I was ready to die with pleasure, did she speak to me, I thought her voice more harmonious than the music of the groves.' When she slips from him for the last time and dies in her father's arms, Dick weeps: 'Stare not reader, for a horse has tears; and his feeling for the moment is as acute as yours.' He even composes a short poem about her. Left idle, he comfort-eats and has to be dosed with a 'black ball' by the farrier. Poor Dick. He ends his memoirs in happy retirement with a family whose sons he initiated into horsemanship and he pens his recollections, hoping that 'the fame of Dick will, perhaps, be more permanent, and at least more sure than that of some of those who have proudly bestrode his back.'

Mary Breese

But if the rougher sex by this fierce sport
Is hurried wild, let not such horrid joy
Ever stain the bosom of the British fair.
Far be the spirit of the chase from them!
Uncomely courage, unbeseeming skill;
To spring the fence, to rein the prancing steed,
The cap, the whip, the masculine attire,
In which they roughen to the sense, and all
The winning softness of their sex is lost.

'Autumn' (1730) by James Thomson

In 1900 or thereabouts, there was a schoolmistress by the name of Miss Howard in Colkirk, near Fakenham in Norfolk, who was so distressed by the death of her beloved donkey that she had it buried with its head protruding from the earth, in case it needed nourishment for its onward journey. When she asked the farrier why God had taken away her ass, he replied, gently, "Cos he wanted him for the angels to ride on.' Mary Breese cannot have been such a sap. I found her in the Staatsbibliothek in Berlin between the covers of a distinctly Californian *Encyclopedia of Amazons* full of reclaimed feminist heroines. The authors had rehashed a description of her they'd found in an 1855 book called *Sketches of All Distinguished Women from Creation to AD 1854* by the New England editor Sarah Josepha Hale. They pulled Mary into the light like old linen from a trunk:

BREESE, MARY,

A SINGULAR character, was born at Lynn, in Norfolk, England, in 1721. She regularly took out a shooting licence, kept hounds, and was a sure shot. She died in 1799. By her desire, her dogs and favourite mare were killed at her death and buried in the grave with her.

Oh, serendipity. The steppes custom of burying horses with their owners as an investment in the next life had persisted, discreetly, even as Christianity began to subdue the old pagan ways and the dancing in horse masks. Anglo-Saxon men and women left horses as heriot or tribute to their lords on their deaths, and right up until the Reformation you can find the well-to-do bequeathing their best horse and its harness as mortuary to their parish church, which sold the beast and kept the cash. The Earl of Buckinghamshire had been buried in a pyramid in the grounds of Blickling Hall, so why shouldn't Mary have been interred like a Norfolk Scythian, a sister in the skin to the Pazyryk ice maiden with her chestnut geldings and her white felt riding boots?

The Norfolk Record Office's computerized databases threw up a Mary Breeze born six miles north and west of Ringland in the parish of Lyng (rather than Lynn) in 1721 and buried, unmarried, in 1799 in Great Witchingham churchyard. Could she still, like Elizabeth I, have been a huntswoman at seventy-eight if she were buried with her horse?

I drove out to the Record Office at Colney and ordered Mary's will, which came in a white-paper envelope, out of which I extracted a sheet of yellowed paper as large as a tea tray, dense with the curlicues of some nameless clerk's best calligraphy. I pored over the lines. It was disappointingly technical, revealing only that Mary had left a few properties in the Lyng and Witchingham area to a nephew called John Smith, of all the names destined to vanish into the records like a tree in a thicket. The will made no mention of her mare nor her pack of hounds.

I telephoned the West Norfolk Hunt to see whether Mary was part of their folklore, but the lady who answered had not heard of her. 'The families that people think of as being the big local families haven't been established very long,' she said. 'You could try a book by Vic Brown called *The Foxhunters of Norfolk*. That might mention her.'

Fox-hunting began in Norfolk in 1534 but when Mary was striking out across the fields around Lyng there was no grand West Norfolk Hunt as such, only scattered private packs who hunted by invitation only. Some of them were very small indeed and it would have been highly unusual for a woman of that era to keep her own hounds, so there was a good chance she would be in Brown's book.

Gentlewomen still hunted alongside men, although the suspicion was growing that perhaps the field was not the place for a lady. In the first decades of the nineteenth century, plenty of the smarter women would be squeezed out of the hunting field to keep them from associating with the lower-class men who were now admitted, although many women and some young girls of all classes persisted in going to meets. In 1797 the *Sporting Magazine* brought its readers news of a twelve-year-old 'female' – shorthand indicating that she was not well born – called Wisdom who lived near Glynde in East Sussex and was such a passionate fan of the chase that she would follow the local hunt for up to twenty miles on foot. Aristocratic daughters, such as Lady Augusta Milbanke and Lady Arabella Vane, whose fathers owned respectable private packs, had been known to whip-in for their papas 'from their very infancy', according to the *Sporting Magazine*'s hunting correspondent, Nimrod.

Mary was barely in the squirearchy and her respectability wasn't safeguarded by marriage, but she was also a woman of independent means, able to keep her own hounds and leave property in her will. She would have first taken to the field as a girl decades before Arabella and Augusta or notorious Dianas such as Lady Lade and Lady Salisbury. Without even a title to her name, she had been famous enough to have been remembered in New England half a century later.

In Brown's book I found a glancing mention of Mary's father, Robert. When she was five, he was working as an otter huntsman to Thomas Coke of Holkham and was master of foxhounds to a local pack. Coke also, Brown wrote, sometimes employed as his agent a certain Miles Branthwaite of Taverham Hall, who had kept his own pack. Taverham Hall I knew, or at least the building that now stands on the site of the old manor, a private prep school whose red-brick chimneys can be glimpsed emerging exclusively from the treetops of its grounds when you ride from Costessey to Ringland. A bundle of verse from 1791 called 'The Taverham Hunt Poems' was held in the Record Office.

The scant facts I had uncovered could be arranged into an outline as arbitrary and seductive as a constellation. I was sure that the next sheaf of old paper would deliver me Mary, a dame of seventy at the time when the poems were written, but surely part of local lore, if not wheeled out to the meet bundled up in blankets. I ordered another plain white envelope from the Record Office desk, which contained a thick pad of scrawled copperplate, copied down double-sided for posterity. There were fifteen sides in rhyming couplets of varying grasp, which started out well spaced and neat, but degenerated into an almost Arabic script by page fifteen. The composer had waged a few battles to tack on crucial rhyming words before he reached the edge of the foolscap and, on losing, had crammed in the outstanding rhyme either above or below the line.

I squinted my way through. The Taverham Hunt kennelled two foxes at the hall, one of whom 'escap'd, and was flown', before they could even set out on a dreary, rain-sodden morning. The raggle-taggle hunt – or, as the poet calls them, 'the Heroes in Buckskin' – included a dandy in tight breeches, a clergyman ('the divine form'), the squire of Great Melton, and a gentleman with 'wig, cap and belt on', all easily waylaid by a breakfast of muffins in the hall. Squire Branthwaite's wife is a Xanthippe who dominates her table, convinced that hunting in wet weather will aggravate her husband's gout. So eloquent is her condemnation of his plans that she threatens to overbalance the entire poem, but she is interrupted when a second woman appears among the muffins and the Heroes in Buckskin:

> Then hark forward! Huzza! A long stride and a bounce
> The approach of our petticoat Nimrod announce
> With her not our Chamberlain's countess can vie
> Nor her fair sister Talbot leap fences so high.

Alas, this was not Mary Breese, but 'Julie', a hearty who takes on Mrs Branthwaite. She's due to travel to Newmarket the next week to hunt, and recommends the exercise as a remedy for gout:

> 'Last winter I tried my persuasion on <u>Billy</u>,
> Who when plagu'd with the gout will like all men be silly,
> And talked till I own'd I was wearied with talking
> To convince him that riding was better than walking:
> Well – and would you believe it? He never would try.
> For he said he was sure he knew better than I!'

Julie, who is made of stronger stuff than her poor Billy, declares:

> 'I'm sure Lady Sals'b'ry against Weather is steel'd
> And to her or no other in hunting I'll yield.'

Julie's idol was Lady Salisbury or 'Old Sarum', who led her own pack at Hatfield House in Hertfordshire with great moxie for forty-four seasons, unconcerned by the fact that the hunt followers included mere farmers and horse dealers. In 1787, The Times reported in awe that 'Lady Salisbury may be considered as the modern Diana; for of all the huntresses of late, none can come up to her … It was computed Lady Salisbury had galloped upwards of 40 miles.' A contemporary political cartoon shows her in a ragged sky-blue dress – the livery of her hunt – with her shredded white petticoats exposed, her grey hair wild and down to her waist, and a fox's brush brandished aloft in one hand. At considerable vintage she was out a-hunting on a tall, milk-white horse, to whose saddle she was tied. A groom rode alongside her, calling out, 'Damn you, my Lady, jump!' at each fence. She was burned to a crisp aged eighty-six, in a fire that destroyed the west wing of Hatfield House. I applauded Julie's choice of role model.

There was sadly no more mention of Julie in the poem, except that, when the Taverham pack set out, with the remaining fox, 'Mr Reynard', in a sack on someone's back, she was mounted on a mare called Diana. The hunt finally got under way in Ringland, where the fox was released behind a hedge and, after a moment's indecision, took flight for some miles, only to vanish into the Costessey plantations. Nobody wanted to jump the boundary fence, so home they went over Costessey Common, presumably to more muffins. There was no mention of Mary Breese nor any character who resembled her. There was nothing left but to seek out Mary where she had gone to ground.

I drove to West End past the track to Costessey Common, just down the hill from the old plantation and along the long, winding lane to Ringland, past the driveway to my first riding school, long since demolished and replaced by Sir Alfred Munnings Road, a new housing development of tasteful maisonettes and flats in pale-yellow brick. I passed the entrance to the Stubble Field, which had been plugged with a metal five-bar gate. Up the slope south of it lay the Easton Reeds through which the Taverham Hunt had careered 'at a terrible pace' before losing the fox in the plantation. On the other side of Ringland, I cut across the Fakenham Road and bored up the narrow lanes, overhung with green, that led to Great Witchingham. Horse droppings were piled on the tarmac like miniature cairns. Mary was within earshot of hoofbeats, at least.

I parked just down the road from where the Church of the Assumption stood in the crook of a T-junction. It was one of those semi-rusticated, musty, Norfolk flint churches with a note in the porch promising services every third and fourth Sunday and evening prayer once a week. An apron of graveyard spread out into a corner of the junction. Pushing open the grey, weathered wood gate, in the lee of the tower I found a large headstone patchworked with a mustard-yellow crust of lichen and pads of velvety moss bedded in vigorous, thick-bladed grass, dotted with buttercups. A minute, tan snail was making its way up one side. Mary was not crammed in too tight a berth with her neighbours but neither was there enough space for a horse and a couple of hounds. Sacrilegious woman, her pagan heart unknowable: how did she become famous in New England?

Two cherubs held an open book above the inscription:

In memory of
MARY BREESE
Spinster
Daughter of
Robert and Susannah Breese
Who departed this life
Sept 22 1799 aged 78 years

The rest was lost to weathering and grass. I wrapped my fist around a sheaf of grass, twisted it so I didn't haul the roots out and ripped it up with a squeak.

I drove back to Costessey with the handful of grass on the passenger seat, twice crossing the path taken by the Taverham Heroes in Buckskin, parked the car in my parents' drive and set out on foot, with the grass in my fist, down Windmill Lane. I passed the field where Tav had lived for a stretch when I was a teenager and where a still smaller me had hung on the fence, trying to entice horses over for puckered apples rescued from the bottom of the fruit bowl. A sign tied to the gate asked passers-by not to feed the horses without permission of the owner. Plastic feeding-ball toys lay here and there, abandoned by the horses. I passed on, saving the grass for the next horse.

As a child, I had mentally mapped this network of tracks and fields between Costessey and Drayton, horse by horse, knowing each field by its inhabitants and their tidbit preferences, a triangulation that served me well enough. When the tarmac gave way to a sandy, flint track, I knew that the wedge-shaped field sloping away on my left used to house another pony I'd fed, and that I'd galloped there with Tav. I turned right at the fork where there's a view over the green belt to Drayton and continued on down the track to the next point of interest on my trail, the Peruzzis' yard. The Peruzzi ponies had always been sequestered behind wire-link fences more than six feet high, but you could poke a twist of grass through to their waiting lips. Now a sheer corrugated-metal wall had been erected behind the wire, blocking the sight of the stables and overshadowing the path.

I walked on, emerging from a funnel of two hedges to the crest of a bare hill and the view across Costessey to Norwich, the spire of the cathedral still dominating the low city skyline. Corn camomile like stringy, overgrown daisies flourished at the track edge, alongside yellow ragwort with black-striped caterpillars curled under its bitter leaves. The track carried on downhill to my next stop, the corner of a field where the Railway Line met a spit of Gunton Lane at the edge of New Costessey. At one time there used to be a chestnut Arab and a small white pony here that would take a carrot, if you still had it after walking past all those other ponies. The brambles before the fence had grown monstrously into a thicket as big as The Chair at Aintree, fronted with dead nettles, so I walked on along the old railway line, which had been rollered and re-gravelled into something too hard for galloping. Weekend cyclists in bicolour Lycra and helmets crunched past in pairs and single file, man and woman, eyes ahead, not talking to one another or acknowledging my 'Good afternoon'.

This was the stretch of the Railway Line where Tav, worsted in a confrontation with a terrible pram, executed a perfect half-pirouette and galloped for a quarter of a mile, hemmed by the hedges. I passed another field, half reed-beds and marsh, with a rotting old railway carriage that used to be a shelter for ponies but was now empty. On the next stretch of the Railway Line, the tree coverage parted and the Wensum valley flattened out on either side like a book laid on its spine and pressed almost flat.

As there had been no rain for months, the blackberries on the purple-stemmed hedges that overhung the track were stunted, only four or five large juice sacks to a fruit, so that when I pinched one I crushed it onto its white core instead of pulling it free. Mum and I once took Tav brambling, intending to reach the higher fruits that hadn't been sprinkled with dog pee. As I picked, Tav craned his head up and champed on bunches of blackberries, then, with a sideways movement of his nose, stripped the stems – fruit, leaves, prickles and all, dribbling purple froth.

The Railway Line ran under oak trees again, this time on an embankment, and the fields to either side of the track fell away. Down to the left were old cow meadows, now encroached at their borders by new fields where horses grazed behind white electrical tape. I slipped down the steep, dusty bank to my right, checking myself by swinging from the slim tree trunks that curved up out of the slope to the brittle, old lianas of ivy.

There at the bottom of the bank, in a dirt semi-circle worn by hooves and kept clear by the shade of the trees, stood an imperious little Appaloosa pony, waiting. He was both brindle and spotted, iron grey, blue roan, pure white in patches. Black spots the size of old pennies spattered his coat, a few running together in erratic doodles, as though someone had put a finger to one of the dots on his cheekbone and drawn a wavering line across his temple. I uncurled my palm and the grass sprang up, only a little crushed. I tucked my thumb under my hand as I was taught, then stretched it flat between the wires of the fence to make Mary's offering.

Gräfin

After riding every day for over a fortnight, Pamela began to feel very much at home in the saddle. I rather think she fancied herself, just a little, as a horsewoman, and had day-dreams in which she pictured herself riding at Olympia.

Pamela and her Pony 'Flash' (1936) by Antonio P. Fachiri

In Berlin, I went back to the riding club for two more private lessons on Zofe. My muscles protested at first and then, surprisingly, recovered rapidly from the shock. My sense of balance began to seep back and I jounced less when I tried to hustle the mare from trot into canter.

I bought a useful-looking paperback entitled *Reitschule für Anfänger* (Riding School for Beginners) and sat down with the dictionary to translate the lesson running order and the commands of the *Reitlehrer*, which, I was surprised to see, matched exactly those at my riding club. Everyone must call out 'Tür frei, bitte,' when they wanted to enter the *reithalle* and wait for the answering call of 'Tür ist frei!' 'Ganze Bahn' meant, as I'd guessed, to use the whole of the school and 'Halbe Bahn' was straightforward – work in only half the space. A circle was only a *Zirkel* if it took up half the manège, but a *Volte* if it were smaller. To 'change through the circle' one had to trot an S-shape through the centre point, ending up on the other rein. An 'offenen Volte' was a half-circle, while the 'Entwicklung des Schenkelweichens aus der Ecke' was entirely new to me, whatever it was. The most I'd done in my childhood lessons was to circle, change rein, rein back and do the odd serpen-tine. The author went into an explanation of several formal dressage terms, but did not mention jumping. I didn't need to jump just yet, but was finding the lessons on Zofe a little repetitive, so I let the whole riding project slide until, fortified by my new vocabulary, I decided to join a group lesson in the new year.

I turned up at the club one early January evening, wearing tights under my jodhs for warmth like a jockey and clutching my old skullcap, which I'd brought back from Norfolk at Christmas. The shell flexed if you squeezed it firmly enough, and a hole had been nibbled in the padded maroon-nylon lining by something unidentifiable. The black silk had lost its elastic, so I'd glued it to the Aertexy surface of the helmet, unfortunately setting the button on the top an inch forward of the cap's apex, so it looked as though it was eager to be off. I'd lost count of the number of times over the last eleven years when I'd hastily pulled a coat off the hook that the skullcap also hung on, sending it tumbling to the tiled hall floor with a great 'bock' like an empty coconut. Responsible riders replaced their helmets after each fall. Responsible riders spoke the same language as their instructors.

The office was closed again, and there were four or five women already busy grooming and tacking up horses. A woman with wavy hair and a friendly face behind her glasses was nipping between them to check girths and to chat, so I took a guess that she was the *Reitlehrerin* and told her helplessly that I was here for the five o'clock class.

'*Wie heisst du?*'

'Susanna Forrest.'

'*Ich heisse Ynes.*' She flipped through a computer printout of horses and riders and we realized that no one had booked a horse for me. '*Du kannst reiten?*'

'*Ja, als Kind hab'ich viel geritten, und letzte sommer . . .*'

'Forrest Gump?' she grinned, suddenly twigging. She disappeared into the barn and then re-emerged. 'Forrest, oder Wald? You can ride Gräfin. Erika, help her tack up Gräfin quickly.'

A line of horses and riders was forming across the yard from the school door, ready for the lesson. Erika was a universal type, one of those girls who hangs around in stables and will give the biggest horse a slap on the rump when he barges her or call him a daft bugger to show you that, though she might be all day in the barn forking up soiled straw that makes her eyes smart and soaping saddles till her nails are soft, she's nonchalant about it, this horse business.

I followed her into the tackroom, hefting the saddle on one arm, as she slung loops of bridle, rein and martingale over her shoulder like a hawser and strode off. I knew there was a cobby grey, whom I'd spotted on an earlier visit and thought was probably the forgiving, broad-bummed sort suitable for a rider of unspecified abilities, the sort who would bustle around the ring and canter, when poked, as if her hooves were set on a bow-shaped rocker. Muttering away, Erika pushed back the metal-barred door to reveal Gräfin.

She was huge, filling the loose box, her waterproof rug like a destrier's tabard. She was also beautiful, the glossy black of a lacquer-work cabinet, polished and nourished till the highlights of her coat were white under the barn light. As Erika wrestled the stiff rug off her hindquarters, I saw that the mare had a brand on her near quarter, indicating that she was a pedigree warmblood of some kind. I hovered in the doorway with the saddle, thinking I'd never ridden anything like Gräfin. She was not Zofe or Tav. She would not tolerate a yank in the mouth or being bounced on by some idiot who couldn't keep her feet in the stirrups. I felt the old kind of excitement that I'd had when the girls at the Costessey riding school let me ride Petita, the Arab, and I'd take it as proof that I was a real rider.

Erika was pulling on the mare's bridle, chuntering away. I lifted the saddle carefully onto the sheeny back, which came up to my chin, then dropped the girth off the offside and ducked down to help

Erika, who held the loop of the martingale for it. She knotted the two stray leather straps attached to the martingale around Gräfin's neck.

I led the black mare out down the aisle, pushing back the door that was swinging open, worried in case it smacked her hind quarters. Erika gestured to me not to bother, as blasé as if Gräfin were some old, seen-it-all nag. At the mounting block Ynes tugged the girth and Gräfin flashed her ears back.

'We'll try!' said Ynes, cheerily, without waiting for me to stumble into the explanation I'd practised of not being able to understand much German.

Gräfin's neck curved in front of me, her mane lying so smoothly over the crest that it was like a barrelling wave. Ynes patted the mare and led me to the door of the *reithalle*, calling out, 'Tur frei!' Six or seven other riders were milling around the school in a chaotic Brownian motion, some clockwise, others anticlockwise, some trotting already, some circling, one cantering. I wasn't sure what to do and opted to walk quietly round, getting a feel for the mare. Spotting Zofe being ridden by a moustachioed man in a body warmer and glasses, I turned Gräfin towards her, the mare striding animatedly with her ears pricked.

Ynes called me into the centre and tugged open the knot of leather straps looped round Gräfin's neck. I saw that the martingale ran up between her legs from her girth and split into these two leather straps, which Ynes now passed through the bit rings and looped back to secure under the saddle flap. Gräfin's head was bowed into place. I had never ridden with side reins before; they seemed like stabilizers on a bicycle. Once, following a tip in a pony magazine, I'd tried to make loose 'grass reins' for Tav from bailer twine to stop him diving mouth-first into every verge, but they would have snapped quickly in an emergency and these *dreieckezugel* or 'triangle reins' were a quarter of a centimetre thick. Gräfin rattled the bit in her mouth, annoyed. I wondered what was supposed to happen if she stumbled and needed to put her head down for balance.

As we walked back out to join the ride, she chucked her chin. The reins slacked and snapped. I let her work off her irritation with my sympathy. The reins seemed to preoccupy her, and as I tucked her into line behind a woman on a bay gelding I thought that perhaps they stopped her seeing ahead of herself properly. Every time the horse in front swished its tail or the woman on him tapped him with her stick – something she did frequently and seemingly for no reason – Gräfin would fling up her head against the side reins as if startled. I reached forward, trying to hook out a piece of mane rucked under her headpiece, and she plunged away.

Any horse who came up behind her or to the side of us caused her to pin back her ears and snake her head. Feeling her muscles gather to kick, I'd push her on. I hadn't wanted to be bored, but now my attention was divided between Ynes's instructions, Gräfin's rapidly rotating ears, the horse behind that got too close to Gräfin's twitching quarters, the bay in front and that damn woman with her whip. Once I saw her turn in her seat and, with a satisfied twitch of a smile, slap the gelding as he walked blamelessly in file. I was used to individual riders performing the occasional canter or circle solo, but in the reithalle we did everything as a troop. I was a beat or two behind the others when they all peeled off the track simultaneously in voltes, which meant that I had to squeeze at Gräfin to finish our circle and slot back into file before the horse behind us got any closer.

We were told to canter in file in a circle at one end of the school. When I sat to push Gräfin into canter, she seemed to grow, doubling in length and power until her stride was so long that it was like riding some sort of regulated sea monster, breasting and plunging down waves. My body was used to a pony's scurrying gait, or to Zofe's amiable, half-assed scuffle. It felt as though the black mare would cover the school in four strides and never make a corner. I sat haplessly amidships, trying to hold her body together with my legs, and to gather front and back as I'd been taught. Finally I gave up and let her carry me round, struggling just to sit out her stride smoothly. I wanted to placate the black mood on the end of the reins.

After one circle she coughed and panted throatily, deciding enough was enough. That was my last canter for the lesson. While the others – including, I noticed with chagrin, Zofe – circled easily at a canter, I flailed on Gräfin's back, kicking and squeezing and bumping as she trotted longer and longer. Ynes kept calling 'More contact!' while I clutched again with legs that were failing and hips that were beginning to twinge. What strength did it take? I felt guilty for riding badly. The mirrors on the school walls revealed my toes turned out and my chin in its ridiculous black cup, half broken where I'd belatedly tried to pull it off the strap during the ride over on the U-bahn. When the ordeal was over, we slumped back into stride with the rest of the horses, Gräfin's radar still twitching in case any of them strayed too close.

As we led the horses in single file out of the ring after the lesson, Ynes gave them each in turn a sugar lump from a little tin with Marlene Dietrich printed on the side. In the stable I went through another slapstick routine of removing Gräfin's saddle, trying to swiftly brush away the tidemarks of dust pushed out by her saddle cloth and re-rug her before she could get a chill. For all her theatrical coughing, there was no sweat on her. She turned sweet, letting me pull her ears and kiss her nose.

I walked back to the U-bahn on hip joints that throbbed in the cold wind, reflecting that it wasn't so bad; it was just that I had things to learn. Perhaps I was suffering from some kind of arrested development because, after all, when other riders had moved on from ponies to horses as teenagers, I had regressed to riding a friend's pony, mooching slack-reined around the countryside, before giving up altogether. At the point when I should have turned riding into an effort worthy of an adult, I'd taken a step backwards instead.

I didn't have the body memory required for sea-monster riding, but that didn't mean I had to remain permanently stuck at pony level.

Each new horse is a challenge, a new biography to open. I had thought I had Zofe down pat, but Gräfin was a fresh enigma. I couldn't reduce her to the palm of my hand, as Erika did, and make her nothing more than another horse. Tiny balls of hail filled the air, obscuring the view to the U-bahn like the white-out of a lost television transmission. The hail blew in swirls around me, blotting out everything, then hitting the pavement and bouncing two, three times before melting into the concrete.

Jeunes Filles Bien Elevées

If you were the daughter of a hundred earls, you would
be mounted on a Shetland pony and shaken into a good seat
long before you outgrew short frocks, and afterwards you would
be trained by your mother or older sisters, by the gentlemen
of your family, or perhaps, by some trusted old groom, or in a
good London riding-school, and, no matter who your
instructor might be, you would be compelled to be
submissive and obedient.

In the Riding School: Chats with Esmerelda (1890)
by Theo. Stephenson Browne

Women's emancipation, it could be argued, to the horror of
modern liberators, began in the hunting field.

English Fox Hunting (1986) by Raymond Carr

Princess Charlotte, the Prince Regent's daughter, loved to scare her
governess out of her wits by whipping up her pair of grey ponies
and driving them across a rutted field, calling out, 'Nothing like exercise, my lady!' Another courtier noted that her seat was 'beautiful – no
fear of course – gallops and leaps over every ditch like a schoolboy'.
When, in disgrace over a broken engagement contracted as a teenager,
she was packed off to Weymouth with an entourage of disapproving
ladies-in-waiting, she bemoaned herself 'deprived of my masters, my

ponies, my everything'. After her tragic death in childbirth in 1817, prints of an engraving of one of her favourite ponies, Spangle, were offered to the public by an enterprising artist.

As a small girl, her successor Queen Victoria rode for an hour every morning after breakfast in the grounds of Kensington Palace, on a pony or a donkey. Aged thirteen, after a ride with her mother one Sunday morning, she wrote in her diary, 'Rosa went at an enormous rate; she literally flew.' She had a preference for a horse called Tartar – 'I quite love him,' she scribbled, 'excessively pretty, and of a very dark brown colour; he has a very springy charming canter and action, is full of spirit, and yet as quiet as a lamb.' She galloped him in Hyde Park and rode him fearlessly past omnibuses and through London traffic. Riding was her only escape from a stuffy, sequestered upbringing.

On being crowned queen, Victoria swiftly appointed her riding master, Fozard (perhaps of the Foubert family), as 'Her Majesty's Stirrup Holder' – a position she created for the express purpose of thus dubbing him. N. P. Willis, seeing her riding in the park at this time, said, 'She rode with her mouth open, and seemed exhilarated with pleasure.' She was painted riding her horse in a levade and jumping in a riding school; she hunted on the paths that Queen Anne had had cleared in the woods near Ascot for her *calèche*. According to the lore of the rocking-horse makers J. Collinson and Sons, when she visited their Liverpool workshop she rode a dapple-grey rocker side-saddle. Henceforth all their horses were dapples.

Further down the social scale in Victoria's reign, where a girl had a will to ride she usually found a way. In the 1850s, a twelve-year-old called Catherine Walters begged rides and lessons from livery stables, although she was only the daughter of a customs officer, raised on the Liverpool docks and half Irish at that. Still in her teens, she made her way to London where they nicknamed her 'Skittles' because of her dead-eye aim in the bowling alleys. In her prime as – so Anthony Dent charmingly puts it – an 'open air poule-de-luxe', she became mistress to the Prince of Wales, Napoleon III and the poet Wilfrid

Scawen Blunt. Gladstone attended her tea parties. Catherine worked as a 'horsebreaker' for a London dealer, exercising his animals in Hyde Park, and even trialled horses for the Princess of Wales. When she moved to Paris the French swooned over her skin-tight 'princess' habits and the fine English horses she drove in the Bois de Boulogne. After a full career as both a demi-mondaine and a rider, she retired, a cosseted, still-adored old lady, dying in 1920 in her own house in Mayfair, in the arms of a man who'd fallen in love with her when he was twenty and she forty.

In Dublin, a more genteelly situated young lady named Nannie Lambert also had to take matters into her own hands to get her riding education. Already horse-mad and an inveterate passer of tidbits to the working horses in the city streets, she borrowed mounts from tradesmen and dealers, and riding habits wherever she could find them. Later she recalled with feeling 'all the queer saddles I had ridden on, the countless odd skirts – rascally, young, or disreputable horses – before I could afford to hire 7/6 worth of something decent to carry me, out of my own private pocket money'. In her twenties she was lucky to have the tuition of a great sportsman, Allan McDonogh, and became, with her married name of Power O'Donoghue, one of the best-known authorities on riding for ladies.

Four-year-old Edith Somerville – later one half of the novelist duo Somerville and Ross – found a kindred spirit in her grandfather, an old buffer straight out of the pages of an R. S. Surtees novel. One day he decided to begin her riding lessons and, wrapping up the little girl in a blanket, propped her on a horse and stepped back. A short while later, horse and child were disentangled from a garden swing, none the worse, it seemed, for the experience. A mere year later, Edith's grandfather was sneaking her out behind her mother's back, in top hat and skirts, to follow hounds.

A child who began his or her riding career in more conventional fashion as an infant would be spooned into a pannier hung from a pony or a donkey's side. There is a photograph of Princess Alexandra,

the wife of Edward the Prince of Wales, wearing a crinoline shaped
like a handbell and leading a pony half hidden by an enormous wicker construction strapped to its back, with a toddler's head poking out
of each side, like joeys from two pouches. Nannie Power O'Donoghue
disapproved of these baskets, thinking that the small children suffered
'an hour's jolting, with their poor little heads bobbing pitifully about'.
On visiting one saddler's shop, she was shown a patented child bucket that could be secured to the top of a pony's saddle and which, she
said, appeared to be a kind of brazier. An accompanying illustration in
The Common Sense of Riding shows the terrible consequences of using these
contraptions: a child equestrian, with a face like Tenniel's Humpty
Dumpty tumbling off the wall, falls to his doom from his stumbling,
wild-eyed pony.

In any case, said Mrs Power O'Donoghue, a girl should wait until
she was sixteen to ride, to spare both her spine, which might grow
crooked on a side-saddle, and her nerves.

I object, as a rule, to children riding. They cannot do so with any safety, unless
put upon horses and ponies which are sheep-like in their demeanour; and
from being accustomed to such, and no other, they are nervous and fright-
ened when mounted on spirited animals which they feel they have not the
strength nor the art to manage, and, being unused to the science of controlling, they suffer themselves to be controlled, and thus extinguish their
chance of becoming accomplished horsewomen.

Less than a year ago a sweet little blue-eyed damsel who was prattling by
my side as she rode her grey pony along with me, was thrown suddenly
and without warning upon the road . . . She fell! And the remembrance of
uplifting her, and carrying her little hurt form before me upon the saddle
to her parents' house, is not amongst the brightest of my memories.

When they had advanced through the earliest stage of their equestrian education, the junior rider would then be plonked on a 'pilch',
or soft, frameless saddle, and led about on horseback by their mamas

or a groom. The editor and author Diana Athill, learning to ride in this fashion in Norfolk in the 1920s, explained that '"Sit up straight", "Keep your heels down", "Don't jab her mouth", were instructions given not in the form of "riding lessons" but in the same way as "Don't talk with your mouth full" or "Shut the door after you".' The quality of this tuition depended, of course, on the skills and patience of the mother or groom overseeing it. Nannie Power O'Donoghue was resolutely opposed to grooms as teachers, for 'Servants are rarely able to ride a yard, and their attempt at teaching is proportionately lame.' They have, she said, no 'more idea of how a lady ought to manage her horse, than of instructing her in the etiquette of the dinner table, or the intricacies of the valse'.

Few paid any attention to Mrs Power O'Donoghue's fears; rare was the wealthy parent who kept his daughters away from horses. In any case, there were plenty of girls who, like the Queen herself, thrived as children on horseback and were every bit as fearless as their brothers. A mother might arrange for a child to 'follow' the hunt in a cart by road and, later yet, go out cubbing in her wake, learning field etiquette as she might learn the correct fork to use and jumping in the handiest places chosen by her dam. The famous huntswoman, 'The Squire' Maude Cheape, even prepared diminutive drag hunts around Hyde Park for her daughters. When they were in their teens she had them whipping in for her Bentley Harriers. Gustav Doré's engraving of *Rotten Row, The Ladies' Mile*, shows in its foreground two girls with manes of long blonde curls. One has a white wing on the side of her beret and a pure, solemn face like Alice Liddell. The other, watched over by a gentleman in a topper, has a great crop of curled black feathers on her hat and a farouche little pony with its teeth bared.

Parents who were not concerned about their daughter's health or nerve had to consider her heart too. Nannie had warned that 'fathers and mothers who permit their daughters to be taught by stud grooms ought not to wonder when these personages impart another and different style of knowledge to the pupils'. A sensation novel of the period, *Aurora Floyd*, had a flashing-eyed heroine who eloped with the groom who taught her to ride.Worse still, although riding schools had developed into commonplace institutions in cities, they continued to teeter on a line of respectability: the teachers must be masters and preferably reputable, former army men. Nannie, again, disapproved: 'Many of those who call themselves riding masters are little better than grooms.'

The American author Elizabeth Carr defended good establishments in her 1884 handbook, *The American Horsewoman*, although she acknowledged that 'considerable gossip, including some truth, as to illiteracy, rudeness, offensive familiarity, and scandal of various kinds has in past years been associated with some of the riding-schools established in our cities.' There were teachers who encouraged young ladies to leap from horseback into their waiting hands, or who took advantage of the moment when they cupped their hands for a lady's foot as she mounted.

The Queen magazine recommended a Mrs Alice Hayes, who gave lessons in London at Ward's Manège for a guinea an hour in partnership with her husband, himself an army veterinary surgeon and an authority on horses.The magazine's correspondent visited to see a lesson in progress, writing afterwards, 'I can most conscientiously advise any mother to send her girls to her if she wishes them to at once become perfect horsewomen while remaining perfect ladies.' Mrs Hayes started off younger girls riding in a 'gymnastic costume' of dark bloomers tied under the knee, with long tunics over them, so that she could check the position of their legs; her pupils wore their hair loose but half-tied back with a ribbon. In three lessons she had the young girls mounted on a 15.3hh horse, 'galloping gaily round and round, with radiant faces and flying hair', at the end of Captain Hayes's lunge rope, their hands resting not on their reins but on a whip they held across their legs – look, Mama, no hands – leaping wicker hurdles till they were 'mighty proud of themselves'.

Mrs Hayes had been a medical missionary to lepers before she married Captain Hayes and then spent seven years rough-riding for him in India, Ceylon, Egypt, China and South Africa, on ornery Waler horses and Arabians that had been considered unrideable. In England she hunted over the formidable Leicestershire and Cheshire countryside. She was Nannie Power O'Donoghue's rival, disagreeing on several niceties of tack and horse management, not least on the correct age for a child to begin riding – Mrs Hayes thinking it depended on the child. Mrs Hayes riled Nannie by attacking an article in an Indian newspaper that she claimed, wrongly, the Irishwoman had written. She published her own riding manual, The Horsewoman, in 1892.

Nannie and Alice were prominent among a new generation of female writers instructing their own sex in riding; previously most equitation manuals for women had been written by men. This was the era of the etiquette bible, and of a new breed of equestrienne. Many of them were not aristocrats to the manor born, 'mounted on a Shetland pony and shaken into a good seat long before you outgrew short frocks', but perhaps the daughters of army captains, or tradesmen or other genteel parvenus, who could not rely on the guidance of a mother who had perhaps barely ridden, and almost certainly had not achieved the social benediction of hunting. The invention in the 1830s of the 'leaping head' – a forked pommel over which the right knee hung and beneath which the left leg could grip snugly – gave women a more secure seat with which to jump, freeing them once more to return to the field.

'To be well is to look well,' intoned The Queen magazine's regular riding columnist, the old cavalryman 'Vieille Moustache', in 1874. Riding was no longer 'confined to those only whose names figure in the pages of "Burke" or "Debrett". Within the last twenty years the wives and daughters of professional men and wealthy tradesmen, who were content formerly to take an airing in a carriage, have taken to riding on horseback. And they are quite right.' Nannie, Vieille Moustache and Mrs Hayes catered to these new horsewomen, instructing them in ways of finding the correct underclothes, purchasing a suitable horse and negotiating the intricate and fiercely held rules and conventions of the hunting field. A deadly snobbery often pervades the texts; riding had the lustre of social cachet only if one could be a consummate lady in both saddle and stable. As one of Mrs O'Donoghue's chapter headings spells out, 'COURAGE INDISPENSABLE — TASTE A NECESSITY'.

Meanwhile, 'Impecuniosus' of *The Field* magazine explained that fathers must carefully monitor their daughters' riding style:

In my own limited experience I knew an unfortunate instance in which a young lady, very pretty, very clever, of good family, in every way desirable, lost her chance (which had been more than promising) of the '*parti*' of the season, merely by the unfortunate notion that she would like to ride one of his horses. Being rather nervous, she held her reins very short and her hand on the nag's mane; her right arm was bent and she was all on one side. A thoughtless friend remarked casually to the *object*, 'Who's that girl! Looks like a teapot, by Jove!' The resemblance was undeniable; the convinced and horror-stricken admirer fled from town to Scotland by that night's limited mail, and when he returned he was 'père de famille'.

The American author Theo. Stephenson Browne poured scorn on those whose skills did not live up to the promise of their dress:

Nothing is more ludicrous than to see a rider clothed in a correct habit, properly scant and unhemmed, to avoid all risks when taking fences and hedges in a hunting country, with her chimney-pot hat and her own gold-mounted crop, her knowing little riding-boots and buckskins, with outfit enough for Baby Blake and Di Vernon and Lady Gay Spanker, and to see that young woman dancing in the saddle, now here and now there, pulling at the reins in a manner to make a rocking-horse rear, and squealing tearfully and jerkily: 'Oh, ho-ho-oh, wh-h-hat m-m-makes h-h-him g-g-go s-s-s-so?'

No ladies' riding manual was complete without a laundry list of the correct wardrobe for modest equestriennes: dark, nunnish, plain habits of 'best Melton cloth', which must cover the ankle and on which 'no braiding nor ornamentation of any sort' was to appear, over good doeskin or chamois breeches, for which Mrs Hayes 'invented . . . a removable pad, which has met with the approval of several hunting women'. There is cattiness about soiled white kid gloves, exposed, frilled petticoats, tasselled whips and vulgar silk hats 'with a velvet rosette and a buckle at the front' or great red bows worn about the neck. Worst of all were the horrifying unmentionables of 'Leather breeches for ladies' use . . . too unsanitary to merit consideration'.

And yet, and yet: in among the frippery and the petty requirements of social protocol beats another message like a bass drum – that in the horse world those very ladylike encumberments could be shed like dandelion clocks. If girls were subject to more restrictions in their day-to-day lives than boys, there was also a pay-off. Horse riding came, like the fairies to Sleeping Beauty's crib, to grant a paradoxical set of gifts to Victorian girls. Although riding was respectable and quite the thing, girls who rode well would be praised for physical bravery and daring, risking life and limb on side-saddles that could snare a skirt, with stirrups that might trap a little booted foot and cause a child to be dragged to its death. They could take on and outstrip men, while remaining ladies. They were commended as having a special feel and gentleness for horses, but must also dominate the brutes. It is hard to imagine a heroine in Dickens whacking a rearing horse on the poll with the butt of her riding crop, as counselled by Mrs Power O'Donoghue.

These manuals were full of thrilling tales of their authoresses' courage, for, while they made great display of their propriety, Nannie and Alice also saw no contradiction in regaling their readers with tales of runaway horses that leaped stone walls six and a half feet high to land in farmyards, or buckjumpers who tossed around their riders like rag dolls but never threw them. They were the original 'hard women to hounds', authentic heroines esteemed by sportsmen and loved by their horses.

Nannie Power O'Donoghue was the first rider – full stop, with no allowance made here for sex nor side-saddle – to ride clear over the steeplechase courses at Baldoyle, Fairyhouse and Punchestown on consecutive days, on her bay hunter Pleader. Her gentleman pilot had a refusal that put him out of the running, but she went on, taking the challenge only to prove that Pleader was 'too clever to put a foot astray'. When you find yourself a helpless passenger on a bolting horse, she advised, it is better to ride for a fall rather than to let yourself be dragged or to career into a road. 'Of course the experience is fraught with excessive danger,' she explained, 'but it is not certain death.' In Ireland she rode nose to nose across country with one of the most formidable and beautiful women of her day, the Empress of Austria, 'who dearly loves a little bit of rivalry'. The two ignored the Empress' pilot and charged a great hedge together, with Nannie taking a purler as her horse somersaulted clean over her. She was up, back on him and away again before realizing that her rein had been broken and her stirrup lost. She was still in at the death and took the fox's brush.

In *The Horsewoman* there's a tiny photograph of Mrs Hayes in Calcutta, riding side-saddle on a surly-looking zebra that had been broken in just an hour earlier and who rests one hind hoof like a warning. She said he had a trick of kicking without lowering his head but also a coat as soft as 'finest sealskin'. The zebra objected to posing for the camera, which he considered 'an infernal machine destined for his destruction'. 'He was far too neck-strong to make a pleasant mount for a lady,' explained the blasé Mrs H. 'Kickers, as I have already said, should never be taken into any hunting field . . . I believe I am the only woman who has ridden a mountain zebra.'

There it was, in print and on the bookshelves, as well as in the subscription magazines for which Nannie wrote a column, or which sent reporters to see Mrs Hayes in action. Everywhere there were examples for young girls of common-or-garden ladies who did extraordinary things. How would a teenage girl react to reading about the self-written adventures of women travellers such as Lady Florence Dixie, author of *Across Patagonia* and later the *Morning Post*'s correspondent in South Africa, or Ethel Tweedie, who wrote *A Girl's Ride in Iceland*, or Isabella Bird ('There never was anybody who had adventures as well as Miss Bird,' observed *The Spectator*), or Emily Low, who in 1857 published *Unprotected Females in Norway*, an account of her travels with her mother, in which she wore baggy trousers and rode astride on a little dun, striped Norwegian Fjord pony?

And might that same girl find in *The Times* a report on a meeting of the British Association in September 1890, where Miss Dowie was cheered by the audience of gentlemen as she told a tale of her latest expedition?

Wild cats, bears, and wolves exist in the Carpathians, but there were no other obstacles, said Miss Dowie, to a girl travelling alone from London to the Russian frontier. Miss Dowie met with no inconvenience. She wore an easily-detachable skirt over knickerbockers; she carried a knife and a revolver, and when riding she rode cross-saddle and bareback ... Miss Dowie said that she had met with several accidents, such as being nearly drowned while bathing in strange rivers, and dislocating her shoulder by a fall, but she regretted that she had never met a bear face to face.

'Not long since,' wrote Vieille Moustache, 'I saw a little girl, about ten years old, riding with hounds on a mite of a pony which was as clever as a monkey. The little heroine took a line of her own (no doubt she knew the country well), and kept her place among the foremost for some time.' Sadly, however, in this case fortune did not favour the brave: 'presently she disappeared, and we found her impounded, pony and all, up to the back of the latter in a piece of rotten ground which had let them in like a "jack in the box".'

New equestrian sports were emerging, too, and girls staked their claim to enter the ring alongside boys. In 1886, ten-year-old Maude Williams competed in a children's 'leaping' class at a major London horse show, with a pony called Little Joey. With the crowd laughing and cheering her, she cleared her obstacles with her shoulders round her ears and a great grin on her face, to finish second to eleven-year-old Master Stillwell.

These girls who devoured travellers' tales, alongside the works of Mrs Hayes and Mrs Power O'Donoghue, would be the mothers of the women who would grow impatient and hurl away their sidesaddles in the 1900s, and the grandmothers of the first pony girls of the twentieth century, who would ride astride from the beginning on felt-pad saddles, in breeches and gaiters. On horses they were braver than princes. Greater attention was now paid to girls' riding lessons than to boys' and as a result, many commentators noted like Trollope in his *Hunting Sketches*, that the female of the species proved superior to the male:

Women who ride, as a rule, ride better than men. They, the women, have always been instructed; whereas men have usually come to ride without any instruction. They are put upon ponies when they are all boys, and put themselves upon their fathers' horses as they become hobble-dehoys: and thus they obtain the power of sticking on to the animal while he gallops and jumps, – and even while he kicks and shies; and, so progressing, they achieve an amount of horsemanship which answers the purposes of life. But they do not acquire the art of riding with exactness, as women do, and rarely have such hands as a woman has on a horse's mouth.

One last tale to share, then, from Vieille Moustache:

Some years ago I chanced to be at the school of a fashionable riding master in London, when a class of young ladies was going through a ride. In the gallery from which I was observing them was also the mother of one of the young ladies who was riding, and of another much younger, who was standing by her side watching with the most intense interest the riding below. The younger lady was not more than ten or eleven years old . . . she did not speak, but I could see from the glitter of her large dark eyes, and her changing colour, that she was heart and soul with the fair equestriennes.

85

After watching the girls leap a 'gorsed bar', some hurdles and a miniature brook, the child burst 'into a violent fit of sobbing and weeping, she clutched her mother's dress, and cried convulsively, "Dear mamma, let me ride, let me ride."' Her mother and sister obliged by leading her around the ring on one of the horses, whereupon the confident miss told the master that she could trot. Thinking she would soon learn the folly of overconfidence, the man gave her her wish, and she not only sat it perfectly, but asked to canter and did so, 'in very good form'.

Vieille Moustache thought the master wrong when he had the groom bring out one of the hurdles and lay it at an angle to make a modest jump for her. However, here 'again our little friend electrified us all' and

before the riding master had time to check her, the little girl's eye lit up just as I had seen it in the gallery. She caught the horse fast by the head, hit him with her heel, put down her hands, and sat as though she had been hunting for years. It was too late to stop her ... with my heart in my mouth I saw the horse go at the hurdle ... his daring little rider had roused him thoroughly, and he jumped high enough to clear a big fence, and far enough to take him over a small brook ... her lithe little figure was bent from the waist, precisely at the moment, and she landed safe ...

This young lady is now one of the most brilliant horsewomen in England. Her genius (if I may be permitted the expression) joined to close application and the best of opportunities of riding good horses, enabled her in a brief space to far outstrip all her youthful competitors, and in less than twelve months after the time I speak of she could execute most of the 'bending lesson' at a canter as well as a professional rider, while over the country with hounds she was always close to her pilot, than whom there was no better man. This when she was barely thirteen years old.

The girls were coming.

Saving Beauty

[Black Beauty's] effect upon adolescent girls has
always been one of unbearable anguish . . . It is read obsessively,
as though it contained lessons which must be learned,
no matter how painful.

The Old Brown Dog (1985) by Coral Lansbury

The first grown-up book that I read – or, more accurately, heard –
at the age of four, was Black Beauty. To ensure my silence on long
car journeys, my parents bought me a two-cassette, abridged version
of Anna Sewell's 1877 'autobiography of a horse', read by Angela
Rippon, with the silhouette of a black horse wheeling, at liberty, on
the cover. With my ears muffled with sponge headphones and the
tape recorder whirring by me on the back seat, I learned that to be
equine is not just to run and be free, but to suffer. The theme music
of great kettle drums overlaid by plangent brass tones was the very
sound of a horse labouring uphill. Angela's husky, posh voice told the
story of the gelding, Black Beauty, and his doomed trajectory from a
good home with Farmer Grey, and then Squire Gordon of Birtwick
Park, to lady's mount, tortured carriage horse in a bearing rein – a
thin leather strap that cranked the horse's head intolerably high –
hired jade and on down through the hellish circles of late
nineteenth-century London, where he breaks down in the shafts of
a laden cab and is eventually rescued. He ends his narrative safe in the
hands of three kindly old ladies and his former groom, Joe Green.

Into my ears poured sufferings more vivid than any fairy tale. The chestnut mare, Ginger, has a bit forced into her mouth by a gang of men, and is beaten when she struggles to free herself. Beauty is galloped over sharp stones by the drunkard Reuben Smith, and his hoof splits 'down to the very quick' before he flounders, breaking his knees and dashing the groom to the ground. The stable in which Ginger and Beauty are lodged burns down, and Angela's voice rose over the crackling sound effects of the rushing fire that consumes the hay loft. When Beauty and the mare are saved, the relief I felt was tainted by the thought of 'the two poor horses that could not be got out' and 'were buried under the burnt rafters and tiles'.

A younger Joe Green, out of ignorance, gives an exhausted Beauty a great draught of cold water and leaves him unrugged, with the result that the horse is stricken with pneumonia: 'Soon I began to shake and tremble, and turned deadly cold,' Angela moaned. 'My legs ached, my loins ached, my chest ached.' Other horses have their tails chopped off or are flogged uphill with unbearable loads, or are pierced right through by the shafts of other carriages in crowded London streets. Captain is caught in the Charge of the Light Brigade, where he gallops on ground slippery with blood and hears the groans of horses with their legs shot away. Merrylegs the pony is beaten by boys who think he is 'like a steam engine or a threshing machine, and can go on as long and as fast as they please'. I listened, wide-eyed.

It wasn't just the pains of being a horse that transfixed me but also the brief, glowing pleasures. Although Black Beauty was not written for children, it relates the same cycle – of comfort, unjust mistreatment, deprivation and then comfort once more – that you find in the stories of Noel Streatfeld or Joan Aiken. The 'clean, sweet and airy' loose box he is given at Birtwick Park was bedded with thick, shining straw that I could have curled up on, by his side. I wanted to taste warm bran mash laced with beans and oats, and eat apples in an orchard. There was no escaping identification: Anna Sewell described so vividly every detail of being a horse, who must accept the bit, 'a great piece of cold hard steel as thick as a man's finger', in his mouth, and learn the unaccustomed heaviness of iron shoes on the hoof, or the slow agony of having your head strapped back, hole by hole, with the bearing reins as her ladyship bullies the groom from the steps of her great house, and knowing, as Max the other carriage horse warns you, that it will shorten your life.

The greatest heartbreak, the worst of what literary critic May Hill Arbuthnot calls 'Black Beauty vapours', was not for Beauty. Beauty is the Patient Griselda of the horse world, doomed to suffer until he can be saved and rewarded for his unquestioning obedience. No, far more acute was the miserable life of Ginger, who knows only cruelty before she comes to Birtwick Park, and who rears up and strikes when they try to haul her head back with the bearing rein. Ginger was 'the great indignant feminist' as the poet Ruth Padel called her – more like Margaret Thursday and Pippi Longstocking and Jinny Manders. You willed her to battle for her freedom as Beauty would not, while knowing how it would end for her. Her spirit and body broken, Ginger tells Beauty, 'I wish the end would come, I wish I was dead. I have seen dead horses, and I am sure they do not suffer pain.' The last we see of her is her corpse lolling on the knacker's tumbril.

Anna Sewell herself would indignantly face up to any driver she found ill-treating his horse. In the novel, a lady stops to politely but firmly ask one of Beauty's masters, Jakes, not to beat the gelding as he labours uphill. She tells him, 'We have no right to distress any of God's creatures without a very good reason; we call them dumb animals and so they are, for they cannot tell us how they feel, but they do not suffer less because they have no words' – a paraphrase of Bentham's affirmation. At Beauty's nadir, it is a little girl called Grace who speaks up for him although she cannot save him. 'Papa, Papa, do take a second cab ... I am sure we are wrong, I am sure it is very cruel.' Horses, I learned, could not save themselves from abusive humans, but must be rescued from these horrors by other, more compassionate humans. I needed to be better than Jakes and the grand lady at Earlshall, and to be the one that saved Ginger and Beauty over and over again.

With love of horses came a duty of empathy, and the pony books that followed Sewell reinforced the message: the girls and boys who yanked their ponies in the mouth and cut them with whips were villains, and the unfeeling, we were told, could not ride. Riding instructors asked, 'How would you like it if you had a sack of potatoes lumping around on your back?' when you failed again to rise to trot, or they would throw their hand up in front of your face to show you why a horse flung its head back when you thrust out a hand to pat its forehead. The critic Alison Haymonds was right to say that 'the world of horses has an uncompromising code of ethics that descends directly from *Black Beauty*.'

Anna Sewell was born in Great Yarmouth in Norfolk in 1820 and grew up in a Quaker household in a close relationship with her mother, Mary, who wrote educational chapbooks influenced by Rousseau and his British followers. When Anna was a toddler, the family moved to London, where they lived across the road from a cab-horse rank. In the summers Anna travelled by stagecoach back to Norfolk where she stayed with her grandparents at Dudwick House near Buxton, which later became the model for Birtwick Park. Anna learned to ride on local lanes and began her horsy education in the stables. As *Dick, the Memoirs of a Little Poney* was still in print during her childhood, and as it fitted so closely with her mother's own views, it is tempting to wonder whether the young Anna was familiar with Arabella Argus's equine autobiography. Dick's and Beauty's lives follow parallel courses from good to bad homes and finally to salvation.

As both teenager and adult, Sewell was periodically invalided out of her normal, active life by what may have been lupus, according to her biographer Adrienne E. Gavin. Her mother said that her disability 'made riding and driving a necessity; and so it came to pass, between her and her own horse, and horses in general, a mutual confidence and friendship sprang up, and she learned all their secrets'. As Gavin pointed out, there was also empathy: Beauty, as a horse, and Anna, as a spinster and invalid, were moved from home to home, both having to deal with crippling injuries and both often left isolated from friends.

Towards the end of her life she returned to Norfolk where she lived in Old Catton, just outside Norwich, and owned her last pony, a fat grey like Merrylegs who was humoured by his mistress when he refused to walk over cobbled streets in the city. When she became too infirm to drive, he was passed on to a good home and she settled to the company of fictional equines, writing steadily between intervals of sickness. The resulting novel was a model for all the pony books to follow, half dramatic narrative and half guide to horse care, so detailed and comprehensive that Edward Fordham Flower, the driving expert and author of many pamphlets on equine welfare, exclaimed on finishing his copy that 'it is written by a veterinary surgeon, by a coachman, by a groom . . . How could a lady know so much about horses?'

Between Anna's birth in 1820 and her death in 1878, shortly after *Black Beauty's* publication, the industrialization and urbanization of Britain had grown apace. The labours of horses had multiplied as they moved into the cities to keep the arteries of trade and transport flowing. By 1893, the social campaigner W. J. Gordon reckoned there were 300,000 equines in London alone, from the Hanoverian 'Creams' who drew the royal coach to the donkeys kept in Mayfair to provide milk for consumptives. In his survey, *The Horse-World of London*, he estimated that over a hundred thousand horses would have passed in and out of the Square Mile every working day. There were cabs – two-wheeled hansoms, 'the gondolas of London', and four-wheeler growlers, drawn by horses with names like Mud, Gaiters, Eight-sharp and Necktie; trams, omnibuses, costers' carts, coal horses, milkmen's horses, butcher's ponies, smart carriages driven by matching pairs, drays making deliveries to pubs, the scarlet-painted post vans, refuse wagons pulled by formidable Shires. There was even a hearse drawn by a team of coal-black Friesians called John Knox, Bradlaugh, Dr Adler and Cardinal Manning.

The light draught-horse mares, who pulled the 3¼-tonne omnibuses, worked six days a week, hauling up to twenty-six people for twelve miles a day before their team was changed. The weight was not the worst of it; that lay in the stopping and starting, when the horses had, from a standstill, to push themselves into their collars and heft the bus into motion. To stop it again, they had to throw themselves back against the bus, aided by the driver's brake. The slightest slope added to the drag.

'Think of it, ye exigent women, who rather than walk a yard will stop an omnibus twice in a minute,' warned W. J. Gordon. A driver told campaigner Henry Mayhew, 'the starting after stopping is the hardest work for them; it's such a terrible strain. I've felt for the poor things on a wet night, with a 'bus full of big people ... there's no cruelty to the horses, not a bit. It wouldn't be allowed.'

Two of every three 'bussers' died in harness, either when their hearts gave out or due to an accident. Once they were in service with an omnibus company, they never saw a field again. 'Trammers' had a harder time of it; the tram rails were often blocked with debris, through which the vehicle had to be dragged. They managed to survive a year less between the traces. Britain's 'vanners' collectively hauled the 84 million tonnes of goods transported by rail each year to their final destinations, over streets that were littered with glass and nails that a horse could pick up in a hollow hoof. All the while they would be threading in and out of the traffic, as Black Beauty described it, 'amongst carriages, omnibuses, carts, vans, trucks, cabs, and great wagons creeping along at a walking pace; some going one way, some another, some going slowly, others wanting to pass them, omnibuses stopping short every few minutes to take up a passenger'.

They toiled under the eyes of a new breed of middle-class

campaigner fresh from fighting the slavery of humans, who were talkers, pamphleteers and writers of articles in the press, complaining about bull baiting and bearing reins. In 1822 the MP for Galway, Richard Martin, finally broke through with his proposed bill, which made it a punishable offence to 'beat, abuse, or ill-treat any horse, mare, gelding, mule, ass, ox, cow, heifer, steer, sheep or other cattle'. These animals at last fell under the protection of the government.

Two years later the Society for the Prevention of Cruelty to Animals was founded in London at a Covent Garden coffee house. Although its first attendees were all male, from the earliest days of the animal rights movement middle-class women were highly involved at nearly all levels. They wrote moral, educational books about cur dogs and birds that were killed to decorate hats; they donated money and, like Anna Sewell and her mother, they lectured the working classes as well as their own peers. They sponsored trophies for the best-kept animals at the working-horse parades in Liverpool, Bristol, London and Manchester. They went out into the streets, again like Anna, to berate and, of course, educate working men who overloaded their carts or kicked their dogs. Mrs Power O'Donoghue took a cabman to task for maltreating his horse and afterwards became his best customer. Mrs Hayes took advantage of her trip to Russia to note how well the cab horses looked and how their drivers cared for them. The campaign for the Christian treatment of animals became a socially acceptable form of political engagement for these women, as though the protection of animals lay in the female domain. Only feminism drew more ladies to its cause.

Anna had meant *Black Beauty* to be circulated among horsemen and out it surged, borne by animal rightist organizations, to workingmen's clubs, to cabmen's dinners, to grooms and to charity schools. When Sewell died she was waiting for the proofs of a school edition; by 1880 education for children aged ten and under had become not just free but also compulsory, creating an audience hungry for new material. The book's simple, didactic style – honed by Anna in years of teaching in working-men's clubs and Sunday schools – and its homilies on kindness, temperance and patience rewarded made it an acceptable school text. Its original Norwich publishers, Jarrolds, called it 'a Bible for children'. It ran into five editions in under twelve months.

One of *Black Beauty*'s readers, a well-to-do spinster called Ann Lindo, was galvanized into taking direct action on behalf of the Gingers, the Captains and the Beauties. She borrowed grazing at Sudbury, just outside London, from friends and sought out horses, mules and donkeys in need of recuperative care. Their owners were lent substitutes until their animals had recovered. The first convalescent she found had drawn a cab. Miss Lindo's 'home of rest' was the first of its kind and would become the Horse Trust, the first charity in the world reserved for equines alone.

As a girl born in *Black Beauty*'s centenary, I found Anna Sewell's thumbmark everywhere. That year the novel was named the favourite book of ten-year-old British children in a major survey. By 1995, it was estimated that 40 million copies were in circulation, in every language from Volapuk to Braille, and generations of children had been raised on Sewell's diet of empathy, sympathy and morality. In 2003, when the BBC Big Read searched for 'the nation's best-loved book', voters put *Black Beauty* at number fifty-eight, polling alongside *Pride and Prejudice* and *Anna Karenina*. The grounds of the house belonging to Anna's brother Philip, on St Clement's Hill, had been donated to the city of Norwich as a park and her niece, Ada, furnished them with a commemorative horse trough. The barn in which Bessie, Philip's horse and a possible model for Beauty, had been kept was converted into the Sewell Barn Theatre, where I attended school plays. I was given a Breyer model set of Beauty, Ginger, Duchess and Merrylegs for Christmas in California, and I galloped them on the lawn under the redwood trees.

Ann Lindo's Horse Trust had in turn inspired scores of sanctuaries and rescue centres for equines. My fortnightly *Horse and Pony* magazine ran photographic advertisements showing emaciated horses in Cairo, their coats raddled with sores and galls from their harnesses and infected insect bites, teetering on their feet between the shafts of crude carts loaded with bricks. Other sanctuaries proffered photographs of horses with hooves as grossly overgrown as Struwwelpeter's fingernails, tottering on splayed, wracked legs, or ponies tethered in halters so tight that they had bitten into the flesh, which was infected with maggots. The Tettenhall Horse Sanctuary in Wolverhampton had an advert dominated by the silhouette of a horse hung by the neck from a black bough, its forelegs trailing unnaturally by its sides, a hand holding a dagger and a tombstone. 'A Horse died in agony at Willenhall when sick thugs used a children's rope swing as a noose to hang it from a tree.' Tettenhall favoured the hysterical: 'PLEASE COME QUICKLY! BOYS ARE RIDING THIS HORSE WITH A PIECE OF ... BARBED WIRE IN ITS MOUTH AS A BIT!'

I had a pull-out poster of the Famous Four – a donkey called Holly and three ponies called Spring, Aladdin and Apache, all of whom had been saved by the local Horse Rescue Fund from the notoriously ill-run sales in Norwich – and also an annual for the *Follyfoot* TV series that I'd found at a jumble sale. Monica Dickens had visited the Horse Trust to research *Cobbler's Dream*, the first novel set at the Follyfoot Home of Rest for Horses. I even took a coin to the Yellow Pages and furiously scratched out the entries under 'Horse Slaughterers and Abattoirs'.

Norfolk and East Anglia seemed exceptionally rich in horse rescue centres, being home to the International League for the Protection of Horses (now called World Horse Welfare) and to the Walbancke family's Horse Rescue Fund. Graduates of the Horse Rescue Fund included a riding-school pony I knew called Orlando, fetched out of the Beaulieu Road sales in the New Forest with a belly full of worms; Sasha, who had to be removed from a flat in a tower block by the lift; and Woody, another rescued foal who became a local dressage star.

My mother took me to a new sanctuary, Redwings in Frettenham, where we saw fields full of horses picking at grass on a bare hill. Redwings was growing rapidly at the time and insisted on being the last home of any horse, pony or donkey that arrived at its gates. The rescue centre grazed its horses for a while on the old grounds of Dudwick House, where Anna Sewell had ridden as a child.

In early 2010, I went back to Redwings to discover horse rescue on an almost industrial scale. The old management had been replaced by a major charity administration with full accreditation and a board of trustees. Now they were keeping 1,000 horses on 1,200 acres on five different sites, with four full-time vets and six veterinary nurses on a staff of just over 200, three-quarters of whom were women. They regularly raised over £8 million a year in donations and, as British animal rights legislation became ever more extensive, they took in an increasing number of horses, ponies and donkeys. When I visited the command centre at Hapton Hall on a grey, late February day, I discovered an English country house with wainscots, rush matting and ornaments, and a well-polished range in the kitchen. It bustled with life as officers fetched equipment for a fleet of horse ambulances that was heading to Wales to collect thirty-odd semi-feral hill ponies.

'We took 130 horses in 2008, and in 2009 we brought in 260,' said one of the workers in the external welfare office. 'That's because of the Animal Welfare Act – it means that you can remove a horse if it looks like its situation isn't going to improve and it will suffer in the future. You need the say-so of a vet to do it, so if Redwings has one on site, the local authorities can give the green light to remove the horses straightaway.'

When a member of the public calls with concerns about a horse, pony or donkey, a welfare officer takes down details and logs the case with a number. They ask them about the situation: where is the horse? How many horses are there? What state are they in? Is there food and water? Any obvious sickness or injury? If it sounds like a valid case, one of three field officers is dispatched to investigate. If the horse is out of the range of these officers, Redwings can call on one of scores of volunteer equine welfare advisors who will go out to make an inspection. A map of Britain on the office wall was peppered with pins indicating their locations. Adam, the welfare officer, called up a computer database with detailed records of the 300–400 calls taken each year. He and the press officer, Nicola, were deputed to take me on a tour of the site and introduce me to Redwings staff.

In the veterinary centre we were greeted by Roxanne, a wildly enthusiastic vet. She showed me the operating theatre with a great black plastic mattress onto which the conked-out horse is lowered, spine first, by a winch that has borne it through from the padded 'knock-down room' where a general anaesthetic is administered. There was a ward of indoor stables and a second, fresh-air yard of boxes for less acute cases. There I found a tiny skewbald Shetland called Peaches, curled up on a bed of cardboard scraps, as softly fluffy as an angora rabbit. In the clinic I watched as Rosie, an old roan Clydesdale mare, lolling under sedation, had an abcess in her jaw flushed out by a team of veterinary students. Two nurses standing on upturned buckets struggled with the tangles in the mane of a colossal white Percheron, Charlie, who was in disgrace after chewing through the field shelter at the visitor centre at Caldecott.

Next door lay the barn where the feed was kept: Weetabix for colicking horses, eggs for those that needed building up and ginger biscuits for the donkeys. In the same barn there were six great white baths for mixing high-fibre pony nuts, forklifts for shifting hay bales, charts of each horse's dietary requirements and piles of numbered feed buckets ready for the tractor that would take them out around the fields. All Redwings horses love tractors and will pursue them eagerly.

As we rolled out past the big brick veterinary centre in one of the charity's four-wheel drives, field after field spooled by with solid post-and-rail fencing like the most expensive Newmarket stud. High up in the vehicle, we passed cheery, waving men on the maintenance team who were assessing some of the fencing. Fresh water gurgled in automatic waterers in every field. The horses and ponies lived out all year round in herds; they were largely native ponies and cobs, shaggy, with trailing manes to block out the worst of the wind, and thick coats, their chins hairy against the damp February chill. There were herds of stumpy Shetlands, some of them rugged up in water-proofs, heads down to suck up the grass. I saw one little skewbald rubbing its arse luxuriously on a fence post, and a barnyard filled with donkeys who came pressing up to the gate, ears waggling. There was a team of women in anoraks and hard hats in the next field, the 'checkers' who drive out on a buggy and inspect each horse twice a day. At night, a second team goes round to look over each horse at least twice more. Another group were collecting some of the 10,000 droppings produced daily by Redwings horses.

At the rehoming centre, where some of the horses are schooled for riding before being adopted out, a young woman called Lucy circled Mister, a grey gelding, in the outdoor school, while in the barn the resting horses whuffled and called out for their next feed. The re-homing manager, Emma, who also taught international-level young riders, told me the work was incredibly rewarding. Her team, she said, were 'fearless. Sometimes you don't know what the trigger will be for a horse.' There was a collection of donated tack waiting for use or resale and a child-size doll with pigtails that they used to back the miniature ponies and Shetlands.

Most of the horses who arrived at Hapton followed a steady process, from quarantine and veterinary care to recovery and either retirement or rehoming. Adam took me to their intensive care unit, or rehabilitation centre, to watch the staff work with some of the worst cases that came to Redwings. Because they have such extensive resources, he explained, many of the most serious abuse cases end up in their care, passed on from other charities. There was nothing physically wrong with the ninety-six horses who lived in this section of the Hapton grounds, but they no longer trusted people.

We ducked out of the freezing drizzle into a large barn divided into yards. Sarah Hallsworth, the Redwings rehabilitation officer, and her team were working a trio of grey ponies who had to be parted from one another and herded into separate pens. Adam and I stood out of her way before a wire 'round pen' like a miniature gasometer, sixteen to twenty feet wide and six and a half feet tall. In it stood Norris, a little pony with a thin layer of wet mud ottering his fur as high as his belly; a warming coat of the stuff obscured any dapples on his pale, mottled, steel-grey coat. Norris's long mane straggled below the curve of his elegant neck as, head up, he stared anxiously over my shoulder at his companion in the next enclosure and snorted – a sharp exhalation with a rattle of fear that echoed round the corrugated-metal walls of the barn. His ears strained forward to catch what was happening, his neat forehooves braced, his body tense. He cocked his tail and a fresh, loose stream of dung cascaded out onto the rubber matting. He snorted once more and, unable to stand it, rushed forward to career round the pen at a trot, driven by the hatched-wire sides into a small circle, his unshod hooves muffled on the soft floor.

Then he stopped and froze again to watch as the woman slipped a headcollar onto Archie, the smaller and tubbier grey in the open pen. Archie put his nose into the headcollar neatly like a model pupil, his little round black eyes like a seal's under a forelock that reached to his nostrils. He nibbled at the leading rein as Jess, a quiet young woman in mud-splattered overalls and a crash cap, leaned down slowly and deliberately, with a steady, definite movement, to gently squeeze Archie's cannon bone. As he lifted his hoof sharply for her, she immediately released the pressure. Behind me, Norris snorted again, once more with that strange rattle, and I felt the uncomfortable sensation of being close to someone trapped and in distress.

Sarah stood with her arms folded, chatting to me about the three grey ponies. 'Archie's still a stallion, and he was quite aggressive when he first came in. He would turn his butt on Jess and try to manoeuvre her away. Roxanne, the vet, couldn't inject him, even in the crush, he was so terrified, but he's come on really well. He could definitely be rehomed as a kid's pony eventually.' She broke off to address Norris, who was haring round once more. 'Don't be silly, Norris, we're not going to hurt you. It's all right.'

Earlier I'd watched as the third little grey pony, Morris, who now stood watching in another open pen, performed a neurotic *pas de deux* with Jess, in movements bafflingly minute, translated for me by Sarah. 'She's using very submissive body language,' she had said, as Jess, her head dropped, moved sideways towards Morris's shoulder. 'When he moves' – the pony took a few steps away, ears twitching in rapid semaphore – 'she tells him off by using eye contact, eyes on eyes – quite aggressive.'

Jess raised her head and looked full face at Morris, whose whole body was a ripple of communication, one ear on her, one turned away, a dilation of nostril, one hoof raised.

'She's saying, "No, that's not what I want you to do." And when he stops and does what he should do, she takes her eyes off him – that's the reward.' Morris stood as Jess approached and permitted her to stand by his head, still sideways on, and slip a leading rein over his neck. 'She's having a conversation with him,' said Sarah, breaking the silence. By the end of his fifteen-minute session Morris had, calmly enough, allowed Jess to rub the backs and fronts of his legs with a stuffed rubber glove on a stick. Released from his headcollar, he had snuffled up a reward of feed shaken out of a beaker onto the floor.

It was a little over two years since Morris, Archie and Norris had been removed, with 108 other horses, ponies and donkeys, from the farm of a dealer called James Gray in Amersham, Buckinghamshire. Tip-offs from members of the public brought RSPCA inspectors to Spindles' Farm to find the corpses of thirty-one horses rotting where they'd been tethered, having starved to death. Their necks had fallen back at an unnatural angle, their leg bones were folded under ribcages picked at by birds, with rotting flesh clinging to the vertebrae. Someone had bothered to make piles of clean horse bones and skulls, which lay in ossuaries about the property. By the corpses in the stables, in the bare fields, were living horses slowly dying. The floor of the stalls was fetlock deep in dung, while the soles of the horses in the outbuildings were rotting with thrush. Those outside had rain scalds oozing on their sides. Gray and his teenage son had been witnessed dragging one live horse by its head and tail into a trailer. An RSPCA inspector said that the yard was absolutely silent, as though the horses had given up.

Small wonder that Norris vibrated with fear in the cage behind me. A number of the horses at Spindles' Farm had to be put down on the spot, after which several horse rescue centres from around the country sent in their teams. Redwings was the largest single contributor, dispatching a team of thirty skilled nurses, handlers and vets plus a convoy of eight horse ambulances. Those animals with a chance of survival were loaded on shaking legs, or even carried bodily into lorries, and driven carefully back. Redwings ended up with sixty-one of Gray's horses. The case caught national press attention, and a second fleet of horse lorries, filled with donations of horse equipment, drugs and food, was dispatched in Operation Esther, named for a donkey foal taken from Spindles. The farm was dubbed 'an Auschwitz for horses'. Theories bubbled – that Gray kept the horses for blood donations, for smuggling drugs past sniffer dogs under horsebox floorboards, for meat, for money laundering – but when he was found guilty, all that could be known for certain was that he simply dealt in many horses and did not care if they starved.

'Norris was bonkers when we first got him,' said Sarah as she watched Jess give Archie his treat for behaving so well. 'He's the only one of the three who was gelded, so that's probably got something to do with it. It breaks your heart – what was done to him?'

She picked up a broom and a scoop for the three dribbly heaps of dung that the pony had produced and let herself into Norris's round pen. Norris drew back to the far end, swirled to face her and watched as she began to sweep up the droppings, talking to me on the outside of the pen all the while. Then the pony broke again and went ricocheting round the pen, his flanks grazing the sides and sending up a tinny, jangled noise like piano strings abruptly pawed.

'He did a wall of death the first time I got into the round pen with him,' noted Sarah, stepping out of his way. 'There now.' And the pony stopped, his quarters to me, his gaze locked on Sarah, who stepped over to the panel of the pen that Jess had pulled open and handed her the scoop of dung and the broom. Then she pulled the panel to and stood in the drum with Norris.

In the round pen, a horse can always run away and it will never be cornered, nor is it able to corner a person. Sarah began to work with Norris as Jess had with Morris and Archie, but the pony faced off to her, determined to keep her directly in front of him. There was no slow progress up to his shoulder.

'He's the most nervous pony I've ever seen. He breaks all the rules.' Norris shifted his weight from one side to the other, uncertain and looking to bolt. 'He wants you in front of him where he can keep both eyes on you, so you have to take an aggressive stance almost, and he's terrified of having people on his near side. That must be where the abuse took place.'

The rehabilitation team are inspired by 'natural horsemen' such as Monty Roberts, the most famous of the horse whisperers, and Kelly Marks, drawing on their philosophies of using a horse's own body language to communicate. The ponies in rehab must learn during their stay to be haltered, led, have their hooves handled by the farrier and to suffer a rug being slipped on their back.

'Really simple things you take for granted, you just can't do with these,' Sarah had told me. 'You go up to them and pat them and you have to scrape them off the ceiling because they think you're hitting

them. You have to train them to be patted. You have to train them to
eat carrots. You have to teach them every single thing.'

The difference between her and Norris was palpable – her calm,
his horror. The feral horses are often the easiest to work with, as they
have no experiences of humans. It's the horses who have been abused
that take the longest to learn to trust. Some of them never truly do
and remain at the rehabilitation centre. Some thirty will never leave,
like Spirit, who was attacked by dogs, had fireworks thrown at him,
was beaten with chains and finally electrocuted. When they put Spirit
in the round pen, he scraped his sides raw, fleeing desperately around
the perimeter. Recently he has allowed Sarah and her girls to rug him
in his field.

No one has touched Norris, unless he's been under sedation, since
he arrived in Norfolk. They simply haven't got close. He lives out in
one of the rehabilitation centre's fields with Morris and Archie, and
is slowly being introduced to a more benevolent type of human
handling. 'If you teach them well, they never forget it,' Sarah assured
me. 'They just want to please you, it's all they want to do. They're not
naughty or vicious. They don't kick.' Under his insulating mud coat
Norris was in good nick, his belly nicely filled out and his hooves,
the pale yellow of old ivory, were finely shaped. James Gray had a
good eye for a horse.

Jess had passed Sarah a slim wooden pole with a padded end
wrapped in gaffer tape, from a bucket containing an assortment of
stuffed rubber gloves on sticks. She reached out with this arm
extension without moving from the centre of the pen, where she
followed Norris with small, steady steps and brought it down on his
withers – no easy move as the pony was still trying to stand head-on
to her. He stood, legs stiffened, curling his neck around the probe to
sniff nervously at the pole and snort. Sarah moved the pole back and
forth, scratching him the way that horses do to one another, hitting
a knot of nerves that respond by lowering the horse's heart rate.

Unable to stand it, Norris surged off round the pen again, wet tail lashing on his hocks. As he raced she kept the pad on his withers till he stopped, nostrils heaving, and then she pulled the pole away – his reward. Then she stepped forward again and pressed the sweet spot gently with the padded stick. He sniffed at it, inspecting it, then pushed it away with his nose.

'He's really controlling himself there,' said Sarah. 'He wants to run. Good boy.' She rubbed some more. 'See? You're not dead.'

I realized that it wasn't simple fear that kept Norris pinned. Like Spirit, he could have run and run around the round pen, but there was an equally strong desire to be with Sarah, to investigate her and perhaps to facilitate the moment when the little cup of horse mix was poured on the floor. He did not know what she wanted; for all the horse body language she used, her behaviour must still have been baffling to him and yet he stayed.

When she herded him slowly so that his nearside was towards her, he quivered as I'd never seen a horse do – not the quick shiver to shake off a fly, but as if to shake off the whole of this terrible nervous energy, this fear that could be expended only in running, when running brought him back to where he began, with Sarah still in the centre, talking quietly to him and to the other humans. His ears flickered wildly and he gave off a hollow, rasping snort once more. He cowered, his hind legs gathered under him and his spine rounded like a greyhound's, then clashed into the fence. He broke again and ran low to the ground, slipping a little on his unshod hooves, the pad on his withers never releasing.

'Calm down, stop being a muppet. Don't get your knickers in a twist.' Sarah talked groom's nonsense to him. 'He's just the most irrational one I've ever come across,' she told me.

As she spoke, Norris stopped and turned to her once more. She moved slowly towards him along the pole, as though it were a rope she were climbing, hand over hand, to reach him. The little grey stood at right angles to her, head once more flexed around the pole, sniffing at it, not spinning, not running, but craning almost, his body on a seesaw between flight and a desire to be with Sarah. As she came within a metre of him, the pony leaned almost imperceptibly towards her, a tiny shift of weight on his hooves, a little commitment. His muzzle went out, past her hand on the pole, to inspect her arm and even brush at the sleeve of her fleece.

She was right next to him now, almost standing in the curl of his neck, and reached out her left hand along the pole and touched him once, gently, on the head, as it was nearest, then stood back and took the pole away.

'That's the first time he's let anyone do that,' she said with some emotion and pride in her voice.

We all breathed out. Jess handed Sarah a cup of food, which she tipped on the floor for Norris who, ears flashing, rapidly lipped it up, glancing up now and then to watch what Sarah was doing as she left the cage. I wondered whether Norris was relieved that, when he had trusted the human, nothing terrible had happened. As Sarah had promised him, he was still alive.

Jess opened up the round pen and the gates between the three enclosures. The three ponies surged together and, as the barn door was opened, set out at a trot back to their field.

Diminutive Dianas

Her nose was blue,
And her pigtails two
Hung damply over her shoulder;
She might have been ten,
Or guessing again —
She might have been twelve months older.
. . . She took up her place
At the tail of the chase,
Like a ten-season lord of the leather.

'The First Whip' (1915) by Will H. Ogilvie

'The International Horse Show, which opens at Olympia on Monday, June 6, bids fair to be more successful and brilliant even than those which have preceded it,' claimed The Times on 13 May 1910. The 'Yellow Earl' Lord Lonsdale had founded the show in 1907 in an effort to transform the British horse show, as he had done the football game and the boxing match. Before Lonsdale tightened the nuts, these affairs had tended to centre on the competitor at the expense of the often bored audience, who might have had to watch a single showing class go on for an hour or more. Always a showman, the earl crammed in a tremendous number of classes for riding, driving and 'leaping'. While his aristocratic mana enhanced the occasion, it was the thrills in the ring that drew society to Kensington in Royal Ascot week. Three hundred thousand would attend to see

2,750 entrants do battle for more than £10,000 in prize money. Up in the specially built garden terrace that encircled the auditorium, there might be distinguished guests such as the Khedive of Egypt or the Kaiser's Master of the Horse. Both the Secretary for War and the Chief of the Imperial General Staff would be there to oversee the performance of the British army, competing against continental officers in many of the classes, as the military still dominated horse shows.

At one end of the hall hung a painted backdrop of the Lonsdales' turreted ancestral home, Lowther Castle, under a sky of clouds like piles of scooped melon balls, with the arena laid out where the front lawn should be. Over the tan arena and the spectators' plumed hats hung 3,000 electric light bulbs on criss-crossing wires, some shielded by pink standard lampshades as big as cathedral bells, trimmed with fringing and festooned with ferns, as though a drawing room had floated up and was bobbing under the vaulted glass roof. For the first time, the leaping competitions could continue late into the night even when the summer evening light had faded.

Below on the arena floor was a grotto inhabited by a nymph clutching a dish from which water flowed and plashed in the pool below. A band in a mock-Grecian temple parped out military standards while the scent of grass crushed underfoot wafted up from 50,000 square feet of turf laid throughout the building. Ivy trailed down over the balconies; purple wisteria was fixed to the awnings of the roof; and rose trees, geraniums and baskets of summer blooms stood like a buffer between the audience and the arena floor. Over 50,000 plants prettified the white-painted trellises of the stands in heady, overblown profusion, and at each break attendants ran out to replace blooms that had flopped in the dusty atmosphere. The jumps for the 'round the course' competitions were framed by high, white wings and surrounded by hydrangea bushes so dense that when one rider was pitched out of his saddle he was lost from view in the shrubbery.

The new king and queen had insisted that the 1910 show go ahead despite the death of Edward VII, perhaps hoping, like the Secretary for War, that the British army officers would put up a better show than usual in the leaping classes. In those early days of showjumping, the British prepared their horses by ripping over the countryside after a fox and, in the confines of an arena, were easily outridden by continental officers on well-schooled mounts. There was some grumbling that the 'railway crossing' in-and-out was a trick fence, as bold jumping horses tended to come to grief there, but at least there was no obstacle so monstrous as the one that had appeared in 1909, composed of two field guns ranged muzzle to muzzle and protected by a row of dummies in scarlet military jackets and busbies. This year, however, the king and queen were rewarded and the Secretary for War could breathe a sigh of relief when Lieutenant Geoffrey Brooke of the 16th Lancers saved the nation's honour by winning the Daily Mail Cup on his talented, gutsy mare, Harriet.

When they were not engrossed by the endless classes in the arena, which ran from 9.30 a.m. to midnight, spectators could promenade around the arcade of trade stalls, lined with palm trees, that circled the ground floor behind the stands. There were gold cups, bandages, patent veterinary medicines, Peat's harnesses, Mr George Schomberg's riding whips and superior horseshoe nails. The Regent Street jewellers laid out discreet displays of trinkets such as silver or bronze hounds and horses, or cigarette cases with hunt scenes on the lid by the caricaturist John Leech. There were carriages in lime green or old rose with matching upholstery, and a brougham that converted into a landau in under a minute. Gentlemen's outfitters offered every make and mark of top boot, while one tailor had employed two ladies to model habits – one of them mounted side-saddle, the other astride – on horses who fidgeted and jibbed as a crowd gathered to call out and ask their riders which seat they preferred. Women who rode into the arena before the king, however, had to do so side-saddle.

Olympia ran classes for mounted policemen, for stagecoach teams and for officers' chargers. There were competitions for tradesmen's horses such as the municipal workhorse parades sponsored by the SPCA, and for 'the best and neatest handsome cab' (won by Mr H. Talmadge and his mare, Kate), in which all the competitors, accustomed to London traffic, stopped dead as soon as they were lined up nose to tail under the electric lights. Derry and Toms won the light trade turnout class, beating Harrods into second place, while W. H. Smith and Sons had the best London vanner, a sturdy grey. There was even a class for costers such as Mr Leon Williams of Whitechapel, who wore a jacket with 2,000 pearly buttons stitched on in coils and stars, and was accompanied by his donkey. Lonsdale, out and about in his frock coat, brandished a gold-topped walking stick, gave out cigars to the costers and 'engaged' a Pearly Queen 'in the traditional embrace', according to R. S. Summerhays.

Best treat of all were the 'diminutive Dianas on equally diminutive steeds [who] wrestled valorously for silver rose bowls and cups'. 'No class, perhaps, pleased the audience or puzzled the judges more than that for boys' and girls' hunter under 15.1 — the entries varying from a 13-hand child's pony to a comparatively bigger hunter,' wrote *The Times* correspondent. 'Great was the competition among the daughters of Nimrod, the desire for first prize being coupled by an equally ardent desire to "beat the boys"; but in the end the boys, or rather their ponies, for the honours of horsemanship were equally divided between the sexes, gained the day.'

Pen-y-lan Perfection and fourteen-year-old Helen Preece 'skimmed over the formidable railway gates as if they had been hurdles, evoking the wildest enthusiasm from the audience', and took third place. Miss Preece's riding was judged 'beyond all praise'; the teenager seemed, to the newspaperman, 'on the happiest of terms with her numerous mounts'. Her little sister Maude, at the age of six the youngest competitor at Olympia, had a hairy moment when The Mouse bolted down one of the backstage corridors and had to be headed off by an official, but she took fourth place in her class all the same.

In the ridden classes, every girl but one rode cross-saddle, wearing long coats over their breeches, although the *Times* man sucked his teeth at 'the fancy tricorn hats and "cavalier" cloaks devised by one or two fond mamas'. Another little girl, Miss Mills, drove Mr Winan's Shetland Tiny, 'perhaps the smallest pony in the country that has ever been in harness', in 'the smallest of miniature phaetons' with a six-year-old boy riding as tiger on the back. This child's 'importance and solemnity were beautiful to behold, his composure being scarcely ruffled even when Tiny, carriage, and driver turned over into a large flower-bed and had to be lifted bodily out of it by two attendants'.

Women and girls overflowed the thirteen classes that were restricted to their sex and competed without qualm in open competitions. Even the jumping classes fielded a handful of women, who were 'to be seen riding over a very stiff course with a dash and judgment that did credit alike to their horsemanship and their pluck'.

When the change came, it came swiftly and earlier in Britain than anywhere else in the world. The women and girls who crammed the classes at Olympia were also pouring onto the hunting field. In some cases their numbers doubled, as ladies who had broken into hunting in the late nineteenth century now introduced their daughters to the chase. During the First World War women took over the running of some packs of hounds when their husbands or brothers went to the front, many of them stowing away their side-saddles in the attic.

In 1914, before hostilities broke out, King George V had still refused to contemplate allowing any women to ride astride at Olympia, and the Kaiser had gone so far as to forbid the wives of his officers to mount cross-saddle. However, it was not long before British women were doing their bit for the war effort by training and exercising army remounts, which, of course, could not be done side-saddle. The debate about the use of side-saddles went to ground for a while, only to resurface when the war was over, when *The Times* picked it up again. It became a hotly contested subject for editorials and several bouts of written correspondence, right up until the 1940s, although it played out diminuendo.

'It must be quite twenty years ago that the wife of a well-known R.A. electrified Exmoor by appearing astride at a meet of the Devon and Somerset, an innovation which furnished the illustrated papers with material for many criticisms and witticisms,' commented one editorial. This lady had asked Mrs Alice Hayes's husband for advice on the appropriate cross-saddle for a lady, to Mrs Hayes's distaste, but now *The Horsewoman* seemed out of date. 'Other days, other ways,' said *The Times*; 'after five years of war it would take something very startling in the way of feminine costume to arouse comment even on Exmoor . . . We may expect to see a very strong cross-saddle contingent with the Devon and Somerset this winter.'

In 1922, Marjorie Bullows became the first adult woman to enter the ring at Olympia riding astride, and two years later she achieved the first clear round by a lady rider. Even Nannie Power O'Donoghue, now in her late seventies, allowed that perhaps a slim young girl might be able to sit a cross-saddle with dignity. Ivy Maddison in *Riding Astride for Girls*, published in 1923, made mock of the lace-antimacassar proprieties of the ladies, saying, 'Twenty years ago a girl who rode astride was looked on as a hoydenish creature with a shocking lack of modesty whose only reason for adopting this style must be a desire to ape masculine ways and make herself duly conspicuous.'

Maude Cheape's daughter was the first woman to ride two winners at a single point-to-point meet. Eileen Joel won the Newmarket Town Plate in 1925, riding astride and leading home a field in which women were in the majority. One of those on her tail was Iris Rickaby, whose son, Lester Piggott, would accomplish as a professional jockey what his mother could not legally have done until the 1970s. The Masters of Hounds Association had to decree that women could compete only in ladies' point-to-points, such were the number of women who entered the open races and threatened to beat men. It was not long before discarded side-saddles were to be seen, incongruous, on the backs of seaside donkeys, with holidaying children clutching the leaping heads.

'That the world is out of balance and lop-sided we know without being reminded of it by the side-saddle,' wrote Lord Brabazon of Tara in 1947, in the last throes of the side- versus cross-saddle debate. As women and girls began to right themselves in the horse world by sitting square in their saddle with a leg on each side, so a great reshaping of society was under way. The first wave of feminism brought victories and overturned the legislation that had kept women as second-class citizens. In 1918 all women over the age of thirty were granted the vote, cheered on by the suffragettes who in 1912 had been accompanied by a mare called Butterfly when they marched from Edinburgh to London. Ten years later, they had parity of voting with men.

Girlhood was changing too, as the efforts of nineteenth-century education reformers provided new opportunities for young women. Between 1901, the end of Victoria's reign, and 1920, the tally of girls who passed on to secondary education had increased ninefold. Middle-class girls who had worked as wartime nurses and VADs began to have ideas about careers, as well as thoughts of stenography jobs and bedsitters. A new, more literate, more modern and empowered girl was emerging, enjoying a similar curriculum to that of boys, although working-class girls still received an education that was inferior to that of their better-off sisters, a situation that would not change until after the Second World War.

The role of the horse was also being redefined, but while women's futures opened out, the horse's uses fell away. The later stages of the Great War had established the tank as a dominant force on the battlefield, rendering the cavalry horse obsolete, while motorized transport eventually superseded the draught horses that hauled artillery and supplies to the front. The motor car was eating up the life's work of the vanner, the cabber and the tradesman's horse.

Horse-drawn omnibuses were gone from London streets by 1911. Middle-class families replaced their all-purpose, ride-and-drive horses with cars and gave their stables over to garages. The coster's donkey was retired as working-class equine ownership declined, and the tradesmen horse exhibitors at Olympia would drop away year by year.

On farms, tractors were supplanting the great Shires, the Punches and the Clydesdales, while the canal horse's fate was sealed. However, it wasn't until 1954, in that year's *Pony Club Annual*, that Margaret Lang reported on one of the last trips taken around the Regent's Canal by a horse-drawn barge, gently drawn by Mary, whose tail was plaited and bundled up with bright-coloured wool. Similarly, the number of pit ponies below ground began to dwindle as they were gradually retired. Horses still worked on the railways as short-distance haulers of rolling stock, but their numbers, too, inevitably decreased. The last horse working on the railways retired as late as 1967, to a valedictory parade at the Horse of the Year Show and a new career opening fêtes.

The working horses no longer needed in the early decades of the twentieth century were packed into 'sausage boats', bound over the grey, roiling North Sea for the continent, where they arrived on the Belgian quays starved, unsteady and exhausted. Three months before Lonsdale's show opened at Olympia, the *Illustrated London News* had published pictures of gaunt, wild-eyed horses being pitched about the hold of a ship in a gale, and of their corpses being piled up by a crane, teeth bared in a rictus and hipbones poking through their hides. Those that survived the journey but could not make the long march to the abattoirs had their throats slit where they stood. Villagers closed their curtains as the sorry procession of worn-out nags stumbled by.

In 1911, an Englishwoman called Ada Cole was visiting her sister in a convent in Antwerp when she saw the horses. Appalled, she bought a camera to record the gruesome spectacle, and on her return to her cottage at Cley-next-the-Sea on the north Norfolk coast, she began to campaign for the wretched English horses to be well treated, or at least humanely slaughtered. In the war she served as a nurse in Belgium, only to be arrested and imprisoned as a spy by the Germans. She escaped Edith Cavell's fate before the firing squad to return to England and take up her fight for horses once more.

Ada founded what would become the International League for the Protection of Horses and under its auspices established a slaughter-house in Lincolnshire to persuade owners to spare their horses a last gruelling journey overseas. Among her supporters were Anna Sewell's nieces, Grace and Ada, the painter Alfred Munnings, and a host of cavalry officers who rallied, helping her to push for inquiries and for new legislation. The law stated that horses should undergo veterinary inspections both before boarding and on arrival, and if they were injured in a storm or fell ill they should be dispatched with a humane killer that was kept on board ship. Even so, when the Ministry of Agriculture was finally badgered into sending an inspec-tor to Belgium in 1921, their man was left 'filled with horror' at what he witnessed.

Ada spoke before an audience at the Albert Hall that year:

You can watch the end of these old horses; you can see it any week in Belgium. The horse is led into the yard, a man holds it by the halter, a butcher drives a knife into the horse's breast, he plunges, falls, struggles on to his feet and falls again. All this time the blood pours out. This goes on for some minutes; at last only his tail moves and he dies ... We cannot prevent the Belgians from killing their own horses in any way they please, but we will not condemn our own horses to a lingering, agonising death.

She made the voyage in the 'sausage boats' many times and covered miles on foot, pursuing the horses to their ends in the abattoirs.

The next decade saw legislation proposed and blocked, delayed or only partially imposed. It was never quite thorough enough to reach Ada's goal of prohibiting the live export of horses. She died in 1930 of exhaustion in the makeshift bedroom that she kept next to her office. In 1937 the Export of Horses Act was finally passed, forbidding the shipping of horses over the age of eight or of draught horses valued at less than £25. This turned out to be double-edged, as cheap horses were bred directly for slaughter in Ireland and the UK. The ILPH, now renamed World Horse Welfare and based in Snetterton in Norfolk, continues to campaign for a ban on the long-distance transport to slaughter in Europe. In Ada's memory the ILPH founded a home in South Mimms for retired horses that eventually came under the capacious aegis of Redwings Horse Sanctuary in 2005. Its earliest residents included an old warhorse who liked to listen to military music played on a gramophone in his field.

In the same year that Ada died, another Englishwoman dived into a hellish situation abroad and came out with a lead rope in her hand. Brigadier Geoffrey Brooke, who triumphed at Olympia in 1910 and was one of Ada Cole's supporters, was posted to Cairo in 1930 to take charge of the British cavalry in Egypt. In the streets of the city, his wife Dorothy found abandoned British war chargers – hunters and hacks in a distant dream life before 1914 – dragging wagons laden with stone and cereal, or being flogged to collapse between the shafts of carts. She launched an appeal in the *Morning Post* and received thousands of pounds by return of post, more than enough for her to found a hospital for the old horses. Some 5,000 of them ended their days at the Old War Horse Memorial, where, as Dorothy Brooke recorded in her diary, they found themselves, despite this strange hot land that had become their home, in an approximation of that distant dreamtime: where the stable floor was cushioned with bedding onto which they sank, where the manger was once more full of fodder and grooms bent over them to feed them from their own hands.

At its last gasp, the working horse had found an ally in womankind.

Young Riders

Some children have been cut off from contact with
ponies merely by reason of their parents never having owned
horses in their youth. They crave for a small four-footed
little beast which they can, in turn, fondle and ride, but fear
they might as well cry for the moon as to confide in Dad
and Mum that this is their heart's desire.

Pamela and her Pony 'Flash' (1936) by Antonio P. Fachiri

'I am quite aware that in these days when it is the fashion to be poor,
people think that they ought to be able to pick up a pony for their
child for a very few pounds,' sniffed the author of a 1931 *National Horse
Association Horse Owner's Guide*. As the working horse faded from the
scene, a newly affluent and leisured class emerged as horse owners
and riders. Most of the horses and ponies they purchased would not
turn a profit, nor serve any useful economic function beyond helping hay producers, farriers and vets earn a living, but these horse
owners were content to pour money into the mangers of their
animals with no expectation of financial return.

The new horse people were weekend riders. They paid for lessons
at the booming new suburban riding schools, kept horses at livery
yards and bought manuals like Hugh C. Pollard's *Hard Up on Pegasus* and
Mrs T. Howe's *Owner Groom: Horse Management for Amateurs*. They lived,
often, in what the authors of the 1930s ladies' hunting guide, *To Whom
the Goddess*, deplored as 'bungaloid towns' that encroached on hunting

country. They were middle class all, but of diverse stock. As the colonels and the majors took to tank driving instead of cavalry drill and fell from dominance in the horse world, the new riders were often female. Above all, it would be children who took to the saddle.

Children found themselves addressed directly by the foremost riding experts of the day in manuals such as Major Harry Faudel-Phillips's *The Child's Guide to Horse Knowledge*, or the now Major General Geoffrey Brooke's *Horsemen All*. The equestrian bibliographer Anne Grimshaw writes that between 1946 and 1959 more than a third of all riding books were aimed at children. By the 1960s, 50 per cent of the books on horses being issued in the UK had the word 'pony' in the title and were published for child readers.

These books were fairly comprehensive guides that offered a crash course in equestrianism from mounting to hunting, and endeavoured to give children a basic grounding in horse upkeep, although to the modern reader the advice can seem woefully skimpy. The authors disputed the advantages of the new forward seat versus the old-fashioned, lean-back-and-yank-'em style, and could not be relied upon to agree on the merits of Shetland ponies as mounts for very small children, but they all promoted horse riding as an invaluable source of fresh air and exercise. Major General Brooke drew on his own childhood to assure parents that 'horsemanship is but a healthy recreation: at the same time it helps to build up a child's character.' To his child readers, he expounded, 'As you grow older,' you will realize that each pony you have to ride, from the little one on which you started, to the proud animal that one day we hope you may possess, will teach you something.'

One of the most popular of these authors was Muriel Wace, née Maude, who took her pseudonym Golden Gorse from the memory of the bright-yellow flowers she saw on her first day of hunting as a child. 'In the old days there were plenty of people who knew the best way of buying and keeping a beginner's pony, and the things I write about were commonplaces in most country houses. Nowadays everyone knows about gears and throttles and brakes, but the knowledge of horses is a sealed book, except to a select minority,' she explained in the preface to *The Young Rider*. Wace was an evocative, straight-speaking writer with a knack – one lacking in some of the cavalrymen – of not talking down to a child.

Born in 1881, she was the youngest of five sisters who ran wild, to the dismay of the governesses appointed by their father, who had laid down a rule that all his daughters' lessons should be suspended if a hunt met in the neighbourhood. Once, the girls taught a heifer to be ridden and then to jump; shortly after, it leaped out of its field, followed by the rest of the herd. The sisters all rode astride in divided skirts and Wace was a lifelong advocate of the cross-saddle. As an adult she bought and broke in a small troop of Exmoor ponies – among which was the model for Moorland Mousie, hero of two of her novels – and taught six children to ride on them. 'A child who is happy on his pony's back has something which will be to him a glorious memory that the years cannot dim,' she wrote, with feeling. 'There is no greater pleasure in the world than riding a good horse.'

She recommended the native Exmoor pony as the ideal mount for any child: 'they make first-class children's ponies; they are full of quality, extraordinarily sound and sure-footed, they carry their heads high, which gives them balance, and they . . . are wonderfully sweet-tempered and affectionate . . . the two I am proud to possess will stand side by side in a stall, eating out of the same manger.' The mountain and moorland pony was an easy keeper who would live out on grass all year round – perfect for the amateur horse owner – and a reliable mount for a child who was beginning to ride. The pony found itself in demand, entering a golden age and coming into its own as a mount for the new crop of child riders. A series of national breed societies were established in the 1920s to improve the quality of Dartmoor, Exmoor, Highland and Fell ponies. Showing classes were added for native ponies so they could be judged on their own stout merits and not against polished 'blood' ponies.

Ponies might have been built to specification for the new children's fixture, the gymkhana. Their nippy speed, short stature and high intelligence – if controlled by their rider, this often a big 'if' – saw them dart between obstacles and come within a hair's breadth of the potato bucket before racing back down the course. The gymkhana had its origins in half-time entertainments at colonial polo matches, where grown-up men and women played oh-so-slightly risqué games of musical chairs or chased one another on horseback to snatch pennants. By the 1930s it had become the province of children harrying their mounts in and out of bending poles, or galloping as they carried hard-boiled eggs precariously balanced on spoons. Many of the games were adaptations of children's party favourites like apple ducking and sack races, but my mother's BHS *Guide to Mounted Games and Gymkhanas*, published in 1948, includes the rules for 'mock pig sticking' in which a rider dragged a stuffed sack covered with balloons behind his horse while children and ponies dashed after, stabbing at the balloons with sharpened canes. The author suggested a modest disclaimer: 'The Organiser does not accept any liability for any accident, damage, injury or illness to horses, owners, riders, spectators, ground, or any other person or property whatsoever.' Just as well.

In 1928 the Institute of the Horse decided to establish a number of local branches around Britain that would organize shows and other events for adults. Some of these sub-branches threw entertainments such as gymkhanas and paper chases for children and their ponies. It was becoming clear that children were in need of solid education in horsemanship; they could not be taught by grooms, as increasingly there were none, and once a pony had been purchased many parents stopped paying for lessons at riding schools. The schools were, in any case, of hugely variable quality. At the end of 1929 a junior branch of the Institute of the Horse was established, called the Pony Club, with the aim of 'interesting young people in riding and at the same time offering the opportunity of higher instruction in this direction than many of them can obtain individually'. It cost two shillings and six-pence to sign up, and most of the branches were linked to established hunts. Major Faudel-Phillips headed the central committee.

Two months later the Pony Club had 700 members, and within another year membership had risen more than sixfold to 4,442. Notwithstanding the shutdown between 1939 and 1945, member-ship continued to rise, and in 1947 there were 17,082 children re-cruited to 167 branches in the UK. The first overseas outpost of the Pony Club was founded in Gibraltar in 1930. In my yellowed, loose-spined copy of the 1953 *Pony Club Annual*, there's a black-and-white photograph of the Addis Ababa branch of the Pony Club: twenty-two ponies with children up in a rocky, semi-desert scene, with only a handful of them in sunhats and striped Pony Club ties. They met either at the British Embassy or at the Riding School of the Imperial Guard, and their number included Egyptian and Ethiopian children, as well as European, British and American. They managed fifteen rallies, two gymkhanas, two picnics and a paper chase in the winter of 1950-1 before the summer heat drove them indoors.

A genre of fiction for girls emerged from this new horsy landscape of gymkhana rosettes, Pony Club rallies and cheap ponies. They featured a heroine who started as an amateur and learned either from a manual or with the help of a kindly guide (often an old major). Her pony, a difficult thing at first, is soon won over with patience and kindness, and finally she wins the red ribbon that confirms that she has done right. These fictional heroines plumped out what lay between the lines in the riding manuals, and added the whisper of ambition.

In 1935, Enid Bagnold's most famous heroine, Velvet Brown, ap-peared on the scene in *National Velvet*, rejecting a future of housewifery and child-raising for the dream of coming first at Olympia and taking her pick from a stable of horses that are all hers. She tells the wealthy Mr Cellini of her love for horses, and he scrawls a will giving her all five of his own — Sir Pericles, Mrs James, George, Fancy and

Angelina – then shoots himself. The same day Velvet wins a runaway piebald horse called The Pie in a raffle. With the help of Mi, her father's odd jobsman with a shady past in horse racing, and her mother, who swam the Channel in her distant youth, Velvet does the unimaginable and rides The Pie to victory in the Grand National. I'd already been introduced to Little Women and the gangly, bookish Jo March, who sacrificed her hair so that her mother could travel to see her father in a military hospital; my new heroine Velvet cropped her fine white hair as a disguise so she could win a horse race. Velvet is only a butcher's daughter, funny-looking and prone to daydreams, and yet she foxes the gentlemen of the Jockey Club and outrides the greatest steeplechasing jockeys in the world.

Bagnold – herself a bold and awkward character – created a strange and beautiful book, using richer, more original language than most of the genre books that followed, and she drew on the realities of the horsy, gymkhana-filled childhood that she was providing for her own three children. Mi was loosely based on Bernard McHardy, an old jump jockey and drifter who looked after her children's ponies, and her own horse, a 'terrible piebald' who jumped anything in front of him, was called The Pie.

Joanna Cannan also raided her children's experiences when she wrote the prototype of the more conventional pony book, A Pony for Jean, the following year. Eleven-year-old Jean Leslie is granted Cannan's own dearest girlhood wish when she is given a pony, but it is a ribby and unpromising beast christened The Toastrack. It's up to Jean to overcome her own ignorance and clumsiness to transform the skinny wreck into Cavalier, who wins a rosette at a local show.

In 1934, nineteen-year-old Primrose Cumming published Doney, the story of a donkey, and used the money to buy herself a horse. She went on to write Silver Snaffles, the tale of a magical riding school where ponies can talk and take pains to teach children how to ride well. The heroine, Jenny, longs for a horse of her own, and one day she confides in Tattles, the carrier's pony, who speaks in a voice that 'was the sound of hoofs thudding on the turf, of bits jingling and saddles creaking and of a horse knickering to his friend, all mixed up and making words'. Tattles tells her to go through the door at the darkest corner of the stable, giving the password, 'Silver Snaffles'. There she finds a new Narnia, a 'pony paradise', where Tattles is transformed into his youthful self. At the Extraordinary Riding School she is taught to ride by Tattles and his friend Cock Robin. The baddies are the Yahoo-like Jostlepots, who roar around in motor cars, and are ignorant and cruel in their treatment of their poor pony, Pippin, whom Jenny must rescue. When she goes back through the stable corner to the real world, Jenny finds that her father has bought her a grey New Forest pony, and she calls him Silver Snaffles.

Cumming's contemporary, Sarah Bowes-Lyon, was all of twelve when she wrote and illustrated *Horsemanship as it is Today* for J. M. Dent, but she was pipped for the title of youngest author by Moyra Charlton, who was eleven years old when she completed *Tally Ho, the Story of an Irish Hunter*. They were followed in the next three decades by a string of teenage authors – Daphne Winstone, Lindsay Campbell, Gillian Baxter, Bernagh Brims, Shirley Faulkner-Horne, K. M. Peyton and April Jaffe.

Joanna Cannan had moved her own family from suburban Wimbledon to The Grove, a dower house in the Oxfordshire village of Peppard. There, her three daughters, Josephine and the twins, Diana and Christine, embarked on a thoroughly horsy childhood. The original Toastrack was an old polo pony mare named Countess; the girls sneaked out in the morning in their pyjamas and clambered on her, using a stepladder. They were gifted with an upbringing that combined English army phlegm (from their father, an infantry captain) and an almost bohemian eccentricity and literariness from Cannan, who had dreamed of free love and a career as a painter before falling in love. 'I don't care what you do as long as you're not non-entities,' she told her daughters.

In their joint memoir, *Fair Girls and Grey Horses*, the sisters take turns to tell their story, as they evolved, in their mother's words, into 'intrepid though unorthodox horsewomen' and horsebreakers to the neighbourhood pony owners. They exercised ponies for children who were away at boarding school, profiting from the great pony boom and gaining experience of a motley collection of mounts, for as Golden Gorse wrote in a preface to a 1942 edition of The Young Rider, 'Five children seem to be learning to ride to-day for one who was learning seven years ago.' The sisters earned pin money 'bringing on' difficult animals for a local dealer, and in 1940 opened their very own riding school. Their brother painted the sign: a grey horse's head against a black background.

They whitewashed stones and laid them out in one of the fields to make a manège, and bought a few ponies, including Melody, a Dartmoor mare who promptly gave birth to a foal they named Windfall, and a black Shetland called Angus that let the cat ride around on his back. Among the attendees were the three-year-old Aga Khan and a Guinness or two, although the sisters also ran 'scholarship' lessons for children whose parents were less well-off. When they were in their mid-teens, the girls jointly wrote their first pony book. It Began with Picotee by Josephine, Diana and Christine Pullein-Thompson was published in 1946. They went on to write over one hundred books between them, selling 11 million copies worldwide.

From the 1920s to the 1950s, many female role models still had a limited range and a woman's 'career' was expected to end in marriage, but the heroines of the books that sprang from this new pony culture – the Jills and Jackies in their patched-up jerseys and breeches that cost seven shillings and sixpence – rode on, leaping all the obstacles in their paths and succeeding through good sportsmanship. They had no time to be sappy and girly when they had to save the stables from ruin or rescue a stranded pony from the sandbank before the tide came in. There was nothing forcedly feminist about them either: they just got on with it. Most existed in the same cosy topography of non-specific, largely middle-class Englishness as Chalet School, Mallory Towers or the *Beano*, the realm that J. K. Rowling taps into when she gives Hogwarts a school song and a steam train. It was a world that both did and did not exist. You can sink into the plots and the atmosphere as you might into a welcoming sofa with a plate of hot, buttered toast balanced on its arm.

The ineluctable bond between girls and horses was now firmly established as a cultural reference point, giving us the image of the girl rider in a velvet hunt cap, tweed hacking jacket and jug-eared jodhpurs. Thelwell's cartoons of lumpy ponies and lumpier children ran into collection after collection for decades. As horses took their place in mass-market culture, a new real-life heroine was about to emerge who would confirm women's place in the horse world.

Lost Heroines

If the second phase of the Three-day Olympic Test of Horse and
Rider is too much for girls to undertake, then I would like to
know why we dropped them behind the enemy lines in wartime.

They've Won Their Spurs (1956) by Hylton Cleaver

Next morning I looked round the Harringay course and
scrutinised the teams. They were mostly men. At that moment
there came a sudden glow of determination that no man should
beat me that day. Tosca, the grey mare, was magnificent. We
pulled off the Lonsdale Cup, the Prix Caprilli and the BSJA Spurs.

Jump for Joy (1954) by Pat Smythe

In a chest of drawers in the spare room at my grandparents' home,
Greenacres, I found an illustrated book of fairy tales featuring
princesses with bulbous sleeves and hand-span waists, and three plain
hardbacks that had belonged to my mother, their covers roughed to
hessian, their dust jackets long gone. They were called *Jump for Joy*, *One
Jump Ahead* and *Bred to Jump*. Every twenty-five or so pages there were
plates: black-and-white glossy images of a woman with dark lipstick
and neat curled hair, at an ivy-covered house in the Cotswolds, on a
camel in a desert, walking barefoot on a beach, posing before an oil
painting of Napoleon in Paris and, most of all, on horses. The horses
were usually caught with their forelegs and hind legs snatched up to

clear some monstrous fence, as high as a man and as wide as a car, their ears pricked, and their rider in her black jacket and hitched-up, loose white jodhpurs leaned forward over the buttons of their plaited manes, her eyes fixed on the next obstacle.

In *One Jump Ahead* there's a shot of a prize ceremony at night, where the horses' sweat-dried coats look like watered silk in the flash: she's on the left, holding her whip upright in victory salute, on an alarmed-looking chestnut with two nosebands – Prince Hal – and the white of his eye on the photographer. To her right are three glum male riders in red jackets, velvet hats doffed and lowered to one thigh in defeat. The caption reads: 'At Algiers with Jonquères d'Oriola [Olympic gold medallist] on Voulette, Paco Goyoaga [world champion] on Fahnenkonig, and Hans Winkler [five-times Olympic gold winner].'

And again, 'Tosca falling at Nice': a dapple-grey mare plunges down the face of an earthwork some eight feet high, her body wrenched and hind legs skewed wildly up to clear the top of the bank. The rider is thrown up out of her saddle, coat-tails flying, toes pointed down in her stirrups, but her hands still sparing the mare's mouth.

Pat Smythe had two backbones and a heart that did not know what it could not do. For me, she was bound up with the heroes and heroines of my grandparents' post-war paperbacks: Airey Neave in *Escape from Colditz*, Churchill himself in the *Young Winston's Adventures* and Jackie Sorour, who flew a Spitfire in *Woman Pilot*. Pat Smythe competed at the highest level for over sixteen years between 1947 and 1963, travelling the world and becoming the first international show-jumping superstar. She was British National Ladies' Champion eight times, European Ladies' Champion four times and thrice Sportswoman of the Year: a record-breaker who decorated her Cotswolds home, Miserden, with strings of new rosettes every Christmas. In total, she scored more Grands Prix in more countries than any rider before or since. 'Everyone wanted to be Pat Smythe,' the television presenter Anne Robinson once said, talking of her own childhood in 1950s Britain. My mother dreamed of living at Miserden.

When the Costessey riding school closed, my mother found out that Pat's old groom and right-hand woman ran another establishment in Cringleford, at the other side of Norwich, and took me there for lessons. Paula Sykes did not teach but she lived at the edge of one of the fields in a mobile home. We all knew her by sight, and that she'd mended the broken stifle of the brown gelding, Dominic, with comfrey when a lady drove into him outside Cringleford Post Office. Paula would have been in her sixties then. I had never spoken to her, let alone asked her about her old boss, so now I arranged to meet to talk about Prince Hal and Tosca and Pat.

On a rainy Norfolk winter's evening, I sat with Paula, in her cosy, low-ceilinged sitting room, in which I loomed but which seemed the right height for her. She couldn't have been more than a few inches over five feet, but powerfully built despite a stiff, arthritic hip, which she rolled on painfully. There was a sofa and one chair for each of the dogs: a boxer bitch and her black daughter (the result of an unplanned liaison with Paula's sister's Labrador), who were hard-muscled and as close-coated as otters. A little tortoiseshell cat with white feet solicited a chin rub from me, then jumped onto the arm of Paula's chair, on guard, and watched me. A second, poofy, pale-ginger cat stalked through and decided to opt out of the interview.

A shaggy brown-and-orange rug lay in front of an electric fire with dusty plastic coals. There was a television, shelves of books, horsy board games, copies of *Classic FM Magazine* and *Horse and Hound*, Christmas cards of ponies in the snow and frames full of images of six decades of horses. I recognized a pencil sketch of Dominic with a bay called Flimsy, Pegasus about to touch down over a cross-country fence, and Woody at a show with his owner riding sidesaddle. Woody had been saved as a weanling from the local sales by the Horse Rescue Fund, and delivered into the care of Paula and her friend Donna; I remembered his chestnut face and white neck extending over his loose-box door. Rosettes were strung across the windows, unfaded: pink, blue, red, green, yellow. Over the fireplace hung a painting of a cavalcade of horses and ponies spilling across a landscape.

Paula, undaunted by the gammy hip and refusing help, fetched mugs of tea and old photographs to show me. She had a dark grey bob, with curls pushed back from her face; her nose was strong, her eyes bright blue under swooping eyebrows. She looked stern, but as she talked she could giggle like a girl, and sometimes seemed caught up and shy. She wore slacks and a navy-blue sweatshirt with a 2012 Equestrian Olympics supporter's logo.

Paula didn't intend to work with horses. 'My father was in the Royal Artillery in the war – the First World War – and he loved horses, but I didn't have much experience with them. I had an aunt in Nottinghamshire and I'd go and stay there in my holidays, and she'd send me out on my own on a pony. I knew nothing about horses! I didn't know how to put a bridle on. I didn't know what to put on either end!' Her voice peaked with incredulity. 'But I got keen,' she added quickly.

After school she spent six months working at a riding school in Bedford, where she was regularly sent out in charge of a string of twenty-five riders and ponies. 'I really . . . I mean, I was really not fit to do that!' she laughed and her eyebrows shot up. 'Nothing happened, but I worked jolly hard and did everything. Then I did a course and a BHS exam at Aylesbury at another riding school. I was there for six months and when I looked for a job, the first one I saw was Pat's mother, Monica, advertising.'

After the early death of Pat's father, Mrs Smythe had moved sixteen-year-old Pat and her older brother Ronald from Richmond to Miserden House, offering riding holidays for foreign children eager to learn English.

'She was from a good family, a wealthy family, but they'd fallen on hard times,' explained Paula. 'She became a good businesswoman. There were no flies on Pat's mother. She just got on with it. She was quite a strong personality. I went up to London to meet her before I went for the job and I was a bit overawed by her.'

Monica, herself a fearless, skilled rider who'd broken in polo ponies, encouraged her daughter from the start. From the age of eleven onwards Pat had financed her own entry fees as well as transport to and from shows, saving a pound a week from her winnings so that she could go on competing. In 1947, now eighteen and fresh out of school, she went to White City for the International Horse Show with Finality, a little mare whose dam had drawn a milk-cart. They won their first class. She was immediately selected to join the British team in overseas competitions.

Despite the enthusiasm of the crowds for the international riders and for Brigadier Brooke at Olympia in 1910, Britain had not excelled at showjumping in the 1920s and 1930s. The competitions were lacklustre, the rules higgledy-piggledy, varying from event to event, and most spectators were bored stupid. Michael Williams – father of the commentator Dorian Williams and a founder member of the British Show Jumping Association – was withering about those early days: 'At that stage there was no time element in our national competitions, which, by comparison with those on the Continent, were dull and monotonous, not say endless, with horse after horse sauntering round the outskirts of the ring over a handful of fences all looking very similar.'

The groundwork for the new British showjumping scene had been drafted in 1942 in POW camp Oflag IX A/H, Spannenburg, when three British officers who had represented their nation at showjumping before they went to war – Colonel Mike Ansell, Bede Cameron and Nat Kindersley – came up with the blueprint for success. There would be greater professionalism in training and in the design of courses, time limits to keep up the pace of the competition and better fences. Showjumping became more regulated, leaner, more audience-friendly, more dramatic and less amateurish. Britain joined the circuit where continental Europe was already established, sending more riders overseas to participate.

They got speedy results: the all-male British team took bronze at the 1948 London Olympics, despite never having been closer than seventh before. Women were not allowed to compete.

On her first overseas trip with the British team in 1947, Pat was the only member of the team to jump a clear round in the Grand Prix at Brussels. Between classes she took a glass of champagne in the members' tent, sitting on a pile of stretchers. Someone commented, 'Hope you're not on that stretcher tonight.' She drained her glass, retouched her lipstick and went to fetch Finality for the speed competition. 'Final' jumped like a deer until the last, where, disoriented by the setting sun ahead of her, she somersaulted over, knocking Pat out cold. She came to lying in bed, stripped to her school shirt and knickers, with her male fellow team members standing round waiting anxiously to see if she was all right before, to her mortification, bursting into laughter.

Pat was still chiefly her own groom, with back-up from her mother, but it was becoming apparent that they needed help, and so Paula, or 'Paul' as she was known, was hired. Paula was eighteen and Pat a scant few years older. After six months of looking after the riding-holiday ponies, Paula became Pat's full-time groom when her career took off in 1949, and she was named Showjumper of the Year at the first Horse of the Year Show.

Later that year Pat returned to Brussels to take the Grand Prix on Nobbler, a horse that a friend had just fetched out of the field. The d'Inzeo brothers of Italy and Paco Goyoaga of Spain ransacked the rule book, searching for a hidden clause that would eliminate Pat for being female. Dorian Williams reckons that it was this year that she became 'the most popular lady rider in the world'. 'Here was a girl who had started with nothing,' he wrote, 'who had had none of the advantages or opportunities of wealth, but who could hold her own with the greatest and the wealthiest in the world.' She was twenty-one.

Showjumping was a natural choice for early television schedules, as it was easy to follow for audiences, many of whom were part of the new wave of horse owners. Its popularity exploded as the sport captured the imagination of the British public, whether horsy or not. Pat was the perfect heroine on this new stage. In 1950 at Harringay she duelled with Colonel Harry Llewellyn on his giant Foxhunter, the stand-off that converted the telly-watching British public to showjumping aficionados overnight. As the fences rose in successive jump-offs, the audience often could not even see Finality and her rider behind them. Eventually the colonel and the young woman shook hands to call a truce, to tumultuous applause.

Pat's incredible momentum faltered only once in the fifties, when her mother was killed in a car crash on a snowy Cotswold road in 1952. That afternoon her bank manager telephoned to say that he had heard about Monica's death, and that her overdraft of £1,500 must be repaid immediately. Family and friends rallied to encourage Pat to go on showjumping in memory of her mother, although she had to sell her best horse to placate the bank.

When Pat had begun competing, women were ineligible not only for the Nation's Cup but also for the Olympic showjumping and three-day eventing disciplines. Arriving in Madrid for the 1954 World Championships, she discovered that 'apparently some international rule had been passed', banning women from competing. The sport was still dominated by ex-military men, who became friends, rivals and obstructions. 'We used to call them "the Colonels",' said Paula. 'The women were outnumbered really, quite a bit.' When Pat won the Grand Prix Militaire in Lucerne in 1956, she had to cede the trophy to the French officer who came third. Although she touched only two of 275 fences on Flanagan, Hal and Scorchin that week, scoring more points than any other rider, she was not allowed to be leading rider of the show, only the leading lady.

An astute publisher signed Pat to write accounts of her travels overseas and to produce a series of novels for children, called The Three Jays. She turned out eleven books in four years. Their success gave her financial security for the first time and offered a behind-the-scenes glimpse to her youngest fans.

'Now if you are aspiring to be a Pat Smythe or a Harry Llewellyn, you have today the advantage of learning your initial training through the Pony Club,' wrote the president of the Institute of the Horse, now the British Horse Society, in its 1954 annual. 'At the same time, let us never forget that the Pony Club was initially founded to teach the young foxhunter the care of his hunter and how to comport himself in the hunting field. In these days, when the emphasis is on budding show jumpers . . . remember that foxhunting, if it is to go on, must depend for its recruits on the members of the Pony Club.' Too late. Why aspire to be Lady So-and-So of the Pytchley when you could be Pat Smythe?

Off duty, she threw herself into the travelling that the circuit afforded her, crossing Europe crammed into a 2CV with three other riders, taking her turn at bullfighting in Spain and cow-poking in Texas. She saw in her twenty-first in Paris, watching Josephine Baker perform at the Folies Bergères; at twenty-two she was dining with the Duke and Duchess of Windsor; she shook hands with Franco, had a police escort through Manhattan and was ushered into an audience with the Pope, where she could not curtsey because her leg was stitched up following the catastrophic fall over a bank in Nice, when poor Tosca had trodden on her and ripped her thigh open.

Paula frowned when I asked her what Pat was like. 'I remember laughter. She was not a sad person. She was a good mixer, she got on with everybody and you know, you'd get a bit of jealousy sometimes, from other women and grooms, but she got on with most people. She never said a nasty word about anybody. She never did. She was brought up properly. She just didn't do it.' Paula shook her head. 'I don't remember her ever blowing her top or having a fit. She was very sensible, very equable. She didn't swear, and she was very philosophical.'

Paula made nearly every trip with Pat for fourteen years. The logistics were considerable. Saddles, bridles, martingales, numnahs and saddle cloths, spares (one horse, Flanagan, once ate his martingale), grooming gear, fodder and hay for a week, buckets, first aid for horses and humans, cornflakes, coffee, tea, cutlery, a kettle, bacon, sugar, linseed oil, boots for horses, boots for human, whips, make-up, nylons, pyjamas, a day dress, a smart hat, a riding hat, studs for the horses' shoes, gas for cooking, crockery and bedding for humans as they slept in the box, rugs and sheets for the horses, breeches, jackets, blouses, stocks, spare stocks, books, spurs, extra breeches, a nice cocktail outfit for Pat, hay nets, some court shoes and the earrings that Paula told me she was always losing in the straw of the cattle truck they first used for transporting the horses. In the summer there were as many as four shows to attend in a week.

'At one time in the early fifties there weren't so many female grooms, and when we went to the continent, more often than not I was the only girl.'

Paula frequently won the groom's prize. Pat called her a 'pioneer' and warned the girls who clamoured for a job at Miserden that they would have to have huge reserves of strength.

'I had to learn a bit of several languages to get on because I was the only English person there sometimes. Pat liked jumping abroad so we went quite a lot. Some German, French, Spanish, Italian . . . I've got cuttings from all over the place just sitting in boxes on top of the wardrobe, been there for forty-five years!' Paula gestured towards her bedroom door. 'I meant to make scrapbooks but I didn't have the time.'

You couldn't take horseboxes overseas at first. The show would pay your transport from port of entry, and the horses would be shipped across Europe by train and boat. From the Cotswolds, Pat's horses went to Davos, to jump on a frozen lake, to Algiers before the 1961 coup, to Sicily, to Stockholm, to West Berlin in a sealed carriage, and across the Atlantic by aeroplane or ship to the USA and Canada. Paula went with them, usually alone.

'We used to go down to Folkestone in the horsebox and once you got to Boulogne the trains were waiting, with wagons that were like the ones you saw in *Schindler's List*, with a door at either side so it could be quite draughty. They had a stencil on the side saying they were for eight horses or forty men. You put two horses in there, and built a partition with poles and ropes that you brought, and then I'd have all my stuff and my bed on the other side. You only travelled at night and you were in the sidings by day. Once we were held up at the Italian frontier for two days in the snow-covered mountains, and I had to melt ice to give my horses water.'

A train returning from the tip of Italy to France would shed wagons along the way, as horses and grooms were shunted to other trains going back to Germany, Switzerland or Holland. In the marshalling yards the wagons would be rolled one at a time down a track to the points and redirected to their next train, coasting till they hit the couplings at the back of it.

'It was fairly hair-raising at night. You could hear the bangs as the wagons hit on the other lines, and the horses seemed to brace themselves. You got a bit more force and then, all of a sudden, bang into another wagon.'

Usually she was the only woman travelling. Once she shared a train with the Turkish army team grooms.

'They were the most odd people,' Paula said, pulling a face. At the underground marshalling yard in Turin, one of them tried to get into the wagon. 'You could fix the door so that it was open a gap, but you couldn't lock it from the inside.' She was woken by a snort from Flanagan. 'All of a sudden this Turkish chap was there. Just as he was trying to get in, the train started to move and he was stuck on the outside. That was scary!' She laughed but cringed too, making both the dogs look up. 'Not that they were savages, you know, but I was stuck with him till we got somewhere where he could get off. But he wanted to get in, you see. The horses were standing there, looking, and I thought, thank God I roped the doorway.' After that incident, she carried a knife.

At sea, the horses travelled in narrow crates on the deck. Paula had to crawl in through a little door to give them massages every day and keep up their circulation. On one trip back from the States, she opened the hatch to push in a bucket of food for Flanagan, but instead of finding his chestnut nose and long, mobile upper lip, she found the end of his tail. He'd managed to turn himself right round. She shut the hatch. Later, she returned and the bucket was empty, the nose in search of more food.

'Pat gave this to me.' From somewhere in the shelving unit behind the telly, Paula dug out a silver trophy like a flattened square gramophone horn, dappled with tarnish. 'It came from a "gambler competition" where each fence has a value and you pick your own course. Flanagan was the first horse to score over a thousand,' she rubbed at the tarnish, 'there, 1,030 points.' She fished a scrap of paper out of the trumpet. 'Pat wrote, "Flanagan's great mathematical feat!" He was a sweetie, he really was. And here's a picture of him at Hickstead in 1962 – he ate his way through his laurel leaves. He bit it in half!

'That's me with Tosca and Hal in the yard at Miserden,' said Paula, pointing to a large framed photograph. It was a black-and-white portrait of herself in blouse, tie and cardigan, between a dapple-grey mare, her head raised and eyes on someone behind the camera, and a liver-chestnut thoroughbred, watching the same person.

'She looks bigger there, doesn't she, the grey? He was bigger than her and an ex-racehorse. Pat didn't pay an awful lot for him. He came third in the Kim Muir Chase at Cheltenham and that's where Pat saw him. He had broken down – he was fired on one tendon but that never caused him any bother. And he jumped the record height at Brussels indoors: that was seven feet, four and one-twelfth inches. He was the first horse to win £1,000 in a single competition. That was in Paris. It was unheard of to win that much money. I've got a picture of him jumping the puissance wall in Paris . . . I don't know where it is.'

For a moment I thought she would take off and vanish into the wardrobe full of clippings to seek it out.

Pat didn't pay more than £150 for either the part-Connemara Tosca nor Prince Hal. Tosca, says Paula, was 'a jumping machine'.

'One year, I think it was 1955, she only touched twelve fences in a year. And at Brighton once she cleared 200 jumps in five days. Pat had a very good eye for horses – she bought horses that hadn't done anything particularly and had success with them. She was just really good at it. And she loved it. And she never abused her horses in any way, like some of them used to. Some of the people who were in it for money weren't very nice at all. You'd see the poles hanging under their horseboxes covered with hedgehog skin for rapping the horses' legs as they jumped. And she never, *ever* did anything like that.'

In 1953 the British team were among the earliest to fly their competition horses across the Atlantic. Paula was on board the plane when Bill Hanson's The Monarch panicked and began lashing out, trying to smash the sides of his crate and narrowly missing Hal's head, which Paula struggled to hold clear. An injection of morphia made him worse. 'There was talk about having to shoot him, but we were able to turn back.' The horses had to be fed carrots on take-off and landing, for their ears. In New York, Hal and Pat carried all before them at the Pennsylvania Horse Show in Harrisburg, unbeaten in every class they entered. 'One Girl Defeats All the Americans!' shouted a British headline. Five boxes of fan mail waited at home.

Though Pat depended on Paula absolutely for support with the horses, neither of them could have kept the army on road and rail without Pat's second backbone, Paddy Bury. By the time Paddy was thirty-seven she had worked as a kennelmaid, housekeeper, secretary and an ambulance driver in the ATS, but still felt as though she hadn't found her place in the world. After reading a serialization of one of Pat's books, Jump for Joy, in the Liverpool Daily Post, she sat down without further thought and wrote to ask Pat if she needed a secretary. She posted the letter and then felt like a fool, but a little while later she was surprised to receive a letter from Pat, followed by an invitation to visit Miserden. Paddy joined the team, holding the reins at home, and would work for Pat for the next forty years.

I saw Paddy Bury a few weeks later on a blue-skied December day in the frost-covered Cotswolds hills, the inverse of gloomy, wet, flat Norfolk. Rugged-up horses from the Cirencester Polo Club breathed steam in the silver-green fields near Sudgrove, where Pat had moved in 1962 and where Paddy still lived. Her front room was the size of a biscuit tin, bright and white in the winter sun, filled with furniture and a lifetime's accumulation of objects and framed photos, but so orderly that they did not overwhelm the tiny space. Tea came in a cup on a saucer. Paddy sat in a corner throne in a fawn cardigan, her steel-grey bob caught back with a kirby grip. She was slighter and older than Paula, at ninety-one, but redoubtable, eyes sharp. Pat's two daughters, Lucy and Monica, with tight brown curls and thickly knitted jumpers, sat by the fireplace on little stools. Together we asked Paddy for stories about their mother.

'In those days, "Pat Smythe, England" was enough of an address,' remembered Paddy. One fan from Preston went to as many of Pat's shows as she could. The fan mail came by the boxful: handmade place mats from the forces in Malaysia, hoping for a photo of Pat without a horse; letters by the score from teenage girls who wanted to work at Miserden. In Paris they called her 'l'anglaise avec l'oeillet blanc', as she always had a white carnation in her buttonhole. This was provided for every show she attended, home or abroad, by one gentleman fan.

Paddy produced a file of clippings in plastic covers and flipped through photos of the horses. 'Hello, old friend,' she greeted Flanagan, before finding a headline, BABY OF THE YEAR, from the cover of IllustratedWeek in 1957: Pat in a full-skirted, blue-and-white print dress in a stable with Tosca and her first foal, Lucia, so newborn that her black coat was still sticky. The press, I was given to understand, had been fascinated by Pat.

The press badgered her for details of her love life and when she would marry. Pat admitted to having received 'five dashing proposals in four languages' but wanted to wait for 'a relationship more vital to me than anything [that had] gone before'. Journalists camped outside a hospital while she recovered from concussion inside, hoping to uncover a romance with her host, Lord Belper. Paula had to smuggle her out. In the throes of the Cold War, the Russian showjumping coach tried to persuade Pat to marry one of his team and defect, so that she might be provided with all the best horses and training facilities. She declined graciously.

Another sliver of yellowed newsprint read LOVE AT FIRST SIGHT. 'Did you ever see his eyes?' Pat asks the reporter, of Hal. 'Take a look into them.'

'Yes,' Lucy said, 'Hal was Mummy's great love.' I peered at the article, whose author was overcome with the romance of it. 'Only she can ride him. He'd be a lost child without her.'

'Her greatest sorrow was that he was never chosen for the Olympics,' said Paddy, eyes owlish behind her glasses.

I'd read that the British team coach, Colonel Jack Talbot Ponsonby, had taken a dislike to Hal, calling him a broken-down old racehorse and suggesting that he was likely to refuse, which would have knocked the entire team out of the competition.

'Not Hal!' Lucy, Monica and Paddy chorused, and Paddy waved two fingers à la Harvey Smith to ward off the thought of Ponsonby.

'It wasn't until 1956 that women were allowed to ride in the showjumping at the Olympics,' Paula clarified for me when I saw her again. 'And in 1952 they asked Pat if they could borrow Hal for either Peter Robeson or one of the others to ride. So he went to Ascot and was in training for the games, and they all tried him, but he was a very sensitive horse, really sensitive, and he'd not been showjumped by a man before and he was too bold. They couldn't ride him. Peter couldn't ride him and neither could General Blacker, so they said we could have him back. The Olympic team came to Badminton to compete and give a demonstration, and we were going to take Hal back from there. And when we saw him,' she trailed off, remembering the old horse, 'he looked so poor.' Her voice dropped. 'He wasn't really happy at all. He'd lost weight; he was really miserable. We don't know what they did with him. There were two showjumping classes, and Pat put him in one and he promptly won it!' Her voice switched to delight. 'Just like that! And the Olympic team were all astonished. He was so pleased to have her on his back he jumped out of his skin.'

The British team took gold without Hal.

When Pat became the first woman to ride into the Olympic show-jumping ring at Stockholm, to rapturous applause, she was mounted on Flanagan, with his broad blaze, comical face and thick Irish neck. He wasn't the right shape of animal to clear the massive fences, nor had he the stride that would have chimed sweetest with the distances between the obstacles. However, he attacked the course with gusto and made a solid contribution to the team's bronze medal. At an international competition held at Stockholm over the Olympic fences immediately afterwards, Prince Hal beat all the medallists.

'That was one in the eye for them. It was a bit of a laugh!' giggled Paula, although the colonels, it seems, did not have the chance to make amends, as Hal died suddenly in 1957.

'That was dreadful,' said Paddy, sadly. 'He wasn't well and he went to hospital in Newmarket. Pat and Paula were in America and there wasn't much communication in those days. I had to call and leave a message.'

That night, Pat came second, and as she wept during the presentation ceremony people thought it was because she had lost.

'He was a lovely horse,' said Paula, miles away. 'A lovely horse.'

'Mum wasn't glamorous. That wasn't a word she would have associated with,' insisted Lucy. 'But it was important for her to be well turned out, and feminine, and to be taking on the boys. She wanted to prove herself as a woman in a man's world. She was determined, quite a forceful character, and she had a devoted team behind her. I remember learning that she'd fallen once and broken her collarbone, but got back on and completed the course. I asked Paddy how she did it, and Paddy said, "Sheer determination, my dear."'

Paddy smiled and nodded. 'Sheer bloody determination.'

We turned up a photo of Pat jumping bareheaded. 'She didn't care if she had a hat on or not!'

Paddy had a clipping from the *New Zealand Herald* with a laundry list of injuries Pat had sustained: numerous black eyes, a dislocated thumb wrenched by the reins, assorted 'black arms and legs' from being trampled, tip of tongue bitten off, a gashed nose, a gashed thigh, multiple concussions, a back badly bruised too many times.

'I think that she used her marriage and the move to Switzerland as a bit of a cover story when she retired, although it was true,' Lucy said.

Pat's back and hips were so bad at that stage that she couldn't keep up the punishing regimen of the showjumping circuit. She had both hip joints replaced in her late thirties to combat crippling rheumatoid arthritis. Much later, she discovered that she had a rare, congenital heart disorder; had she been diagnosed as a child, she would probably never have been a showjumper.

In 1963 she married Lucy and Monica's father, the former Swiss Olympic three-day eventer Sam Koechlin. Pat wore lace that had been her prize in the ladies' championship at St Gallen in 1960. Paddy led the press on a wild-goose chase and Paula brought Flanagan to the reception with a top hat wedged between his ears and a white carnation tucked in his headcollar. Paddy stayed on to keep the English side of Pat's life on track; Paula made plans to move to Norfolk and open her own riding school in the suburb of Cringleford. While Pat was on honeymoon, Flanagan came to stay at Cringleford in the box that would later be occupied by Woody. Paddy showed me a ledger Pat had kept of competition results, which began with Flanagan in Algiers and petered out in 1967, with Tosca's children and grandchildren winning at local shows.

'She was at the peak of things,' Paddy told me as I left her at the door of her cottage, her eyes screwed up against the sun. 'She was a one-off really, because it was the beginning of it all.'

I steadied him and he cantered, then trotted then walked. Soon we were in the winners enclosure. I dismounted and unsaddled my horses. As I pushed my way through the crowds I turned to see my horse wheeling high above the crowds resplendant in his blue winne -rs rug and wreath. He whinnyed and I smiled. Because there was no horse on this earth who could beat him, except his brother Shêtan...........

Housework

I am eleven and would like to help out and learn
more about stable management within a two-mile radius of
my village. I have been riding for almost seven years
and could exercise at weekends.

Advert placed by Susanna Forrest in *Horse and Pony's*
Work for Rides column (1988)

I loved Paula's riding school in Cringleford and stayed there for
years. It lay tucked away at the end of a loke that branched away
from a long, solid row of semi-detached houses with pampas grass
in their front beds and two cars on the driveways. The lane was un-
metalled and potholed, running alongside the riding school's fields,
which reached down to the River Yare, hemmed in by hawthorn
hedges and the occasional ditch. The ungainly, hapless gelding Jasper
once sank up to his neck in one of these and had to be heaved out by
the fire brigade.

The yard had none of the weird isolation of the model stables in
Costessey, but was large and busy. There was a line of breezeblock
loose boxes, including the one where Flanagan had boarded, and
numerous later additions of weatherboard-faced stables arranged
roughly in a square around the central yard. Here, Muscovy ducks
with raw pink crops guddled in the mud-edged pools and sorrel
chickens scattered at the approach of the cockerel, running for cover
into one of the hay stores tucked behind a corner loose box.

There were crannies to explore, where you might turn up something like old, curly-coated Noddy in a box by the dingy feedroom, or fawn-coloured eggs still warm in the mess of straw shaken loose behind the bales, or a tiny steel-grey pony mare who hadn't been there the week before. Sometimes the accretion of boxes could look ragtag – the paint too chipped, the mud starting too near to the door, a gap in the tar-paper roof – but the horses all bloomed, their sides round, their coats soft, their eyes lustrous. There must have been twenty or thirty of them, from the piebald Shetland, Tommy Tucker, who occasionally got down and rolled with a child still on board, to the liveries' smart competition horses like Pegasus and Flimsy, who lived in a row of loose boxes on a raised concrete platform near Paula's mobile home.

There were riding-school gymkhanas, and own-a-pony days, and jumping with square yellow-and-white poles, blue plastic barrels and battered wings in the indoor school whose walls were made of a jumble of planks held behind girders. We hacked out past the long rows of semis, over the railway crossing and finally broke onto a country track, where we could canter and chase one at a time round a circuit with a little jump. The instructors would wave us off to hurtle round the narrow track, the pony accelerating as he turned back towards his mates, and either skipping, despite frantic tugs, around the low fence, or taking it in a bound. Then we rode on through a spinney of beeches before coming back to tarmac and lawns. Sometimes my parents took me to the yard on a Saturday and left me there all day to join the population of loitering girls looking for horses to groom.

There would be one ride of girls holding their ponies in the yard, the instructors slipping their fingers behind the girths and tugging, to check whether the pony had blown its sides out when saddled. Derwen chased wisps of hay across the floor, tugging his child along after him. You heard the scraw and whap of a stirrup being pulled down a leather, and saw Joe heading across the yard with a girl hopping along beside him, one foot in the near stirrup, trying to heft herself into the saddle. Arab-y Tango, whom the instructors rode, circled impatiently with his tail held high as his rider called out the order: 'Wimpy first, then Red, Cricket, Joe, Derwen, Smokey and Orlando at the back.'

The telephone had an outdoor bell with a crisp double trill that would be followed by silence, then shouts: it was for Paula, or for Sue. The last ride lingered if their parents would let them, hanging around outside the tackroom with a bridle over one shoulder, its reins just clearing the ground, and a saddle on a warm, sweaty numnah over the crook of one arm. The numnahs would shed moulted white horsehair on their sweaters, from where it was brushed off and redistributed all over dark jodhs that were brown with dust on the inside of the calves. Other girls hung over the door of Pickles's stable, trying to get the old pony's attention as he investigated his hay net. The unlucky trailed back to their parents' cars, stinking of horses, talking of what Joe had done, or how they had jumped a cross-pole, and next week they would try a double, and could they please go for a whole Saturday and . . .?

There were rosettes for mucking out on own-a-pony days when we forked up sodden rostis of soiled straw with a sharp ammoniac tang as corrosive to nasal hair as nail varnish remover. We took the wheelbarrow out to the fields and collected dung that was like soft fruit in the summer, but in the winter it froze solid and went into the barrow with a clang. The muck heap was periodically loaded up and carted off by a local mushroom farm, but most of the time it was formidable, a warm fortification of slow-cooking dung and darkened, rotting straw. A plank leaned against the raw cliff face at the end. You had to take a run-up at it and thrust the wheelbarrow before you, hoping you'd got it straight, and that you and the barrow didn't plunge off the edge of the plank. The best stage of mucking out was shaking down the fresh straw, segment by segment, at arm's length as you walked round the box. When there was enough piled, fluffed-up straw for Rumpelstiltskin's chamber, you banked up the sides and tried to pick the last curls off your sweater. Then you would let in the pony, who trailed through it all ungratefully, straw dragging on his hooves, and rearranged it to his own satisfaction.

Horses were fed before humans. We queued at the feedroom to collect buckets for each pony and mixed porridges of feed with our hands – a black peaty slop of soaked sugar beet, flaked oats, little chips of shining chaff, smashed yellow corn, gooey linseed oil and a scoop of garlic powder. The ponies would move to their doors and curl their necks over them like sea horses, a breathy rumble coming up from their chests, like a whicker played on a thunder sheet, hur-hur-hur-hur. They knocked their knees on the doors and scraped their hooves, making wavelets of straw behind them, weaving from hoof to hoof, straining to follow the scent of the food.

'All right, all right.'

You were bossy and firm as you slipped the bolt and, hugging the bucket to your chest to protect it, reversed into the stable to begin a do-si-do with Derwen, his nose raiding over your shoulder, then pulling back in frustration, making that rumbling again, unsure whether to barge you or to get into the best position at the feeding place. The muzzle followed the bucket as you placed it on the floor and the blunt lips greedily smeared the food into the base; there was a huffling noise as the porridge was funnelled back to the teeth by the lips. After a minute or two, as you stood with your hand on his shoulder, watching, there would be the sound of teeth scraping on plastic and then the pony's head chasing stray flakes round the bucket, licking it with a raspy tongue.

If you were lucky he lifted his head, looked at you as if surprised that you were still there, held his nose to your face and snorted, blowing the last bits of chaff that had adhered to his moustache into your face. Once again you could call him a silly bugger and take away his clean bucket before you got your own lunch.

The tackroom had a whiffy heater with a dimpled copper front and white bars that had been smoked brown at the edges by the gas flames, circulating warm air to dry the quilted numnahs that were clammy with cold sweat and the thick cord leading ropes that had been dragged in mud on some complicated expedition to the fields to retrieve a pony, and were gritty and damp to the touch. We kept our grooming kits there in plastic toolboxes: dandy, body, curry, hoof pick, two sponges (one for dock, one for eyes), an old cadged tea towel for a duster, blue plastic mane comb that came as a freebie stuck to the front of *Horse and Pony* magazine, and hoof oil that I liked to uncork and sniff when I wasn't near the stables. Like old grooms, we sat on wooden boxes full of old rugs and blankets under the saddle racks and bridles hanging on rounded pegs, and sucked down mugs of hot, strong tea with UHT milk, or Ribena that was sweet and sharp on the teeth, and talked some more about horses.

The Horse that Only
I Could Ride

Consolation from imaginary things is not an
imaginary consolation.

News from Somewhere: On Settling (2004) by Roger Scruton

I often dreamt I was a horse, and I know exactly what it
feels like to be one. I even know what it feels like to be able to
twitch the skin on my shoulder and shudder away a fly.

Period Piece (1952) by Gwen Raverat

The voice down the phone from Sydney was soft and breathy, like
having a pony exhale gently in your ear. It paused often, looking
for the right words.

'I loved horses. When I was growing up in north-eastern Australia
we didn't have any horses, but a couple of hundred metres up the
road there was a paddock and these people had horses. I used to go
and grab handfuls of grass to feed them. I was quite little at the time
but it struck me how gentle they were, and there was just an instant
connection between myself and the horse. I was about thirteen when
we moved, and I missed that side of my girlhood.'

The line was poor but it didn't seem as though my caller was a
hemisphere away. She went on, 'When I discovered pony play about
ten years ago, I discovered that, hey, there are no rules, and I can relive my childhood and this time I can be the pony.'

148

I had a picture on my computer screen of Shyanne dressed as a pony: she wore a hot-pink PVC catsuit with a flouncy blonde horse tail at the coccyx, a black-leather harness over her head and a bit between her teeth that pinched the corners of her lips. Funny sort of pony.

I said nothing and she sighed. 'It's expressing outwards the way you feel inside. I've always been a pony girl, always will be, I guess.'

When I contacted The Other Pony Club, looking for an interviewee, I had expected to talk to a fetishist. Pony play, to the outsider, is a subsection of the BDSM, or bondage, domination and sadomasochism scene, in which (mainly) women and (some) men dress up as horses and are handled by dommes or masters who chuck their reins and 'train' them. At sites like *Equus Eroticus* and the Other Pony Club, you can see the fantastic trappings of the pony people: sheeny horsehead masks like chess knights, butt plugs trimmed with horsehair tails, rubber bits, body harnesses that buckle at the crotch, pastel circus plumes, cut-down bridles with blinkers and leather ears, bells, hobbles, saddles and sulky carts. Pony girls and boys do everything that 'bio horses' do, whether it's rodeo – 'He managed to throw me off, hard, and I went flying through the air over his head!' said one bronc rider – in-hand showing (the horses curried with real currycombs beforehand), chariot-racing or even foxhunting with human 'puppies' in pursuit of a man-fox who is ceremonially cut from his black rubber outfit at the kill. It is as silly and uncomfortable to watch as a government minister performing a balloon dance straight-faced.

'When I first got the pony boots I couldn't walk in them at all,' continued Shyanne.

Her hoof-shaped boots looked excruciating: the ball of her foot was in the 'hoof', the rest of her sole sloped back unsupported and braced as a 'pastern'.

'You're right up on your toes, it's like being *en pointe*. It does take a commitment. It does take self-discipline. But now I can do anything in them. I can gallop flat out.'

Shyanne's hesitant emotion was something utterly unexpected. I bent my ear to the phone to catch her words and unconsciously tilted my head, like, well, a pony listening.

'Pony play for me is totally nonsexual. I do know that it screams fetish but it's very much a role-play for me – it's part of who I am. Even in real life, if Grace, my girlfriend-mistress, scratches me behind the ear I'll respond, or she'll hold out a piece of chocolate with an open palm and I'll eat it out of her hand. There's nothing weird or perverse about that, it's just really lovely.'

She had, she explained, a little stable at home with hay in it. 'There's also a farm that we go to where we do some proper training, or I'm just allowed to run in the paddock. I can let myself go completely, and stand and face the wind if I like and just exist, in that beautiful pony headspace.'

'Isn't that just like playing imaginary horses?'

I sounded querulous. She was describing a place that I knew very well, albeit at a distance these days. Pony headspace. Well I never. Feeling awkward at knowing what she meant, I asked, 'What's it like, I mean, how do you go into pony headspace?'

There was a long pause again. The faint white noise on the phone line rose and then Shyanne replied, as if she were letting go a deep secret, 'If Mistress and I are going to engage in pony play, we usually give at least twenty-four hours' notice. I start to enter the headspace maybe eight hours before putting any tack on. I'll go for a walk, take a breath, then come home, shower and groom, and then slowly get ready. When the bit and bridle goes in, it's literally a sigh, a breath and then I'm gone. I've left the room.' Her voice shook. 'At the very end it's . . . a release. It's also a descent into a place. I usually cry as I descend through these human emotions and then the world's a little bit different.' Suddenly the words came in a rush. 'When I'm standing there in completely full tack and bit and bridle, I am me and I am raw and I have to feel safe to go there and when I do it's just amazing.' This time the white noise prickled with life and excitement.

'I suppose it's a kind of an escape,' I offered tentatively, boot-faced at the thought of mentally preparing for eight hours to do anything, and then added, 'I think that's what I was trying to do when I was a child. It was just more interesting to be a horse – you could do things you couldn't when you were a human.'

I remembered myself galloping headlong down the football pitch at school at lunchtime with my best friend Cheryl, playing at racehorses with a finishing-straight crowd roaring in our inner ears, and blotting out the fact that some other girls were watching and whispering about some obscure condition we'd failed to meet, like not pushing our knee socks down to our ankles.

'You don't have to deal with lots of crap.'

'Exactly,' said Shyanne, 'and then society forces us to grow up and become adults. I'm sure there's part of you that's still longing to be a pony again, and relive part of a childhood. Come to Sydney. We'll train together.'

When I first became a horse, I could not have pony boots, although I would have wanted them, had I known they existed. I would have liked to clatter on hollow hooves. Instead I went on all fours, the quickest form of imitation. Playing at Black Beauty, I crawled round the neighbours' dining room and collided head first with the table leg, cutting open my forehead. I was delivered home to my mother, groggy and smiling, with a Mr Bump band-aid and a permanent scar. My friend Karen was mocked by her brothers for having scuffed knees. Transmogrification is not without its physical perils.

When I got a little older, I began to realize that hands and knees, while authentic, were limiting. So my imaginary horse became upright and bipedal, the better to jump box hedges and gallop and paw the lawn. It was also easier to throw my head up and whinny like a wild horse, and to see where I was going and avoid table legs. Not that different, really, to what Shyanne was doing in her rubber catsuit.

'Amongst little girls Playing Horses is almost as popular as playing

Hospitals, and popular with some boys too,' noted Iona and Peter Opie in their 1969 survey of children's outdoor games. 'When a child pretends to be a horse or other animals he often becomes, as in no other pretending game, almost unconscious that he is pretending.'

The Queen and her sister used to play at being circus horses, cantering and neighing, even though they had real ponies to ride. The novelist Deborah Moggach could identify what I meant when I brought up the idea of being horsy: 'I whinnied and neighed and galloped around Camden Town and St John's Wood, occasionally tying myself to railings or cropping the grass. I know it sounds weird, but you did ask. And by asking, you obviously understand.' A friend, Kate, said she had grazed out of bowls without cutlery. Someone else recommended tucking a cardigan in the back of your belt, for a tail. Helen's nan knitted her a saddle complete with stirrups and she used her brother's gumshield as a bit. 'My parents were cuted,' said Helen. 'Until I started doing it naked.'

You can also convert your upright Equus caballus into something approaching a centaur. A solitary child transforms her front hooves back into hands that now hold imaginary reins and switches her own leg with a twig she broke from a tree. Two legs substitute for all six legs of imaginary horse and rider. You click your tongue to yourself and canter on. I held the back of my friend Cheryl's belt and galloped in tandem with her over the little walls in the junior-school playground. Another friend, Rowan, made a bridle out of old tack and used a spinning-top whip to drive her pony, Julia, until Julia's mother sent a note to Rowan's: 'I would be grateful if Rowan would stop whipping Julia.'

When rocking or hobby horses were not available, other girls used sofa arms, walls, ironing boards, brooms, walking sticks and mops. In one case a kitchen table named Lusty was tacked up with a coat with string stirrups (Lusty was the brand name of the furniture maker, not the rider's choice). The daring attached skipping ropes to their bike handles before careering off. Velvet Brown, like her creator,

Enid Bagnold, kept in a shell box pictures of horses cut from the *Tatler* and pasted onto cardboard, which she took out on 'rides' with cotton bridles and paper saddles. She groomed them with a scrap of handkerchief, neatly hemmed, and drove a team of her own big toes with tape reins.

In the woods behind our house and at school, cross-country courses were plotted over fallen trees and heaps of branches dragged into place, the distances between them carefully paced. 'It was,' recalled another friend, Chen, 'a bit like Badminton in the school woods.' I balanced flower pots on top of one another in wobbly towers to make showjump wings and painted garden canes with red-and-white stripes, only to discover, when it dripped off with the first rain, that the poster paint wasn't waterproof. I used the *Pony Club Annual* for advice on fence-building, and repurposed an old door from the garage as a 'gate', then recorded the course in a notebook for future reference, tacking a shorter route in dashed lines for the jump-off. Friends were lunged in back gardens and the dog coaxed over the bamboo-cane fences.

Distinct mounts with heights, colours and pedigrees began to emerge. I admired Arabians, so I had one. Then, of course, I needed a racehorse, so I added a few. There was a photograph of an impressive Percheron in my *Observer Book of Horses and Ponies*, so I acquired a stout 18hh gelding with honeycomb dapples and white feathers, with ribbons in his mane to match. I collected Flicka, Banner and Rocket from Mary O'Hara's books, then a full set of Josephine Pullein-Thompson's Six Ponies – Rocket, Romany, Grey Dawn, Rufus, Sunset and Jet. I began to keep track of my stable in a ledger like the one with a list of pupils and horses at Cringleford, with smudged ruled columns of names, colour, height and stud number. When we went to the Burghley horse trials on a riding-school trip, I came home and copied out the name and details of every horse in the competition card into the studbook.

Then I found an Avon catalogue and branched out extravagantly into lipstick names: Plum must be a blue roan, and Bronze Goddess a chestnut Hanoverian mare with a regal muzzle and a leather head-collar with a brass plate. From this stable I took my pick whenever we went for a walk. I needed my dapple-grey hunter, Cobweb, to carry me along the Railway Line, or the piebald Chessboard to jump logs in the woods. For showjumping in our garden or my friends' gardens there was Hey Presto, a bay thoroughbred mare, and for cross-country at Greenacres, Inca, a black warmblood.

When I asked other women for details of their imaginary horses, they described beasts that ran the gamut from garden variety to fantastical. Some were just generic, nameless horses, or simply Fudge, a chestnut gelding. Black Beauty was incarnated over and over, sometimes in a white coat, carrying his riders safely away from horse thieves, or even flying to other countries and escaping bad witches. Ginger was rescued by one girl and lived in a garden shed. Greek battle horses existed alongside Richard the Lionheart's steed, given flesh as a scooter. Wildfire Girl would come galloping when called, while an Andalusian called Kimono had wings and flew faster than the speed of light. Gypsy Foxfire was like Carlotta of the St Clares' books. Midnight Magic, a dark-bay thoroughbred showjumper, was always triumphant in garden Grands Prix, and the old grey mare Mother Horse would patiently follow the car that carried 'her' child.

Horse and Pony ran a regular 'dream pony' feature for the 'ponymad but ponyless', a little column illustrated by the creators' pencil sketches and blobby poster-paint efforts, like Winged Pegasus, a palomino with a black snip, or a show pony called Fraser (formally Moonlight Star) who had won precisely eighty-three rosettes. 'We have a dream to travel to an Arabian desert,' wrote Alison and Eleanor, 'where we would gallop off into the sunset on purebred Arabian horses ... Hers would be called Festival Spirit, and mine would be Whisper Grey after the famous showjumper. I would call him Wizz for short.'

There was a second kind of daydream, one that featured not a specific imaginary horse, but the blessed chain of action that would lead to a real pony. I used to size up our back garden: I knew there wasn't space for an Arab on our suburban back lawn, although Ruth Hollis in K. M. Peyton's *Fly-by-Night* keeps her new pony on a council estate, so perhaps it was possible, although the flowerbeds would have to go – without those we might have at least a quarter of an acre of grazing. I read eagerly the scene in *Jill's Gymkhana* where Ruby Ferguson's Jill Crewe realizes that the old shed behind her cottage is, in fact, a stable with a hayloft, a manger and cobbles; she and her friend Anne Drew spend a satisfying day scrubbing out and whitewashing it. I considered our own garage, sometimes rearranging the tools and plant pots in the little creosoted shed by the back fence in rehearsal.

The heroines of pony books always, as a bare minimum, had at least one pony whose lead rope fell into their hands, *equus ex machina*. Judith Berrisford's Jackie won Misty by writing an essay on the subject of 'If I won a pony' for *Horseshoes*, 'Britain's Premier Weekly for Pony-Lovers'. In the 1950s, 1960s and 1970s, you could win the Kerrygold palomino, the Sugar Puff pony and the Milky Bar Shetland. There were competitions in the *Evening Standard*, *Reveille* and the *Sunday Express* to win ponies. In the 1970s advert for the W. H. Smith Win a Pony contest, a girl posted her entry and an answering whinny resounded from deep inside the pillar box.

I collected tokens from *Horse and Pony* and completed a quiz on stable management published in weekly stages, sending those, along with a photograph of myself jumping a cross-pole on Orlando, to the office in Peterborough. 'It helps,' said H & P, 'if Mum knows how to do a spot of saddle soaping. Is your mum fully trained?' Later I read with heart-stopping envy of the day when the winner went to the stables and out sprang the lady from *Horse and Pony*, brandishing a smart blue Polygram rug, to tell the lucky, lucky girl she'd won the competition. The Win a Pony ponies might never have taken flesh and tested the floor of our shed with their hooves, but they left behind them possibilities as tangible as vapour, so I added them to my imaginary herd, a teeming, super-abundant cavalcade of more piebalds, dapple greys, chestnuts, bays and roans than I could have ridden in three lifetimes.

After I rang off from my conversation with Shyanne, I realized I hadn't asked her why she chose horses as alter egos, because I'd taken it as read that any girl would rather be a horse than a tiger or a fox. At the simplest, child's level of love, you want to become what you love, to merge and lose yourself in them, to know exactly what it is to be them. You want not to be able to tell yourselves apart.

With an imaginary horse you are no longer confined to the sticky back seat of a car on a long journey alleviated only by Mint Imperials. You are free to gallop with its rider across country, breasting hedges and swooping over ditches. Horses make reality better. A horse embodied the liberation inherent in all fantasy, a sense of something powerful that burst, all snorts and enthusiasm, into the everyday and filled up your imagination. Horses take you away from the mundane. The child psychologist Marjorie Taylor interviewed a little girl who would play with a unicorn, to the chagrin of her Christian mother, who thought imaginary friends were somehow a sinful habit. Asked why the child wanted to be a unicorn, her mother answered simply, 'She wants to be free' – just like Shyanne.

Another small girl in Taylor's study of imaginary friends had been separated from her mother during the Second World War and boarded at a nursery for eighteen months. She brought home a pony with red points who slept reared up on his hind legs and escorted her everywhere afterwards, travelling at times in her mother's shopping bag, a portable familiar.

Imaginary horses offered the sweet satisfaction of wish fulfilment when you were stuck in a child's body and lacked any real independence; it was a satisfaction that was vivid enough to alleviate and then, cruelly, to stoke a pang. Had I waited till I was eighteen to compete in the Olympics, I would have expired of longing and boredom. As it was, I could compete not just every four years, but every day of the week if I chose. I had no real pony, but I had a thousand horses from which to choose.

Being a horse gave me not just their speed, beauty and adventures, but, like Demeter, I could disguise myself as a horse to escape undesirables. Although I had friends who lived in our cul-de-sac, they were older or attended the school in Old Costessey. My school was another matter. I wasn't attuned to the social machinations at New Costessey Infants School and, at the age of five, had had the misfortune to return to school from California with an American accent that gave way to a 'posh' one. The politics of little girls shift suddenly. If I tangled with girls other than Cheryl, I quickly lost my way, unable to predict from one day to the next the best course of action. This situation was aggravated by my daydreaming, as I was too abstracted to pick up the signs and a sad bore in my obsession. When charging an imaginary horse down the length of the playing field side by side with my best friend Cheryl, none of this mattered and we always had enough horses to share. I was too ill-coordinated to play elastics, and did not choose to sit on a wall while the boys monopolized the playground for football. I had energy to burn. School would have been unbearable without the horses.

I had more luck finding kindred imaginary-horse lovers out of school, in Old Costessey, who would still jump the bamboo canes and old doors and wrecked fireguards I assembled in the garden, with me clashing the wind chimes to indicate the beginning of a round. The imaginary-horse play continued unabated, even if I had real horses to ride once a week at Cringleford. Burdened by a self-inflicted learning programme about the minutiae of horselore, which involved trying to read every equine book that crossed my path (including tracts on the history of horseshoeing and musty Time Form annuals that my godmother had retrieved from jumble sales), I buckled and wondered – sacrilegiously, fleetingly – whether an imaginary horse were not easier to manage than the real thing. I understood the twelve-year-old letter writer to *Horse and Pony* who said, 'If someone said, "Here is a pony," I'd refuse, because I feel I don't know enough about the care, the food, the diseases . . . I'd never forgive myself if . . . I hurt a pony simply by not having enough knowledge.'

I was becoming aware of the gap between the riding-school ponies and my skills in handling them, and the grander mounts and ambitions in my head. As these imaginary horses retreated from any obligations that might have been imposed on them by the real world, so they took wing and my daydreams became more elaborate, no longer hemmed by the edges of the lawn at home. If everything flawed on earth has its ideal in a platonic heaven, so I built up my giant golden Arabians as I rode and adored Red, a 13.2hh pony who stargazed a little, or some sour old pony at a trekking centre on holiday, squelching through the Lake District. The gulf between real and imagined opened up still further.

Gradually, a single imaginary horse emerged and when I transferred my studbook to a new folder, with a winged unicorn with piggy eyes on the front, this new stallion became horse number one. On a second long trip to California I had discovered Walter Farley's Black Stallion series in the local library. He wrote the first book when he was in high school and at college, calling it 'a dream on paper'. It tells the story of Alec Ramsay, a boy from Flushing, New York, who is shipwrecked on a voyage back from visiting his uncle in India. He is saved by clinging to a great, black stallion who had been put aboard the ship by a mysterious tribesman in 'Arabia'. Alec does not tame The Black, but he is allowed to ride him and, when they return to New York inseparable, to race him against the greatest horses of the time. The Black is an awesome creation, massive, savage, perpetually alert and restless, all but a daemon. He is in constant animation, plunging, wheeling, dancing, pawing, thrashing, a beautiful Incredible Hulk of a horse who breaks boxes and bridles, and who yearns to be free. Alec often passes out on his back, his hands knotted into his thick mane, because the monster is so fatally fast.

If you compare the stuff coming from the pens of Britain's leading pony writers to Farley's yarns, with The Black unbeaten in every great handicap in America, they do seem feeble and domesticated. Enid Bagnold had no problem letting Velvet win the Grand National, but the most that many Pullein-Thompson heroines can reach for is the district hunter trial.

From Farley's books came my own Ground a Fire's form, his career and his backdrop. The origin of his name is lost – possibly I meant that he danced as though the ground was on fire, or ran so fast he set it aflame. I imported Ground a Fire as a two-year-old from the same desert as The Black, and found an Arabic dictionary in Norwich Library that I raided to name Ground a Fire's scions and daughters, Sharr, 'I'ssar, Saqr and Banan. I made my own Arabian a brother of The Black, who duelled with him. He won British and American triple crowns because I was in love with the great racehorse Nijinsky and I rode him in all his races. He ran, I wrote, with 'efortless, long and flowing strides' at the front of the pack, before 'excelerating in the last quarter mile', though always with his head held high.

Ground a Fire is my favourite [I went on, unbowed by spelling conventions]. He's 7 years old and stands a massive 17.3hh. Though he is a thourghbred he looks like an arabian. He is a race horse stallion. He does both flat racing and steeplechasing. He has wins in: the grand national, The English derby, Kentucky derby, Irish derby, 2000 Guienias, Prix de la Arc de Triumph, Belmont Stakes, Preakness Stakes, St Leger, Champion Match race, International Match race, grand national (twice), Scottish grand national, The grand parduvitche Cheltnam gold cup, and the Lincoln … He has a fiery temper only his owner, trainer and jockey can ride him. He reaches speeds of 100 mph. He is the worlds fastest ever horse. He is a LEGEND.

Ground a Fire was sent to stud after his momentous racing career, only to come out of retirement and dead heat with The Black. I bring you these details as they are extensively documented but I'll spare you more. I could show you timetables, charts and a huge family tree – complete with scratchy colour-pencil illustrations, the horses' coats filled in with stabbed, radiating lines – of the descendants of Fire and The Black. I signed off: 'And so the family spreads ...' Though I sometimes 'rode' Ground a Fire, I began to find that it was more convenient to confine him to paper and to daydreams I could call up without moving. On paper he seemed more fleshed out, more detailed and more secret.

I plotted my empire on graph paper, one acre to every two millimetres, and coloured the pastures in green. It was reminiscent of the 300,000-horse farms of the Tang emperors in the seventh century, with vast grazing allowances for each inmate, and my one thousand horses were released from the biro confines of the ledger. At the heart was a field five acres square that housed Ground a Fire, like the central cabin of a panopticon. This was surrounded by 120 barns like the ones on Hopeful Farm, each an acre square, and four colossal storage barns of eight square acres apiece. Then came the paddocks, some as big as Ground a Fire's, others subdivided, making space for a racetrack with one circuit with Grand National fences and a flat course. There was a separate Arabian stud and one for thorough-breds, a riding school, a training stables, accommodation for the grooms with the footprint of the presidential palace in Bucharest, an indoor school (again, cavernous) and, tucked away in one corner, the 'ranch', where I lived. This was the Goose Bar Ranch from *My Friend Flicka*, transported direct from Wyoming, with its Dutch doors and apple-green kitchen floor, and the Green out front, where Nell McLaughlin maintained a little Boston civilization in the West.

In my daydream stories I was not required, like Jo March and seemingly every other heroine in classic girls' literature, to learn to be nice and patient. I didn't have to worry about who was friends with me and who wasn't that week. In them I was a neutral, doing character, who won the Derby and the Prix de l'Arc de Triomphe on Ground a Fire. I trained horses that I would race in my gold silks, and

I prepped my Olympic showjumpers and three-day eventers. I bred my race of gigantic Arabians. I did not dream of being a bride, of endless dressings up and paradings that never resulted in anything, nor of being a boy so I could have 'proper' adventures. I was a girl and a jockey, and Ground a Fire and I made enough money to set up my own stud farm, just like Alec's Hopeful Farm in Walter Farley's books.

My obsession was, I soon gathered, excessive. Once, lingering in the corridor at school, aged six or seven, I overheard one teacher remark to another, 'I don't like that Susanna Forrest, she's too horsy,' and was briefly mortified before I took off in a storming gallop across the playground, Cheryl alongside. I later found a letter from a kindred spirit in *Horse and Pony*, whose English teacher had added a note to her report suggesting she 'vary her composition subject to something other than horses'. 'How can anyone be so heartless?' demanded Jayne, aged nine, and I with her.

The longer my legs got, the less adults seemed to understand the dignities of what I was doing. Running (not galloping) up the wing during a football match, I frowned and swivelled back my horse ears as Mr Shreeve, grinning, called out, 'And it's Lucinda Prior-Palmer coming into play now ...' I could kick backwards and catch my brother in the shins when he wound me up by talking about horse slaughter; I could gallop away from the kids yelling 'Horsy!' Foolishly, I caved in to little-girl politics and galloped away from Cheryl in pursuit of new friends – a mistake. I wound up with two girls who wanted to talk about perms, bras and kitten heels instead of racehorses, and who thought I was silly to throw my head about and neigh. As being horsy in the real world, or at least the school playground, became more complicated, I discovered the rewards of full immersion in my own world.

I used my parents' huge and heavy electric typewriter, changing the plain golfball to the more expressive italic one, fired it up with a hum and then a crunch as I hit the first key, and tapped out the story of Ground a Fire at a canter, without pausing to correct or rewrite. I stole innocently and freely from my horse books and old Victorian hagiographical poems about wind-whipped Arabian steeds in the desert that were unfailingly faithful to their masters. There was a second type of story that was more domestic and confined to things such as gymkhanas, hunter trials and dressage tests, featuring sisters called Diane and Sasha, and Welsh-cross Arab ponies that were temporarily troublesome. These I typed up and posted off to *Horse and Pony*. My own stories I kept.

Nerve

A German Lady who dresses, and rides, *en cavalier*,
has for several days past attracted the attention of the beaux and
belles in Hyde-park. She is well mounted, takes her morning
rides without any attendant, and leaps over the different bars in
the park with all imaginable coolness and resolution.

Morning Post, 3 March 1778

The week after my ride on Gräfin, I plugged up the drive of the
riding club in Berlin, only to find it blocked by a lorry loaded
with enormous rolled bales of straw, like cross-sections of a giant
redwood. Better watch that, I thought, thinking of horses' dislike of
the unfamiliar and their ability to conjure monsters from the
inanimate. The cab was parked by the door of the *reithalle*.

I was assigned Zofe instead of Gräfin and retrieved the phlegmatic
mare from the barn, where she had been waiting, blankly contem-
plating the stable partition. I was confident that there wouldn't be a
problem with the truck.

'I couldn't definitely predict what would happen if a rocket went
off behind Zofe,' I'd told a friend that week, 'but I don't think it
would be much.'

She swung her head to inspect the lorry briefly as I led her past it,
one ear cocked mildly, the other skewed sideways at me. In the
school with other horses, Zofe did seem more fluid and nappy than
before, but when I tried to coax her into a warm-up canter, she cut

the throttle and her quarters filled up with wet sand. I tried again on the next corner, squeezing with my legs and pushing my seat down into the dish of the saddle, willing her to break the choppy movement of her front legs and spring into canter. We went faster into a straggling trot instead, my posting getting more irregular as I bounced off the saddle out of kilter.

I ran through my actions in my head, trying to work out what I was doing wrong – bad leg contact, perhaps, or confusing signals with my hands – but couldn't pinpoint it and had to steer quickly to avoid another rider coming in the opposite direction. At childhood riding schools I'd learned to kick horses, to flap my legs, hoping that my heel would connect smartly but bluntly. Now I'd realized that this was scornfully referred to as 'Pony Club kicking' and was worse by far than a sharp tap with a long, elastic schooling whip. Whips reminded me guiltily of other old riding-school habits, when instructors called out, 'Give him a smack on the bum,' and a short crop went down on the thick fur of a pony's quarters. If Zofe was unhappy, a whack on her thin, fussy skin wasn't going to improve her mood.

A bareheaded blonde woman in a speckless, sky-blue polo shirt and neat black gloves fastened at the wrist was schooling a grey Andalusian in the reithalle as my group lesson formed a ride. The Spanish horse had matching sky-blue bandages, his long mane gathered in a lace braid at the ends and falling on his neck like a cowl. Together they performed perfect circles, switching seamlessly to the inner track to avoid the crocodile of civilians, the woman's hands fixed upright, her horse's neck arched, his face open and concentrated under his loose, grey forelock. Zofe and I bumbled by her, my hands stretched idiotically in front of me.

We were cornering badly up by the entry way when the lorry let out a ferocious gurgle. Zofe started and I felt her cannon bones liquefy as a tremble ran up from her planted front hooves and through me from tailbone to brainstem. Her muscles sublimed from wet sand to air and she lurched sideways, head thrown up, quarters gathering under her to race. Without thinking, I shortened my reins and moved with her, trying not to clamp my calves to her sides. She danced for two strides of canter, then settled back to a trot, head high and eye rolling. She rushed up to within a foot of the horse in front, swarming close to his tail for safety. As we passed the door again, she hopped sideways with her ears trained on the gurgling monster that blocked her only escape route.

I watched her ears anxiously for information and felt her mouth take a pre-emptive hard grip on the bit. I waggled the reins, trying to break the monotony of my hold, and we settled into an acrimonious tug-of-war. Come on, Zofe, I wheedled with my hands: be nice to me, work with me. Now she would canter, but every time we passed the lorry at the door she'd dodge off the track, and I'd sense a sudden alarming lightness, and feel insubstantial on the thick leather-and-wood saddle and half-tonne of scared and gathered muscle under me. Zofe began to object, ears furled and lip raised, to the Andalusian as he cantered past on the inside, and to shy a hoof at him.

As we trotted in file with the ride, she kept on crowding the quarters of the bay gelding in front, so I worked harder on the reins, pushing her deep into the corners to open half a length between the two horses. She made a sudden rush, corkscrewing her head down and bunching behind in a couple of bucks. I surprised myself by knowing what to do: reins short, sharp turn into the centre of the ring and she was forced to halt. Before I'd even thought what to do, I had her standing, neck stiff, outmanoeuvred and rattled, but four-square. After that, I rode her confidently, facing up to her peevishness about the Andalusian and her horror of the lorry, but she didn't appreciate it. She wanted to be, had to be, with her nose in the roots of the bay's tail.

Five minutes from the end of the lesson we were trotting Indian-file when, once more blithely not thinking, I began to turn the mare right in a small circle because I was sick of her clinging to the bay. In an instant I was on the floor, the string reins ripping through my fingers and the thought, I shall be dragged, flashing through my mind. I unclenched my fist and watched from the ground as Zofe cantered off, nose so high that her nostrils were level with her eyes, hooves kicking out like a Charleston dancer. Everyone oohed; the other horses pricked up their ears and shook their heads. I'd been at the back of the ride so no one had seen what happened. When Zofe and I had turned right, she'd baulked, fixing her hooves and spinning left like a quarter-horse blocking a bull, and I'd sailed off.

Ynes asked if I was all right. I felt the bump on my hip, inspected the blisters that had formed and been ripped open in a split second on the pads at the base of my fingers, brushed off some of the sand and said yes. She held Zofe's stirrup as I hopped on.

'It is spring or something?' I asked her.

'*Ein hobble-di-hop!*' she replied with a broad smile and a twinkle.

On my next circuit of the ring I inspected the crash site: a long, smooth patch where the sand had compacted under me, like fine flour pressed with a spoon. The worst had happened, I had fallen off, and it wasn't bad at all really. I fell well. I had grappled with a horse who was trying to bolt. I had been a little overconfident to circle the mare, but we were both fine.

In the middle of the night, after some bravado on email, I woke to the thought that, when I circled Zofe after the buck, I might have turned her smack into the Andalusian.

The next week I rolled back the sliding door of Zofe's stable, stepped in, pulled the door to and began to disentangle the headcollar. At once, the corner of her mouth hooked back in a grimace of disapproval, then went on curling sourly, pulling her ears back as if with a string. Her head dropped low and her ears flattened. I took one step towards her in the confined space of the loose box. She flung her nose up and flashed yellow teeth at me, shaking her head as if I were a wolf she were chasing out of the herd, and all but snarled like a Mare of Diomedes. She took a step towards me, weaving her head and snapping. Never having seen a horse so aggressive in all my life, I scuttled out and hauled the door shut behind me. Zofe was at the bars, looming, teeth as big as dice, ears pinioned.

I turned to a young woman who was sweeping the gangway and had seen the whole performance.

'Das ist ein Problem,' I managed.

She put the broom down and disappeared as I stood dumbly outside the box, and Zofe ranged back and forth, threatening me with terrible things. The woman came back with Ynes, who told me off for being late as the others were nearly ready to go into the school and, tutting, took the headcollar from my stiff hands. She pulled back the door and fished a sugar lump out of her pocket. Zofe stopped making faces and submitted. I wondered about the wisdom of rewarding Mrs Hyde.

Tethered outside her box, Zofe was sweet again, as though the sugar had dissolved the sourness. Sunlight through the skylight filled the orange, red and yellow glinting filaments of her short chestnut coat. She nuzzled me as I bent over to smooth down the Velcro fastening the boots on her front legs.

Despite the inauspicious start, I had a small epiphany in the lesson. I had to trust Zofe, not hang on her mouth and police every twitch, or try to carry her around the ring with my legs. I felt her mouth down the reins as she chucked the bit, and the reins slackened, then grew taut like the jerk and tug of a kite string, as she responded to me. Draw too hard and you pull the kite out of the sky, I thought, as the mare skipped kindly into a canter for me, sweet on the heels of the bay in front.

PATRICIA LEITCH

JINNY
4

NIGHT OF THE
RED HORSE

The Red Horse and
the White Mare

Two small statues were on the altar, one on either side of a
golden bowl. One was Epona. The other, about the same size, was
of a Horse. Its simple shape was made out of metal. The head was
an Arab's head, the tail kinked over its quarters was an Arab's tail.

The old woman's hand moved again, sprinkling more herbs
into the flames. The two statues grew huge. The Pony Folk
moaned with a low terror. Jinny flung herself on to the ground,
pressing her face into the earth to block out the fearful thing that
towered above her. The Horse on the altar was the Red Horse,
rearing above them all, while Epona, an apple in her
outstretched hand, watched and waited.

Night of the Red Horse (1978) by Patricia Leitch

When I was rooting through a wardrobe in my parents' home in
Norwich for evidence of Ground a Fire, I turned up a drawing
on a piece of computer paper. In the foreground – somewhat poorly
drawn and with evidence that an earlier, rather bovine, straight-
edged top line had been rubbed out – was a chestnut Arabian mare,
rapidly and sketchily coloured in with a mix of orange, red and
yellow pencils, in an effort to render the bright fire of her coat,
which resembled Zofe's. The uneven hatching gave her a little
animation, but didn't follow the rounds of her muscles and skeleton,
stranding her flat on the page. One foreleg was raised as she stood in
a pool of golden light from the setting sun, which was lowering in

the dip of the moors behind her. At the crux of the hills was a circle of standing stones and neatly positioned on either side rose cliff faces of rock, like the backdrop for some antique, rustic opera production. The red mare was Shantih, although I was forever to misspell her name with a faux-Gaelic lisp as Shanith and miss the fact that the word meant peace.

Patricia Leitch published her first pony book, *To Save a Pony*, in 1960 and, while many of her earliest novels adhere to the classic jodhs-'n'-gymkhanas template, she evolved into the Alan Garner of the genre. In 1963 she wrote *The Black Loch*, a story that interknit dark, reclaimed and reworked Celtic mythology with adventure and a mouldering Highland castle. The heroine, Kay, discovers that her estranged Scottish family are custodians of a great black water horse or kelpie, which lives in a lake. When the horse is tranquillized and dragged away by a showman who wants to put it on display, Kay must rescue it and escape by night across the moors of northern Scotland. At the time Leitch was living in Renfrewshire and working variously as a teacher, a librarian and a riding instructor, and riding her pony Kirsty on the Kilmacolm moors.

Later, in 1975, Leitch's *Dream of Fair Horses* would break with the pony-book formula altogether as its heroine Gill won and gave up the grey Perdita, the pony of her dreams, and went to live in a commune with her boyfriend, saying, 'We want to live the laughter that makes the bungalows and the cars, the trophies and the rosettes, the desperate possession and the empty success seem like half-forgotten things, skins of restriction we cast off long ago.' It lifted the pony book out of its cosy, bounded, stable-yard existence, of gymkhana heroism and hunter-trial tribulations, and set it down in an altogether stranger, wilder and more open place.

Patricia Leitch told pony-book specialist Jane Badger that in the 1970s she had begun to dream of a chestnut Arabian mare, although the only Arabs she had seen were in photograph books: Lady Anne Wentworth's famous Crabbet horses. This dancing, fiery mare came over the Kilmacolm moors with a new heroine with long, red hair who, like the Arabian, also showed more spirit than was sometimes safe for her.

In *For Love of a Horse*, published in 1976, Jinny Manders is eleven when her father inherits some money. Deciding to start a new life as a writer and a potter, he whisks the family away to the Scottish Highlands. Jinny is passionate, wilful and often troubled, a day-dreamer who is also unafraid of lashing out at authority, or breaking her promises in order to do something she is convinced is the best course of action. Her mother is, alas, rather negligible as a character. Her older sister Petra is neat and officious, wears make-up and wants to be a piano teacher, while her younger brother Mike is a good-natured ally, but he doesn't have Jinny's embattled fervour. Ken, a gentle, hippyish lad whom Mr Manders met in his work as a pro-bation officer, comes with them. He perhaps understands Jinny better than the others, but he is also prone to rather Buddhist, gnomic statements about the earth and the cosmos.

They move to Finmory, a stone house on a clifftop; huge, bare and dirty, it has been squatted by a group of hippies. Jinny takes the bedroom in the attic, with windows on both sides: one looks out to the moors, forbidding and beautiful, backed by mountains; the other looks out over the kitchen garden and a paddock to the sea. On the wall is a crude mural of a horse, painted red with yellow eyes, storming out of a strange thicket of green-and-blue branches and white flowers.

Before she can understand the Red Horse, Jinny unwittingly makes a supplication to it. On their journey to Finmory, the family stop to watch a circus. The acts include a terrified chestnut Arabian mare, billed as Yasmin the Killer Horse, who is whipped around the ring by the sadistic ringmaster. Jinny, having fallen heavily and catastrophic-ally in love with the mare on sight, leaps into the ring to attack her tormenter, bringing the show to a halt and allowing the mare to escape before she can be dragged away.

Safe in her new bedroom at Finmory, she draws the chestnut mare galloping free on the moors and pins it on the wall opposite the Red Horse. A short time later she sees the circus lorry carrying the mare being wrecked in a car accident, and with Jinny's help the Arab plunges out and flees onto the Finmory moors. Jinny tracks and rescues the mare, almost dying in a snowstorm, and brings her back to Finmory, where Ken christens her Shantih. The Red Horse brought her Shantih after all, although Shantih, rather like the peace of mind that is her namesake, proves elusive, frustrating and difficult to understand. Perhaps I thought that if I pinned my own drawing of Shantih to my bedroom wall, she would come to me too.

The Finmory moors unfurled in my mind – the same moors that we did not have in unwild Norfolk and which I craved from trips to Dartmoor or Yorkshire. I rode out from trekking centres on holidays and thought of Finmory as I cantered over the short turf on some dependable native pony, my eyes on the gulleys that ran down the hillsides and were bridged by stepping stones. A hillside in Wales could be black and sodden on a dreary summer afternoon when rain was trickling into your wellies and the fur on your pony's neck had pinched into spikes like barbs on a wet feather. Then, suddenly, when the clouds parted, the bracken would glow, the tors would shine – the rock would be slick with water – and the pony would prick his ears.

For me the Finmory moors were open and endless, spreading on into further moors and into the deep past. They were dangerous, dotted with bogs that could swallow horses whole, and inhabited by deer poachers, thieves and spirits. They were not bounded like the greenbelt fields that surrounded Costessey, and they were traversed on narrow sheep tracks, not the hemmed-in Railway Line with its cyclists and cheery dog walkers. They stood, as Francis Spufford says in *The Child that Books Built*, following C. S. Lewis, on 'the frontier of ordinary life'.

You began reading the Jinny books with what Ken calls 'plastic people' thoughts – the desire for empty success and the desperate urge to possess things that Gill rejected – suckered in by the promise of pretty Arabians and trophies. The ponyish, competitive, collecting me was satisfied with the rosettes that Shantih eventually wins for showjumping and cross-country, but the stories raised bigger issues than I could have considered in my ceaseless imaginary galloping and racing. Far more complex questions were asked of me at Finmory, as they were of Jinny. Where Walter Farley's Black Stallion books and Ground a Fire were all wish-fulfilment, Leitch hinted that to wish for something was a complicated thing in itself. When Jinny declares that she has to have a trophy, because 'It means you are the BEST and everyone else knows you are the BEST,' she's brought up short by Ken's reply: 'Listen to how you weave yourself a web of wanting.'

In other pony books girls learn how to help others, how to look after horses, and not be rash or boastful. Jinny struggles to find a way to carry into adulthood her awe at the world and her intensity, saving herself from becoming one of the plastic people. She must also come to terms with the inevitability of loss – of friends, of horses, of places and even of life. She learns, above all, to let go. When she rescues Easter, a neglected old show pony, she has to accept that, even when the mare is safe at Finmory and hand-fed rich food, she is still tired and ready to die.

Life does not obligingly stand still, and the world that Jinny loves – that of her family, Finmory, Shantih and her friends – is always under threat and never stable. Nell, who buys Jinny's paintings for her craft shop, will leave the town and move to the South of France. The old tinker woman, Keziah, dies before Jinny can ask her about the story of the Red Horse. Finmory is almost sold, and the family is faced with a move back to dreary Stopton, with Mr Manders returning to his hated former job as a probation officer. Shantih is stolen and returned. Finally her breeder, Mrs Raynor of the Talisker Arabian Stud, tracks her down and Jinny must face losing her once again.

By the end of the tenth book, *Jump for the Moon*, she is even able to hand Shantih's reins over to the old woman who raised her, telling her to take her, but Mrs Raynor presses the reins back into her hands and says, 'She is your horse.' By letting go, Jinny gains Shantih. For a reader on the verge of adolescence, at the end of childhood and the familiar, Leitch offered solace in the guise of fantasy: you would grow up, it was true, and things would change, but you could take that rich imaginary life with you.

Finmory's moors are also haunted by the Pony People, an ancient Celtic race who linger as a shadowy spirit presence and whose descendants are the tinkers who still camp in the area. The Red Horse was painted by a tinker girl with red hair like Jinny's. When archaeologists arrive to excavate a Celtic settlement twelve miles away and dig up the Pony People's graves as they search for traces of an old pony cult, the Red Horse wordlessly reminds Jinny of her obligation to him, for delivering Shantih to her. A statue of the Celtic horse goddess Epona has been found nearby by a tinker and left at a small local museum called the Wilton Collection, and the archaeologists want to unearth more artefacts. Unbeknown to them, there is a second tiny metal statue, of a horse god, an Arabian that is small enough to fit in the palm of a hand. The Red Horse wants Jinny to find it and smuggle it into the museum, where it will be reunited with Epona.

When Jinny tries to fight the commands of the Red Horse, she is haunted by nightmares of Shantih sinking into a bog, or the Red Horse's yellow eyes glaring at her from a fire. She has hallucinations of huts that were burned down over a thousand years ago and the Pony People who lived in them speak through her when she is in a trance. Eventually she does as the Red Horse asks, having seen a vision of the Pony People gathered at a ceremony for Epona, burning herbs and chanting as the forms of Epona and the horse god on the altar grow monstrous.

In the ninth book in the series, *Chestnut Gold*, a mysterious man called the Walker who criss-crosses the moors and can gentle Shantih, leads Jinny to a sacred cave painted with a frieze of golden horses who dance when the sun's light hits them:

Mesmerised, Jinny stared down at the Walker. With his words she felt the reality of her everyday world floating from her, as if the doors of a prison opened on to vistas of freedom, and she stepped out into a world of shimmering beauty, a world at once magnetic and terrifying, that spoke so clearly to her inner being that its very strangeness was a homecoming.

The Walker destroys the cave after it is desecrated by a pushy film-maker who wants to expose the mystery to an audience of plastic people, and Jinny must repaint the golden horses at the Wilton Collection, with Epona and the horse god looking on.

Eventually, Jinny's fear of the Red Horse gives way to reverence for its awesome, deep and ancient power – after all, it brought her Shantih when she inadvertently prayed to it. Time and again it hooks her away from the quotidian horse world of showjumping and hunter trials, to show her what lies beyond them, although Epona and the Red Horse always release her back into the everyday world of her family and school, and through them she learns to keep that brighter, more meaningful inner life. When the dancing golden horses she has painted at the Wilton are in turn destroyed, she realizes that they are still in her head and will go on dancing as vividly as before. She learns to have an existence that overlays the two worlds like lamination, the older, richer Celtic world enhancing the modern and showing her which parts of it are false.

Leitch's great strength was to make both those worlds vivid and real. Shantih is a good deal more convincing as a living, breathing mammal than The Black, even with her mystical role. The Pony People are huddled and sad, but human; merely ancient, not sprites or pixies. Leitch's language is vibrant and poetic but never imprecise or clichéd, while Jinny's emotions are fully fleshed out and as convincing as the moors behind Finmory. This realism made the moments of fantasy all the more seductive. The thought came to me that if one day I too reached the heart of a moor, I could slip out of the boredom of contemporary life and growing up, and avoid the plastic people for ever.

In a letter Patricia sent to Jane Badger in 2008, she reminisced over Shantih and Jinny, who were still vivid to her twenty years after the series ended, and asked, 'What is imagination for if not to conjure up the past?' She was still living near the Kilmacolm moors, the inspiration for Finmory moor where she had ridden for years on her pony Kirsty, who was in turn the model partly for the Manderses' borrowed Highland pony Bramble and for Jinny's early battles with Shantih. Jane gave me an address for the care home where Patricia was recovering from a stroke, and I wrote to her to tell her about the hoof prints in Berlin and asked whether I could visit her. She wrote back a short note that, as she was in a single room, this was not possible, but she hoped to get into sheltered accommodation soon.

'Ah freedom, "say not the struggle naught availeth",' she scribbled.

'And you still read the Jinnys?' she queried, as if a little surprised.

'Their Time will come again, they still have a lot of life to be shared.'

'Wonder when the hoof prints rise over the wall?' she asked. And then she signed off, 'Shantih, Shantih, Shantih.'

The northernmost relic of the cult of the goddess Epona is a Roman altar found in 1771 near a section of the Antonine Wall by navvies digging the new Forth and Clyde canal at Auchendavie, seventeen miles from Kilmacolm. It's a roughly hewn stone block cracked in half at the waist and crammed with a roll-call of gods and goddesses including Epona, and the name of the donor, a centurion called Marcus Cocceius Firmus, who was thought to be a bodyguard of Emperor Marcus Aurelius.

Statuettes and inscriptions to Epona are found across much of the Roman Empire, although they are clustered in Western Europe, usually at points where garrisons were concentrated to defend new territory. She is the only Celtic goddess adopted by the Romans, and the only goddess in the Celtic pantheon who is worshipped in the same form both on continental Europe and in the British Isles. She protects horses and, by extension, those who work with them: the cavalrymen, grooms, farriers, cartmen, mule drivers, scouts, deliverers of dispatches, trainers and jockeys.

Epona is one of the old European earth mothers – the Lady of the Foals. She has no exact equivalent in the pantheon of the gods of the steppes, nor in Greek mythology, where Artemis presides over the birth of foals and Demeter sometimes has a mare's head. She either evolved to plug a theological gap in the Celtic pantheon or else she existed before the Roman conquest of much of Western Europe. All trace of her before that period has been lost, although there are wild Welsh and Irish goddess queens, Rhiannon and Medb, who are linked to horses and serve as earth mothers when the occasion demands. The name Epona means the divine or great mare, although she is usually depicted as a human.

You can see her in a case at the British Museum, a blackened copper Roman matron three inches high in a gathered chiton, seated on a throne and flanked by two small ponies or foals with clumsily sculpted bodies. Her hands rest on their backs, one supporting a dish of grain, the other a yoke. Their thumbish heads turn towards her in respect. Often she rides side-saddle, carrying an apple or an overflowing cornucopia. In a very few examples, she, alone of all the goddesses, rides astride. Epona surfaces only a handful of times in classical literature, where she is mentioned in passing and where Pseudo-Plutarch claims nastily that she's the offspring of the coupling of a mare and a man called Phoulouios Stellos, who hated women. No ruined temples dedicated to her have been excavated or found knitting up the foundations of a church; the statuettes of the goddess were found abandoned on the cobble floors of barracks and stables.

She was still worshipped in the fifth century and then was lost by name to the record, her rites broken up and scattered as the cult faded. As little is known about her original rituals, it's impossible to say whether Aelfthryth danced in her horse skull in the New Forest to supplicate Epona or some other Lady of the Foals. The poet and mythologist Robert Graves mentions Epona in passing as one facet of his White Goddess, related to a Danish Mare Goddess at whose feast horsemeat was consumed and horse blood splashed towards the south and east. The novelist Diane Ackerman says Europeans still ritually bled horses on Boxing Day in honour of the White Mare. Perhaps those remnants of horse magick such as horseshoes nailed up in stables, are distantly connected to her, as though horse people still made homage unwittingly.

Despite this slender trail, there has been a revival of the goddess. I found 'Devon, Maid of Epona', a former groom who lives in Pennsylvania, via the twenty-first-century divinatory method of Googling. She'd written several articles about worshipping Epona on Witch Box, a pagan community site.

Epona wants you to talk to Her. If you decide to work with Her, She can bring such beauty into your life. She is a very empowering goddess and She relates well to both men and women. She can give you strength and peace, laughter and healing. With Her you can accomplish amazing things if She is the right deity for you.

When the White Mare gallops into your life, pay attention! Listen! Follow, even if you cannot catch up.

Her hoof prints will lead you onward.

I called Devon to talk about Epona. She had a warm, good-humoured voice and laughed often. She was not remotely fey.

'The whole male God thing just never worked for me. Never. And when somebody suggested that God might be female I started perking up my ears. Then I found Wicca, and Wicca was nice because it was kind of like "Pick one, pick where you belong." And in my opinion if the divinity had designed us to be all one religion, then why did they make us so different? But before I even found Epona she was keeping an eye on me.

'I did not have a horsy childhood,' she went on, 'and I didn't understand why not, because my father was a wildlife biologist and I grew up on 800 acres of wildlife refuge. So there was room for a horse but I was told we couldn't have horses because the mosquitoes would eat them in the summertime. And if you knew where I grew up, you'd understand – it's all marshland. No one had horses – they would have gone nuts in the summertime. I had relatives in Pennsylvania and whenever I went to visit as a child, I think I could tell you every place we passed that had a horse in the backyard. I could tell the way there just from the horses in the fields, and the paddocks, and the houses that had horses.

'I wanted to do anything that involved horses. If I couldn't own them, then I wanted to work with them. And working with them taught me a lot about them, because I didn't have a clue how much work it would be, and they're a lot of work. But it prepared me. I was a good groom. I proved time and again that I could keep on top of things. I could spot colic easily and although horses can die of it, no horse that colicked on my watch has ever died.' That, Devon was sure, was Epona's influence.

Once she had discovered the Lady of the Foals, she says she 'pretty much learned by doing, by working with her, by talking with her – I would talk with her in the car on the way to work – and that was my morning prayers.'

Now she gave me a more hands-on list of suggestions for the worship of the goddess that she's developed: offerings of horseshoes, apples, grain, beer, roses and hippomane, a liverish deposit found with the placenta after some horse births.

'I got hired as an equine midwife at one stable, and that was an extremely powerful and moving experience. I helped the vet and watched the mares give birth, and it was very physical work. When she went into labour you were there in the stall, pulling the baby out of its mother, then feeding the foal colostrum within the first thirty minutes of its life. I'd go to work in the middle of the night and if there wasn't a baby born, I was very tired, but if there was a baby born, no matter how tired I was, I couldn't get to sleep the next morning, I was so keyed up. It was a very magical thing.'

'That's what Epona's about,' I offered, 'the birth of new foals for the year.'

Devon agreed. 'The whole maternal instinct. The rebirth and death, the whole cycle. If you wanna look for a trilogy, she is a trilogy. She is the birth, she is the life and she is the death too. She is the circle.'

Evidently her Epona was as persistent as the Red Horse and the goddess who compel Jinny to do their bidding. What kind of mistress was she, I wanted to know. Wrathful?

'Every time I tried to get away from the horse world, I found myself pulled back into it, so that was her signal to me. Everything was very subtle with Epona. This is where you belong, don't get out of it.'

'What does it feel like,' I asked, feeling daft, 'when she's there?'

Devon considered for a second, and then gave me an example. 'I have a very active imagination, but when I meditate and Epona comes through, it's stuff I couldn't make up,' she said emphatically. 'I remember a certain meditation where Epona came through and halfway through the meditation I thought, This is silly, I'm just imagining this. I'm just a little girl with a little horse dream and you know how little girls are with their horses. And Epona said something like, "Daughter, come to me." And I thought, I'm making this up. Then I got again, "DAUGHTER, come to me," just like she was saying, like any mom, "I'm not going to tell you again!" I was like, OK, got it. I'm not going to wait for the third! When she wants to make her presence felt, she makes it felt.'

'What does she look like?' I asked, thinking of the Red Horse with its terrifying yellow eyes and the black Roman matron-madonna with her foal guards of honour.

'Well, there are two depictions of Epona,' Devon explained, 'one as a woman with green eyes and brown hair, and one as a white mare. Personally whenever I picture her, she's the white mare variety.'

I imagined a grey Arabian mare floating across a field, or a stout white Highland pony with kinked tassels fringing its legs.

Devon believes that Epona can teach you many lessons, and that it's OK to ask her for things, but you must never ask for anything trivial. You should also be aware that she may grant you far more than you bargained for, as Jinny found out. You have to work hard to get your just deserts. I wondered whether Epona could help me keep my nerve at the riding club – I'm the kind of agnostic who greets magpies and will not walk under a ladder, and who swears by the placebo effect of horoscopes and tarot. It couldn't hurt to communicate with the White Mare. I asked Devon.

'Oh definitely,' she was emphatic. 'I would particularly ask her to bring the right horse into your life to help you with that, because it is a partnership.'

How should I go about it?

'If you cut off a bit of your hair and burn it, you will get an answer. I warn people, make sure what you're asking for, make sure you think about it and it's an ethical question before you sacrifice your hair, because when you do that, you will get an answer. It may not be what you're expecting,' Devon laughed, 'but it will be what you need to hear, whether you want to look in the mirror or not.'

Tav

The extension of power offered by a pony, the ease and speed of movement, the tapping of unsuspected courage, the satisfaction of collaboration with another creature and of controlling it in order to improve that collaboration, the joy of fussing over it – of loving it – these, from the age of about eight to sixteen were the most completely realised delights of my life.

Yesterday Morning (2002) by Diana Athill

My mother took the chance to cut a deal when I was eleven. Our friends, the Riseboroughs, had a riding school pony called Mactavish on loan and had asked if I'd like to ride him. I'd played horses for years with their eldest daughter, Carol, although now she was a little old for charging around over flowerpot fences. Tav came from a riding school at Swannington where Carol and her mother Linda rode, whose owner, Mrs Whiting, was selling up and leaving the country. Perhaps, Mum suggested, I would like the chance to ride him once a week and maybe I could give up a few other activities.

At the time, my parents ferried me not just to riding lessons, but also to swimming squad, where I ploughed up and down a pool in a Nissen hut, bored, and to ballet class, where at last the lure of feather coronets and stiff tutus had worn off. I never read many ballet books because I knew early on that, with my rolling insteps and shonky hips, I was never going to be Veronica at the Wells. It was all hop-scrape, hop-scrape, and the smell of floor polish at the Bob Carter Centre was giving way to something ranker; our teacher had suggested that it was time for our mothers to buy us deodorant. Leotards and swimming costumes were ceasing to be something you pulled on without thinking about how you were nearly naked, although I somehow managed to be oblivious to the physical remodelling that was going on.

I had escaped the junior school for a private girls' school, where I'd arrived, with my socks pushed down round my ankles and my skirt rolled up at the waist, to find that the natives pulled their knee socks up, wore plaits instead of perms and were happy to gallop around the wooded grounds and whinny. It was a brief reprieve from the problem of growing up. I slipped gratefully back into Jill Crewe and Mallory Towers, a world where your mother was given a list of suitable shoes and every day you wore a tie that could only be purchased in Bonds department store. You sat at wooden desks instead of Formica tables, and chased around a lacrosse pitch in matching aertex shirts and bumbags. I gave up ballet and swimming for homework, and carried on having lessons at Cringleford, while hacking out on Tav, with my mum in pursuit on a bike with the dog. After a while, she let me ride out alone.

Tav was only nominally a Highland. Nobody knew what he really was. Old Mr Peruzzi, the local scrap-metal merchant and owner of trotters, who knew every pony in Norfolk, reckoned Tav was a 'Highland crossed with something'. Mactavish resembled most a miniature Suffolk Punch. He was the rich marmalade 'chesnut' – as it is spelled in this breed's case – of a Punch, blazing to soft fuzzy red in the winter. Stout and glossy in the summer, he'd break out in a sheen of faint purple dapples. His mane was as dense as a Highland's and fell at will on either side of his neck, but his legs were clean like a Punch's, with a fine skirt of pale-chestnut hair over his hooves. He was sturdy but had no pony barrel belly, although he was an incurable 'good doer' who only lost weight when kept on starvation rations in one of Mr Peruzzi's dirt paddocks.

He had a great, plain skull like the Iron-Age horse mask in the

Stanwick hoard, bony and solid – a horse's head, neither dished like a pretty Welsh pony nor Roman. His eyes were brown with a ginger fringe of short lashes, the brow often gathered and thoughtful, his ears foxy. Mr Peruzzi helped to fill in a few of the blanks in Tav's biography, which was as chequered as Dick's or Beauty's. He'd been purchased as a two-year-old by someone in the travelling community and turned over to their son, so he could practise breaking in. The son had set a solid wooden saltire cross called a dumb jockey on his back and bent his neck to it with fixed reins. When the Costessey vet came to rasp his teeth, he noticed Tav's jaw had been damaged and set badly. He had a thick neck and a strong will, did Tav, which probably led to the injured jaw, although Tav himself was emphatically not 'broken'. He remained a horse of many opinions, not inscrutable but very intelligent – it was not always possible to second-guess him, even when you had known him for years. The traveller's son sold him to a dealer called Siddy Wright, and then he was purchased by a lady who liked to bring on horses. She later passed him on to Mrs Whiting at Willow Cottage Riding School in Swannington.

Here Tav was in his element. He liked to lead the ride, and if anyone was fool enough to open his stable door when he was on a break, Tav would barge past them and canter to the schooling paddock, where he would join in with the lesson. He went to local shows and did a bit of jumping, and turned out to go very handily in a cart. This was another mystery – evidently the traveller's son had tried him in harness a few times. Tav carried a decade's worth of pupils, and years later, when she was hacking out, Carol would be stopped by people who remembered him fondly, even though he had trodden on their toes, or scraped their knees on a gatepost when they weren't paying attention. When the peevish handy-pony judge at the Costessey Show Ground told me she recognized him, it didn't surprise me in the least, nor was I surprised that he'd thrown her, although that was not normal behaviour for him. He was a good judge of character.

He was engaged in a constant study of exactly what he could get away with. Once Carol left her boyfriend holding Tav outside the post office while she went in to get ice creams. She came out to find Tav, ears pricked and mouth drooling at the sight of the cones, and the boyfriend out cold on the pavement after a well-timed head butt. I laboriously built a little course of crocky jumps made of traffic cones and painted drainpipes, and jumped Tav over them. Afterwards, I watched from a hiding place in the stable as he walked round the field, pushing over all the fences with his nose.

Tav was kept in a field that sloped gently down to a deep stretch of the Tud where it flowed under Longwater Lane bridge, just over in New Costessey at the edge of the old grounds of Costessey Hall. At the top was a low, pink-brick stable with three loose boxes, one of which was packed with straw and hay bales. The windows were laced with cobwebs that had collected that fine brown greasy powder that comes off ponies' coats in quantity. There was a battered old freezer with pony nuts in it and a sack of misshapen carrots. The long side of the field looked out over sheep pastures to the stump of Costessey Hall tower, as it strained to clear a choke-hold of dark ivy, and to distant woodland that reached round to Ringland, somewhere near the site of that lost deer park where Queen Elizabeth I had once hunted. On the other side was an orchard where Kitty, a dappled-grey cob mare with white feathers, sometimes grazed with a donkey for company.

On one occasion Tav gorged on windfall apples that fell on his side of the fence. I rode him up to my parents' house, wondering at his sluggishness, and once there he showed no interest in carrots but tried to lie down on the lawn and sleep. I walked him back to Longwater Lane where he stood in the middle of the field on three legs, his bottom lip baggy, his coat dull, drunk as a lord. Every time he tried to lie down, I ran over and pushed him back up again, fearing colic. His hangover lasted for days and he never touched an apple again.

More often than not, though, he was down by the electric tape that kept him from the marshy, river end of the field, where he would soak his hooves till they went soft and whinny for Kitty, whose other paddock lay over the river and across the Recreation Ground, a bland stretch of lawn with a cricket field, a playground and some tennis courts where people walked their dogs or, when the wind allowed, flew kites, which Tav watched. One Christmas, Tav swam across the Tud and galloped amok all over the green, looking for Kitty and tearing great divots out of the pitch.

When the electric tape first went up, Tav was discovered on the river side of it the next day, and had to be retrieved. The landlord, Mr Perrott, who lived in the bungalow by the field, increased the voltage. By morning, Tav was back dabbling in the Tud where it flowed over clover and long grass. Mr Perrott announced that he would 'not be beaten by a horse brain', and added a second strand of tape. Tav appeared once more by the water's edge, grazing briskly. The fence was not uprooted or broken. There were no hoof prints suggesting he'd jumped it, and as the gaps between the two strands and the lowest strand and the ground could have only been a foot wide, the most plausible explanation was a trapdoor, or that he simply disappeared from one side and materialized with a loud pop on the other in all his hairy bulk. Finally, observation revealed that Tav would stand on the lowest tape, thrust his head and neck, thatched by his thick mane, under the top tape and then scoot through with the live tape skimming along his back. Mr Perrott bought more tape and, muttering, spent an hour or two fitting it to the fence, while Tav browsed the short grass on the stable side and watched out of the corner of his eye. This third strand did the trick and Tav was no longer to be found on the river side.

Tav was not the kind of pony to come when you called. You could get him to walk up the field to you, but only if you stood on the brow of the hill outside the stables, waited till he raised his head and looked at you, then pulled a carrot out of your pocket and started to eat it. Then, after a moment's thought, he would walk steadily towards you, head low, ears to the fore, a look of intent on his face.

On hot summer days I'd find him sprawled on his side in the sun, his back to the stable and his belly to the view over the Tud, and as I approached he would poke his nose out to see who it was. I was glad that he didn't see me as a reason to get up and run off, but just went on sunbathing as I crouched down and scratched the white whorl on his forehead. Eventually, with a weary grunt, he rolled up onto his knees and then was up on all four hooves for a shake, making believe that he had no idea I was there to put a halter on him and dipping his nose towards the grass, but submitting at last as if accepting it was a fair cop.

I'd take two steps trying to lead him up the field, then I'd have to take a step back and give him a slap on the rump before he conceded and walked on beside me as though he were Ginger waiting for the knacker's van. At the gate I tied him under the hawthorn tree where I'd left my grooming kit in a plastic toolbox, fished out a dandy brush and went to work. He liked to lean on you when you held his hoof to scrape it clean. When Carol mucked out his stable he'd pick her up by the waistband of her jodhs, or rest his head on her back and sigh.

There was usually a play at refusing to take his bit, until you poked a thumb in the bar of his mouth and levered it open. Then, when I'd swung on the saddle – which was pigskin, half painted a horrible fleshy colour and half worn to brown leather – and dropped the girth over, he'd breathe in, his ribs distended like a dropsy victim, and brace himself for the buckling. He couldn't hold his breath for ever, though, so I'd pull his headcollar off and lead him round to the gate, then plunge under the saddle skirt and hoick at the girth straps till they would go no further. Finally I would pull the stirrups down the leathers, set one foot in the iron and commence hopping before launching up, at which point Tav would take a neat step away from me, but I'd be ready for him and land on the pigskin only a little too heavily.

I would negotiate the field gate from Tav's back, in a casual fashion, swinging him round and dropping the chain over the post, and then we'd set out for Ringland, with Tav sometimes pretending that the Tud was transformed into a life-threatening force as it flowed under Longwater Lane bridge. His only true fears were the air brakes on the number 20 bus and the slaughterhouse in the village, whose walls smelled of pig blood and from where squealing could be heard. We would turn left and head off along West End towards Ringland.

The road through the village was a continuation of The Street and followed the Wensum, which lay on the right behind the Costessey-brick houses with their long, waterlogged gardens. We would pass Kitty's little field; she might come to the fence to nicker at Tav, who would strain his ears and bridle and have to be pushed on. A little further on opposite the gates to Costessey Park was the old Falcon Inn where the painter Alfred Munnings stayed to prepare for painting expeditions. Munnings bought a blue caravan, a gypsy cart, a troop of ponies and a donkey from a Norwich dealer with an aesthete's eye and a businessman's hunch for a client who'd take some difficult equines off his hands.

'Look, Mr Munnin's,' he told him, ''e 'on't 'ev nothing to dew wi' a cart or 'arness, but what a beautiful pony for a picture!'

A Costessey character called Shrimp or Fountain Page, an 'undersized, tough, artful young brigand', played groom and became Munning's muse, although like many muses Shrimp was not without his temperamental complexities. Dressed in the picturesque outfit ordered for him by Munnings, he arrived drunk at the Falcon and fell under the wheels of the cart, which came to rest against his head. Later Munnings had to bail him out of jail.

The inn was now a private house, repainted a fresh white with black-framed windows, but still with a loop of gravel drive out front, as if waiting for the arrival of carriages. Munnings would not have recognized the pebbledash council houses that had sprung up after the war, set back from the road on long lawns. He was repelled by the New Costessey bungalows when he visited in 1947. Sand collected in tiny drifts at the road edges. This stage of our ride dragged as cars queued behind Tav's broad, orange quarters and I would wave them on or halt them to let oncoming traffic pass. The road's faded surface was patched with potholes and a long scar of fresh black tarmacadam where a pipe had been put in. Peering over the fences, I could catch a glimpse of pale-green lozenges of poplar trees and the cows in the river meadows. At the outer edges of Costessey, we'd pass a great field split with dykes and run wild with dense copses of nettles and giant hogweed with thick, ribbed stems. The ponies roaming in it would raise their heads to see Tav pass. At the road's fork, the village finally tapered out and we would head left towards Ringland, and into the countryside, following the route of Munnings's cavalcade.

A pale wheat field might peter through a break in the hedge, swallowed by a profusion of hooped wild grass on the road verge, grown lush on fertilizer. Tav would plunge his nose in, yanking the plaited leather reins through my palms to tear up squeaking ribbons of tough, flat-bladed grass, missing the silky darts of wall barley and the wild-oat stems that challenged like épées. Later, I'd find goose-grass pillules in the fringes over his hooves. Tav was unperturbed by the cabbage whites that flew in quivering loops in front of his nose before settling on the cow parsley or worrying at the tiny white gramophone horns of bindweed flower and cochineal poppies like burst balloon skin. Across the fields the red roof and chimneys of Taverham Hall rose from dark-green treetops.

We'd pass the sand road that used to lead to my old riding school, sometimes with a dusty, growling lorry behind us waiting to turn off to the quarry. All traces of the old yard were gone, the manège lost under a desert of harsh ochre sand staked out by rosebay willowherb, ready to fill the air with its cotton-wool seeds. Tav's ears would sweep back to monitor the lorry as I shortened my reins and refused to kick him on for the driver's convenience.

Further down the road, the hedges became glossy laurel and rough leylandii as we'd pass gardens and houses, and the sand at the roadside gave way to leafmould mulch and yew pins; the hedges and trees reached up and over the road to form a cool, dark-green tunnel. Puddles lingered in the shade. If I stood up in my stirrups I could look over the high fences erected on the river-side of the road and see the Wensum flowing by, as flat and slow as olive-green gloss paint, its far bank jungly with purple foxgloves and thick vegetation that no angler bothered to penetrate. The fences concealed a race of secretive old men who camped in battered, ancient cabins dusted with dark-green algae, surrounded by long lawns barely carved out of a tangle of wild riverbank foliage. They could be glimpsed at leisure in their deckchairs or else performing some mysterious task involving hoarded planks of wood or old tractors. They put up ship's bells for visitors to ring and employed large padlocks to keep out thieves. Peering over the fence, I'd wish them good morning and they'd give me a curt nod, before going on with the business of escaping their wives.

If the flies were bothering Tav, I'd reach for a spray of cream elderflowers and lean forward to cram it under his browband, his ears swivelling at me as he accepted his crown as Queen of the May. The woods on the left were half given over to a dark grove of rhododendrons that must have been another remnant of the hall's grounds. After a few turns we'd emerge into light at Beehive Lodge, a white drum with a thatched roof and black-painted trees bracing its side. Munnings had had use of one of its rooms to stack his canvases to dry. Here he would watch for one Moses Rogers, a Norwich cheese merchant who went fishing from the Wensum bank opposite every Thursday afternoon, dressed in a silk hat and white waistcoat with a flower in his lapel. I usually passed anglers there too, fathers and sons drably dressed in neutral country-coloured anoraks and jeans, settled on fold-out nylon stools with a picnic cooler for their catch.

I didn't pay them much attention, as I'd begin to sit up straight in my saddle and shorten my reins, and Tav to step out more, as we were coming to the Stubble Field. A roodscreen of old trees swamped with ivy separated the generous, open stretch of cropped wheat from the tarmac road. (Once, flying homewards at a clip along the Stubble Field, Tav jumped out through the screen and onto the road, sparks flying from his shoes.) Tav and I would break into a canter on the whispering, hollow straws. He'd be good to me and the bit, and we'd both enjoy ourselves, me up in my stirrups a little, leaning forward over his mane, Tav bowling, his heavy nose pushed out, the thrup, thrup, thrup of a snort in his nose, until he ran out of puff and came back to a raking trot, shaking his head and snorting long, 'clearing his pipes', and me grinning, slapping lightly into the saddle and bouncing up as he was going too fast to post. At the end of the field I'd turn him up the hill along the edge of the woods of Ringland Hills, and at the top corner there was an opening in the trees under an oak branch. As we walked out of the sun and into the cool of the wood, I could look back to see the sweep of the Stubble Field, broad as a racecourse, curving away like the first bend at Epsom.

Tav's hooves would beat the hollow ground with a tum, tum as the foliage closed in overhead. He'd stretch out and snatch great fronds of rotten-smelling green ferns, a sweet poison, so I'd have to lean down to tug them out of his mouth, to his annoyance. Then I'd have my arm hooked by a bramble with its delicate, flexible thorns, which rasped as Tav carried me by, trying to prevent me from confiscating the bracken, leaving a fine thread of blood beads. I'd let the reins hang slack on his neck when the danger of the bracken was past and the path sloped steeply up, and he would poke his nose out happily, stepping faster to meet the steep path, which was really a gully for rainwater, with a seam of sand in the crook of it. Flints the size of sheep skulls had come to rest here and there, with drifts of twig and ground leafmould caught against them.

Among the oaks were silver birches, enormous, ragged holly

bushes and sudden groves of slender trees, sprouted close together. We would rise up the steep-sided gulley as it curled up the hill, passing small hollows like bomb craters, or collapsed and abandoned badger dens. At the top of the hill, the woods gave way to silver-green gorse bushes and I'd pick up Tav's reins as we came to the grass clearing on the very crown of the hill. The view over the Ringland meadows was concealed behind the trees, but I'd canter Tav in a slow circle as though the lumpy clearing were a circus ring. Then we'd head back into the wood, over puddles like day-old stewed tea and past brick-wall fragments half submerged in the path, old forester's huts or piggeries or who knows what.

Munnings painted Shrimp riding the ponies bareback on the uplands, surrounded by a swirl of the yellow gorse that intoxicated him and which was picked up in the yellow kerchief that the groom had knotted about his neck. Exhilarated by the multiplying canvases that piled up in Beehive Lodge, the artist stripped naked in a storm and danced and sang to the tune of 'Nuts in May':

> When we were young the only way
> Was to finish a picture day by day;
> Now we're old and turning grey,
> We polish it off in a morning.

The country with its gentle slopes – barely hills – never satisfied my own need for drama, but the skies did. I could barely see the landscape for them. They were so big that they were overpowering when clear, and like the late wild swimmer and nature diarist Roger Deakin, I found that an overdose of East Anglian skies had the effect of 'becalming' me. When you are already spaced out and drowsy with adolescence, there is nothing to anchor you. It was easier when the skies were filled with blue-bottomed cumuli like barges piled high with cotton, or with enough mackerel skin for a celestial shoal.

I didn't want to be becalmed. I chafed at confinement in stupid teenage nothingness, unable to drive, constricted by the funnel of GCSEs and A levels and UCAS forms, and wished Norfolk into something different. I wanted wilderness and moorland; I knew that there was 'real' country elsewhere in the county, but it lay beyond the range of our wanderings. There were always faded drink cans and crisp packets that the wood could not digest, or the occasional burned-out car, its tyres coming off as though they'd been run through a ricer. On the roads we'd see toads reduced to 2D in mid-leap, their paper-flat arms and legs outstretched and their innards in a neat pink pile by their mouths. Once, as we drowsed our way down the lane that cut between Ringland and the Costessey road, with me singing tunelessly, Tav stumbled and slid on his knees, leaving a pair of foot-long stripes of chestnut hair on the tarmac. Mortified, I led him home and had my hands bitten into bear paws by clegs.

Tav was my fellow explorer; he never baulked at new routes and was happy to be out alone with me. I could take him anywhere I dared, though I kept off crops and never ventured behind 'private' signs as I didn't want my adventures ruined by an adult scolding. Together we explored every wood, every bit of common, every footpath I could find that rose up and away from the roads.

We had half a dozen or more rides, striking out in any direction as long as it took us away from the big road. There was the Railway Line, where I'd once been a pitiful, ponyless girl feeding horses in the fields. There were the tracks up by Moreton Hall, where, one misty winter morning, we stumbled across a muddy field littered with little Nissen huts like an old airfield, out of which exploded a troop of pigs who trotted over, their bare chubby pink thighs rubbing together. Tav started and curled away, and the pigs halted in a row, the weak winter sun behind them catching the long, white, bristling hairs that fringed their ears, lighting them up like haloes. In the summer we paddled in the Wensum. Tav plashed at the water with his fore hooves and dropped his muzzle in it, before flinging his head up and scattering droplets. Or there was the great field the other side of Honingham Lane, with a huge block of rancid silage like a fetid terrine, and a spindly water-spraying system stretching across the arid crops.

My parents had started me on black-spined Penguin classics – Janes Eyre and Austen, Hardy and Trollope – so in a literary mood, Tav and I sought out a lonely loop of track round open fields on the other side of Ringland that served in my mind as Haworth, with its own isolated rectory, or the long, bleak, black-soil stretches beyond Taverham heading to Marriots Way, which made me think of Tess D'Urberville wrenching half-eaten swedes out of a frozen, hundred-acre field. The landscape didn't in any way resemble Dorset, but as a state of mind it gave good frisson. The mill at the other end of Costessey could have been the Mill on the Floss, where Maggie Tulliver drowned with her brother, and I looked out for the old machinery spikes I'd been told lay under the surface.

In the Blackbreck plantation there were red-trunked pines and velvet, stunted, starburst grass, dew-ponds and dark, windowless huts. Paths stretched away out of sight between rows of trees so rigidly and densely planted that staring down one aisle made your eyes buzz like an optical illusion. I was never quite sure if I was allowed to be in there, but the close trees muffled us, and I found a little course of jumps that someone had constructed from fallen branches. Tav would attack them with gusto and then, his blood up, bolt. Once he exploded out of the wood and off a bank onto the road like a startled cock pheasant in his bright-red winter coat, landing twenty yards in front of a car with a loose piece of thick wire tinkling round one leg.

Twelve years after my last amble on Tav, I sat on Gräfin in the middle of the ring at the riding club as Ynes hooked three fingers under her girth, then pushed my leg up out of the way and disappeared under the saddle flap to tug it up. The mare's neck stretched away and plunged down in front of me, bowed by the side reins, her mane lying as precisely as Clark Gable's kiss-curl. Her ears winced with the tightening girth, and little fractals of anxiety began to unfurl in my mind – *Will she kick? If she kicks what will I do? Can I hold her? What if I can't hold her?* – each one of them budding and bursting into replicant fears. I hadn't expected such a swift change in myself after my fall from Zofe.

'She's in a bad mood,' I observed.

'*Mausi*, why a bad mood?' Ynes asked the mare, then grinned, clucked to her and sent me out onto the track, where I rode unfocussed and badly. Gräfin had her own preoccupations; once again she was absorbed by her private battle with the side reins, snatching her chin back, then throwing it forward and snapping them, or starting when the lady in front tappy-tap-tapped her horse or it swished its tail in annoyance.

She was peevish when the other horses came close, and their riders would admonish us both with a 'Gräfin!' – as though there were anything I could have done to make her happy. Everyone else was on horses, while I was on a big, glossy sea monster, a creature from another element. I should have made offerings to Poseidon before I pulled on my boots. I scratched her withers to soothe her as we walked. We looked good in the school mirrors, although I was sallow and grim.

We still always cantered as a ride and only in a circle in one third of the ring, never for the length of it. The nine horses in a class made a complete hoop when we cantered a centre circle round Ynes, a zoetrope or a frieze of flickering horses: black, grey, chestnut, bay, one gawky, one thickset, one snorting, one farting, two tossing their tails, one breaking into a trot, one on the verge of careering. There was an altercation between two horses by Gräfin and me, and she bunched and half bucked and, this time with no instinct but panic, I turned her into the centre of the zoetrope and stopped her there. My diaphragm had thickened to two inches of rubber, barely elastic, and I choked like an hourglass with a stoppage. Fear is the biggest, blackest horse; I felt it would have swallowed Gräfin with a gulp.

At the end of the lesson, I slid off onto flimsy limbs. The mare pricked her ears and tried to rub her nose up and down my back, the way Tav used to. I fussed her, kissed her, pulled her ears and said, 'You silly old mare, you sour old mare. What's the matter?'

'I'm so nervous, and she seems worried by the other rider's whip,' I began to tell Ynes in bad German.

'Ja, ja,' she said, unconcerned, 'and she does it when they swish their tails too.'

Afterwards, I hauled off Gräfin's tack and tied her outside her box in the barn so she could attempt a conversation with the pony next door. She pricked her ears as she heard me tear the wrapper from a packet of mints. One for her and one for the pony, who was so squat that he had to crane his muzzle up to the level of the stable door. I poked the mints directly through the bars, into his snuffling lips and yellow teeth.

I talked to Gräfin as I tried to buff the clods of yellow sand from the school off her hooves, then picked out each one in turn, though there was nothing in them. I ran the plastic brush on the back of the hoof pick round the frog. Sparrows swooped between the barn rafters in imitation of swallows.

I went to work with the body brush and currycomb: two swipes with the brush on her neck, one rasp of the bristles on the curry to clean it, then two more swipes, leaning hard against the muscle as she leaned back against me and propped up a hoof. The pony shuffled around in his box and checked his manger for the umpteenth time, in case the oat fairy had visited.

I skimmed off the fine particles of dirt that made a bloom on Gräfin's coat, revealing the expensive shine underneath – ebony, velvet, satin, every pony-book cliché. I thought how lovely it would be if I could go on grooming horses for ever and never have to ride them. She wasn't the Loch Ness Monster after all. I fed one more mint to the pony – it was like feeding an elephant when all you could see was the trunk – while Gräfin nuzzled jealously, and the scent of herby horse breath and sharp peppermint oil was heavenly. Then I dug for the extravagance of a red, organic apple I'd hidden in my hat bag and held it out for the mare. She sank her teeth in and chewed away two thirds, leaving the other third in the palm of my hand as I waited patiently, the apple wallah. She champed scuds of foamy saliva and dribbled on my sleeve. I left her in her box, having kicked the straw around for her to even it out where she'd roiled it up.

As I walked back to the U-bahn, I realized that nothing much had happened in the lesson, except that I had been very afraid. That was all.

The Beast

One of my classmates at my new school, a shrewd, studious little girl with tight brown curls and gold-rimmed glasses, embarked on writing a kind of *Decameron-cum-Confessions-of-Fanny-Hill*, with one erotic story for each member of the class. Each tale was thoughtfully tailored to its subject. She had a precocious flair for hackneyed erotic themes, and when I got my turn with the notebook during its brief circulation before being intercepted by a teacher, I discovered that in 'my' story I rode out on horseback with a man and we tumbled off into the leaf mould together to make passionate love. Shades of Mellors.

Oh how far the cliché reaches, and now, at eleven, with new knowledge gleaned from sex-education videos featuring a gambolling family of nudists, it came creeping into my consciousness. There was, it seemed, something about girls and horses and girls who liked horses. It was not just the objection of my primary-school teacher to the fact that every story I wrote for her was about horses. This was an intrusive, insinuating new implication. The snickering at the title of the Ruby Ferguson book, *Jill Enjoys Her Ponies*, leering references to

Catherine the Great and a sudden friskiness on seeing riding boots
and whips. The whoops coming from a passing car of teenage boys
when Tav stopped to pee in the road, with me stranded awkwardly in
my stirrups waiting for it to be over. It came with adolescence and it
stayed.

'Isn't it true,' one man in Berlin once asked me, curiosity pricking
round the corners of his mouth, as he seemed sure that he would
finally have the definitive answer to What Women Want, 'that when
women ride, they have orgasms?'

'It's actually all about sex, isn't it? The women and horse thing?'
another Mr Mybug said, confidently.

I thought of one little girl I'd been told about, whose parents were
oblivious to the real reason she loved to ride a carousel horse every
day, and of Anaïs Nin's short story, 'The Model', in which the
heroine's garter comes loose mid-gallop and wreaks havoc in her
knickers. The same heroine later has a wild ride on a mechanical
horse with a prominent pommel while posing for a painting of a
woman riding with wild abandon.

The mythical association of horse with sex is ancient, probably
pre-dating their domestication. The horse that was sacrificed to the
sun or the sky god by the Scythians ensured meat and prosperity, and
was therefore required to be fertile. Epona was a mother goddess.
Queen Aelthfryth danced with the ponies in the New Forest to
ensure there would be more foals, and we appear to have inherited
the symbol, without any innate understanding of what first created
the association. We conflate the libidinous stallion and lustful mares
that unnerved the poet Virgil in the *Georgics*, not with power and
wealth but with the randy equestrienne who rides all day and is not
yet satisfied.

'Did you know horses lead to divorces?' asked Lord Arran in the
Sunday Times in 1967. 'You've no idea how sexually promiscuous they
are in the shires. It's all that jumping up and down on horses that
does it. They get over-stimulated.' In women, an abnormal love of

horses is taken as an indicator of abnormal sexuality and of immoderate, inappropriate appetite.

In Władysław Podkowiński's 1894 painting, Frenzy of Elations, the canvas is filled with a dark, tumultuous storm from which emerges a black stallion, rearing and suspended or perhaps plummeting through the turmoil. His eye is a blank, goggling ball; his mouth a grotesque, outsized leer, dribbling foam; and his legs are as feathered as a satyr's. A naked voluptuary straight out of an absinthe advert clings to his neck, her face upturned and her eyes closed in opiate bliss, golden hair flying behind her, her white breasts pressed into his mane. It was too much for its artist: after it had been on display for thirty-seven days, Podkowiński attacked it with a knife.

In the literature of the early sexology of the same period, women who pour their energy into beasts, instead of their homes, their husbands and their children, are deviants and nymphomaniacs; their excessive devotion to the equine is part of the symptomatology. Miss D, a tomboy who grew up to be an 'invert' in British author Havelock Ellis's Studies in the Psychology of Sex, said, 'Before I could walk I begged to be put on horses' backs.' For German sexologist Baron von Krafft-Ebing, the 'female urning' or lesbian was one who was drawn to horses because they represented male toys and soldiery instead of dolls and girliness. 'The masculine soul, heaving in the female bosom, finds pleasure in the pursuit of manly sports, and in manifestations of courage and bravado.' His beautiful patient, Miss X, despite having 'a large bust and the appearance of an exceptionally handsome woman', refused the attentions of would-be suitors and was 'strikingly mannish in her manners, had masculine tastes, loved gymnastics and horseback exercise, smoked, and had masculine carriage and gait'.

Krafft-Ebing also recounts the tale of Alice M, aged nineteen and 'belonging to one of the best families in Memphis, Tennessee, USA', who was passionately in love with a Freda W ('also of the best society'). Alice had sent her an engagement ring, begging her to elope with her to St Louis, where she would grow a moustache and get a job, and they could live as man and wife, but Freda had begun to be interested in boys. Alice's attempt to kill her love by pouring laudanum into her mouth when she was asleep proved unsuccessful, but she later fatally slashed Freda's throat with a razor. Alice M had had her own pony and loved to care for it, 'riding about the paddock astraddle on its back like a boy, without a saddle'.

Then there's what Krafft-Ebing called 'stuff fetishism', the feel of pony skin, coarse tail hairs, leather, the smell of sweat. The trappings of sado-masochism are also those of horses: for those who want to be abused, there's a whole wardrobe of accoutrements in the tack-room – gags, bits, martingales, cruppers, fearsome crops and spurs. Horse-training manuals are full of the language of subjugation and mastery. The poet Ruth Padel compared *Black Beauty* to pornographic narratives like *Fanny Hill*, calling Ginger's breaking-in her 'deflor-ation'. In Weimar Berlin they called the whores who took a flogging *Rennpferde* or racehorses.

The horsewoman can be a fresh source of titillation as she swishes her crop impatiently – any dominatrix with mettle wears riding boots. There was a witch in Kennet valley in the late 1800s who used a carter from a local farm as a mount, appearing at his bedside and bitting him with a magic bridle before galloping him in horse form to join her sisters at their coven. In medieval apocrypha, the elderly Aristotle lets the young, beautiful Phyllis saddle him and ride on his back. Krafft-Ebing had a patient called 'Z' who 'dreamed he was a proud, fiery steed ridden by a beautiful lady. He felt her weight, the bit he had to obey, the pressure of the thighs on his flanks; he heard her joyous, beautiful voice.' He artfully manipulated the lady he lived with into saying she would like to try this for herself, and then she rode him, beating him, scolding him and fussing him for forty minutes at a time. She rode astride, in 'short closed drawers reaching to the knee', with gloves and hat in place.

*

When it became clear after the Second World War that little girls were the most devoted members of the horse cult, the Freudians stepped in to make explicit what the earlier generation of sexologists had hinted at. In *Normality and Pathology in Childhood* (1965), Anna Freud tapped down the nails, one by one:

A little girl's horse-craze betrays either her primitive autoerotic desires (if her enjoyment is confined to the rhythmic movement of the horse); or her identification with the care-taking mother (if she enjoys looking after the horse, grooming it, etc.); or her penis envy (if she identifies with the big, powerful animal and treats it as an addition to her body); or her phallic sub-limations (if it is her ambition to master the horse, to perform on it etc).

The child psychoanalyst Bruno Bettelheim, writing in her wake, had the best interests of the little girls at heart:

Imagine what it would do to a girl's enjoyment of riding, to her self-respect, if she were made conscious of this desire which she is acting out in riding. She would be devastated – robbed of a harmless and enjoyable sublimation, and reduced in her own eyes to a bad person. At the same time, she would be hard-pressed to find an equally suitable outlet for such inner pressures, and therefore might not be able to master them.

So all this then, the little girls 'galloping gaily round and round, with radiant faces and flying hair' in the Hayes riding school, the child whom Vieille Moustache saw begging, 'Dear Mamma, let me ride, let me ride,' the girl-cavaliers at Olympia with their 'ardent desire to "beat the boys"': all this was repressed sex and maternal instinct, erotic obsession and a lack of babies? Why else, I suppose, would females pour so much energy and enthusiasm into some-thing? It cannot be for the reasons that they themselves give, for how could they know their own minds? It must be sexual, except that . . .

When I learned the association as a pre-teen, riding-school ponies were not suddenly transformed in my eyes into what they'd been all along, hairy, obstreperous, misplaced penises and instruments of sinful association. They remained just ponies whose personalities I knew, whose quirks and whose speed I enjoyed, with whom I hoped to win rosettes. If I was robbed of something 'harmless and enjoyable' by the revelation, it was that core, childlike unselfconsciousness in my enthusiasm. Now I was uncomfortably aware that to others I was a smutty punchline, lusting to roll around in the leaf mould with a human stallion.

This, it has to be said, is not just the fate of equestriennes – it happens to all teenage girls, whatever they enjoyed as children. Gymnastics? My, how bendy you are! – nudge nudge. Football? Well, you know what they say about women footballers. Walking down the street in school uniform? A provocative act! Don't you know the effect you're having? Just as a girl's physical transformation at puberty is beyond her control, so are the fantasies of others.

The erotic is often in the eye of the beholder, and Freudians can find the sexual in a ticking clock and an overcoat. When a female patient was afflicted with constant vomiting, Freud explained that it was merely that as a teenager she had wanted to churn out infants with a multitude of men, and that she was punishing and protecting herself by rendering herself unattractive through weight loss. When a psychologist challenged Freud to find a sexual interpretation for his recurring dream of climbing stairs, Freud's rejoinder was that stairs were 'undoubtedly a symbol of copulation', because one got out of breath and stair climbing was rhythmical. As his critic Richard Webster put it, 'His observation is not dissimilar from the proposition that, since alligators and elephants both have four legs, alligators are actually elephants.' The mental acrobatics tell us more about Sigmund Freud, the man, than his patients or the greater human consciousness.

The neat logic, which in Professor Freud's 'organic analogy' conflates a penis with excrement and maintains that women desire babies because babies are penises, must mean a horse is a turd, a phallus and a baby all at once, and so all the pleasure and all the elation and power the little girl feels must be erotic. A horse is not merely a swift, four-legged, hoofed mammal but the ultimate sex toy, which fools you into thinking you're not having penis envy at all.

Do I protest too much? Well, there's the infuriating, infallible Freudian trap: if you deny it, they say, you mean it all the more. The psychoanalyst hogs the last word from his patient. My argument is complicated by the fact that a horse is obviously, in itself, a sexual being. As Angela Carter pointed out when she examined Georgia O'Keefe's voluptuous flower paintings, O'Keefe's images are sexual because stamens and unfolded petals *are* sex organs. And while a horse is just a horse, it is also male or female – rampantly so, on occasion.

The action of riding astride can certainly resemble a sexual act, the rider with their legs parted, their pelvis rocking back and forth in rhythm with the animal, but does that mean it is, actually, any more physically sexual than climbing stairs? As for the idea that, as my Mr Mybug maintained, women have physical climaxes when riding, then think of my own riding lessons and what they would have been like with eight self-conscious teenage girls oohing and gasping their way through transitions. And what about Olympic cross-country riders? Do you really imagine that someone in the throes of a climax could steer a hot horse through an obstacle course of solid timbers and ford rivers? All swooning and fainting like that Anaïs Nin heroine?

There is a certain blankness of thought that comes from riding actively, intensely and well, when the rider's concentration is so focussed on the horse that the mind might as well be diffused through the entire body – I'd felt a hint of it the first time I rode Zofe – but it is not a *petit mort*. Not all sensation and passion is confined to sex. Girls do not stop riding, as one pseudo-theorist suggested, because, having access to boys, they no longer need to masturbate.

Little girls might want power and ambition for their own sakes, and not for the trophy of an imaginary willy.

But within that horse love of little girls is a great aesthetic appreciation of the equine form – those endless drawings and gazings (not that these efforts are exclusively female, by any means). Melissa Holbrook Pierson wrote beautifully about the physical appeal of the horse, conceding, 'All love is at base sexual, or perhaps even deeper at base the social is sexual, and since we don't know where these things begin and end in our daily life, we are not about to demarcate them when it comes to girls and horses, either.' Perhaps.

One friend confided that her first erotic dream stemmed from reading Elyne Mitchell's *The Silver Brumbies of the South*, which features the creamy wild stallion, Throwra, leading his band of mares. Both Throwra's Golden and Jewel, a thoroughbred mare drawn into Thunderhead's band in Mary O'Hara's *The Green Grass of Wyoming*, are like white women seduced by an outlaw sheikh in a romance novel when the stallions come to call for them in the night and spirit them away.

I was contacted by another woman who told me that she and her husband liked to role-play as stallion and mare in bed, but she thought better of being interviewed, and the bedroom door, having opened a chink, was closed once more. In *Forbidden Sexual Behaviour and Morality*, the psychologist Robert Masters quotes a patient of Schrenk-Notzing: 'a woman who, while masturbating, phantasised herself being covered by a stallion'. Lucrezia Borgia watched with debauched delight as four stallions fought to breed two mares, while Sir Philip Sidney's sister, the Countess of Pembroke, had horses brought to mate in front of her house for her viewing pleasure.

Mostly, however, the accounts of women sexually entranced by equines are proposed by men. If there is a basic sexual root to girls' love of horses, it comes garnished and obscured by male fantasies – and Freud and Bettelheim are only drawing on a long history. Do you trust the poet Juvenal when he says that Roman matrons kept donkeys for their pleasure, like the 'tender and highborn lady' who seduces Apuleius' Golden Ass? Do you think Pliny was too credulous when he repeated the rumour that Semiramis, the original whore of Babylon, loved her horse so much that she copulated with it? Do you think that the canard about Catherine, the Empress of All Russia, is drawn from life, or extrapolated from the fact that she rode astride and took human lovers without apology? The sexuality of the horse and its prepotency are fascinating to many men, and the male fantasy of being a stallion is a more diffuse cultural meme than any female fantasy of being a nymphomaniac seduced by one.

The horse becomes a super-phallus, a source of admiration and anxiety. 'I know two things about a horse,' as the saying goes, 'and one of them is rather coarse.' Perhaps one Freudian concept, that of projection, has its uses here. Male horses are a source of sexual jealousy in some human males: in an old Indian myth, men used to have penises 'fifteen hands long' until one young blade, refusing to wait till his girl had finished cooking rice, poked his member through a hole in the kitchen wall and she, exasperated, doused it in boiling water, chopped it off with a spoon and gave it to her horse – the Just-So explanation for Why the Horse's Penis Came to Be So Long.

One horse ripper arrested in Germany in the 1990s turned out to be a paedophile who had abused many small girls. He was drawn to attack the animals because, as a biologist investigating the phenomenon reported, 'Little girls give a lot of love to horses and there is therefore a psychological connection with children. Paedophiles thrive on that tenderness shown by children and animals.'

A 1968 pseudo-psychology textbook, The Beast Seekers by H. L. Bagley, gives a 'case history' of Marsha B, a twenty-four-year-old secretary who lives on the outskirts of a large American city. As a child, she once saw a stallion with an extraordinary penis:

I never saw anything like this. The horse went from there way down to the ground ... Maybe I was having a hallucination ... it was the most fascinating, fantastic, beautiful thing I had ever seen. It appeared to be many shapes. At one point, it appeared like stars, at another point, circles, then it appeared to be held together by twine of different colours.

When she grows up, Marsha buys a white stallion called Miska and they consummate the relationship, living out her fantasies and presumably those of H. L. Bagley too, on a stormy night when 'nature sensed something ominous in the air'. She is, Bagley tells us, 'worshipful of his penis', which must have been even more cosmically awe-inspiring than that of the stallion she saw as a girl. 'I was a virgin as far as men were concerned, but I wanted Miska,' she sighs. Martha, one presumes, is a pseudonym within a pseudonym for Bagley, or else she has done a vast amount of acid while reading poor nineteenth-century erotica.

Bagley does not think it was merely a carnal appeal, insisting:

Women's psychic make-up is inextricably woven with larger animals, especially horses, who penetrate the woman's psyche via dreams. To many women, the horse symbolises the unbridled passions and the strengths, as well as the life-giving force of the subconscious mind . . . This psychic attraction can become so great that it encourages expression on the physical level.

Bagley's pseudo-Jungian fantasy – like the old coin with the brazen Whore on one side and the demure Virgin on the other – is that women are both hot for mystic phalli and also possessed of such a delicate, nebulous sexuality that they can never physically crave from the id. Having promised the reality of 'animal lovers' and 'beast seekers', he still cannot bring himself to believe that they exist. Once again, a male theorist has wrongly expressed and glossed over genuine female sexual feelings, for there are women for whom horses are not a suppressed erotic sublimation, but a true one.

Krafft-Ebing was the first to make the distinction between 'bestiality' – sexual congress between humans and animals – and what he called 'zooerastia'. The former, though 'monstruous and revolting', was not necessarily a sickness, merely the result of 'low morality and great sexual desire, with lack of opportunity and natural indulgence'. Havelock Ellis concurred, calling it 'the sexual anomaly of dull, insensitive and fastidious peasants', which 'flourishes among primitive peoples and rural communities'. Freud and the sexologist Alfred Kinsey also saw it as a result of the prohibition of normal sexual relations. It could equally be, of course, a mere financial arrangement, as Carla C told Dr Harold Greenwald when interviewed for *The Call Girl: A Social and Psychoanalytic Study*: 'Black, white, what difference does it make? I'd screw a zebra for fifty dollars.' Bestiality was done for physical relief or financial gain, but zooerastia, which would become 'zoophilia', is what Martha B shared with Miska – a relationship that went beyond physical relief, that might be termed romantic, as well as sexual. They do exist, these women.

In the early noughties, Dr Hani Miletski, a clinical sexologist and psychotherapist, researched a PhD on zoophilia in the virtual paddocks of the internet, offering understanding and reservation of judgment in return for shared accounts of zoophiles' lives and loves. She found considerably fewer female 'zoos' than male (although her sample could have been limited by the internet's demography). The women interviewed were also more cautious about sharing their stories. They were less voluble, avoiding bragging and had become irritated by the approaches of thrill-seeking outsiders demanding details.

Six of the eleven women who filled out her questionnaire had had oral or masturbative sex with stallions and one with a mare. While all of them were sexually attracted to dogs, horses were the next highest animal of preference – nearly three quarters of the women named them. The animals were, for most of the women, lovers, beautiful creatures and friends, fond memories, not props to be used, although they were a source of physical desire too. The respondents were largely heterosexual and had also found pleasure in normal sexual relations with men. Nearly one in three of them had suffered sexual abuse as children.

They had known from an early age that they were drawn to animals, in quite the same way that I had known that Red and Dandy and Mikalo et al. were not prancing dildos. The median age for their first zoophile experience was nineteen – roughly the age when the pony-mad girl of cliché, who falls in love with horses aged four, loses interest in them. The 'zoos' commented that it had seemed 'natural' to them to be attracted to animals, seeing their orientation as being as instinctive as hetero- or homosexuality. 'Zoos are regular people who happen to prefer animal partners,' one of them wrote, cheerfully.

The numbers of self-confessed zoophiles were also tiny: Miletski was not in a position to make a wide survey of the general population, but referred readers to a study of 1,900 Americans by Morton Hunt on behalf of the Playboy Foundation in 1974. This put the percentage of women who had had any kind of sexual contact with animals at 1.9 per cent – while for men it was 4.9 per cent. Fewer men were 'into horses', but more of them were literally into horses, which makes you wonder why the idea of a man and a horse does not give rise to the same innuendo as that of a woman and a horse?

So what is it, then, that causes girls to talk obsessively and rapturously about horses and their love of them? What is it, if it is clearly not sex?

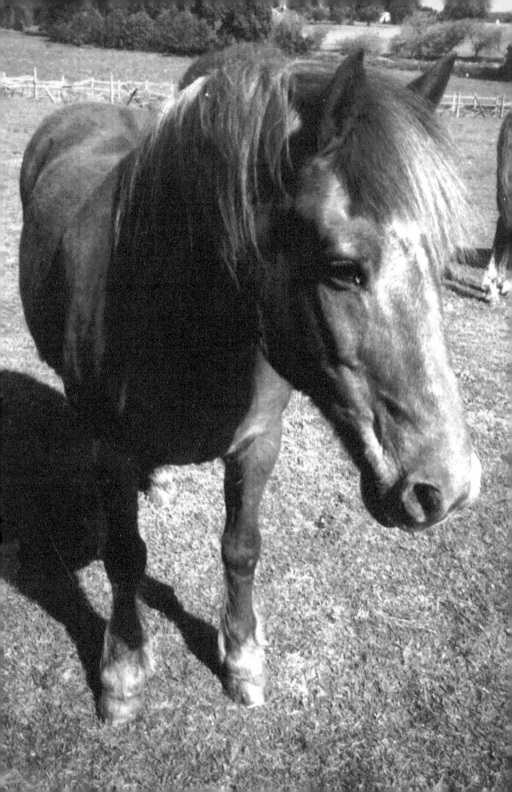

Love

With a striking of hoofs, sparks flying on the flints, a
piebald horse, naked of leather, wild and alone, slid almost to
his haunches and stood stock-still, shaking and panting.
He lowered his head.

'A suitor for Velvet!'

A suitor for Velvet. The horse glared at Mrs Brown.

National Velvet (1935) by Enid Bagnold

A t the riding schools at Costessey and at Cringleford, we had had
no choice of horse. It had been like lining up on the lacrosse
pitch or the netball court and waiting for a team captain to choose
you and your blue knees for her side. In the grubby, tea- and dirt-
smeared ledger in the tackroom, there'd been a list of the girls riding
that hour and, next to their names a pony. You didn't get to swap and
wouldn't have dared to ask, even if an unlucky stroke of the biro
meant you would be plodding at the back on old, tufty-coated
Noddy, or relegated to the little skewbald Cheeko.

In the Berlin riding club we were all grown-ups, so we could make
requests, although of course I couldn't because I only knew Zofe and
Gräfin, and now I was terrified by the thought of riding either of
them and, worse, embarrassed by that disproportionate fear. Besides,
the other women in the class always rode their own favourites – the
lady who smacked the bay obviously preferred to smack him rather

than any other horse. In any case, even if I had managed to stop arriving late, I had begun fatalistically to assume that I would never have dibs on any horse but Zofe, whose name was written just once on the lockers in the ladies' changing room, perhaps out of a sense of fairness rather than heartfelt affection.

I was pondering all this the next time I sloped up the drive with a rising sense of foreboding about what the next hour held. I found some of the other riders already grooming their horses and stopped one who was coming back from the tackroom to ask which horse I was riding. She smiled.

'*Der grosse Schimmel*,' she said. The Big Grey.

She led me down the gangway of the barn past two rows of the metal-barred boxes and, grabbing a headcollar from the peg, slipped a bolt and pushed back a door. She led a horse out and, for all my nerves, I laughed. I laughed because I had never seen, let alone been expected to ride, such an enormous animal.

The big grey came out of his box with his not inconsiderable ears pricked and a 'Hello, now what fresh entertainment is this?' expression on his immense face. Between two banana-sized ears was his poll, a prominent bump topped with a mouse-grey frizzed puff of forelock, like a home perm gone wrong. Halfway down his nose a stripe appeared from nowhere and meandered down to his lips, shading into palest pink. His coat was white, the skin under it slatey, and he was blotched all over with brown and yellow stains where he'd been wallowing on his dirty straw bed. He had a few flea speckles and hooves like fruit bowls under slim pasterns.

He took a mint from me, and politely and deferentially requested a second as I ran a hand down the long, deep groove of muscle in his neck. I could not see over the high ridge of his bony spine; his lungs must have been the size of twin manta rays. He was at least 18hh, taller even than Ground a Fire. So I found myself confronted, at the age of thirty-two, with my wildest, fondest childhood imaginings, belatedly delivered in the form of a great albatross of a gelding with a kind expression and a gentle fascination with the peppermint scent coming from my coat pockets. It was a joke, a wonderful, gawky joke. The cloth was whipped off the magician's box and there he was, the Pferdberg, his ears at ten to two, eyes showing mild interest. 'Heigh ho!' This is what you wanted!

As I bent over to scrub away at the smudge on his chest, he bowed his head and lipped my hair and back in affectionate boredom. Then, over the next five minutes, he deftly untied his own halter rope, clawed a chunk out of the stable door with his incisors and finally, as I held one of his hind hooves to pick it out, ponderously scraped a fore hoof on the concrete floor while balancing on two feet.

For once we were ready before the others, and I stood with him in the gangway, scratching him between the ears and grinning as he dropped his head to my shoulder to be fussed, the way Tav used to. On board him in the reithalle, I felt as though I were wearing glasses of the wrong prescription. The change of perspective was dramatic: the ground receded, the other horses shrank, and his head, at the end of his giraffe neck, was as distant as the bow of a supertanker viewed from the bridge. I calculated that if I fell off even as he stood there, I wouldn't escape with less than a broken collarbone, but I felt safe up top. I trusted his good humour and his laziness. He did not mind the other horses; his ears were either pricked or parted sideways in a semaphore 'na ja' – 'heigh-ho'. His canter was lolloping and when we circled with the others I had to draw him wide in case he galumphed up their tails and into disaster.

'He's sweet!' I told Ynes in surprise.

'I thought you'd like him,' she grinned, patting the Pferdberg. 'He's my favourite, the big white bird. You're both tall.' She pulled a face at the gelding, who regarded her intelligently. I went home and thought about him all week.

We do fall in love with horses – there is no escaping that cliché, at least – and it is not platonic love, but a deeply romantic one. We choose them or we say that they 'chose us' for the same reason that we find ourselves drawn to lovers; there is a click in the head, a moment of recognition borne of life experience, of misguided sentimental notions, genuine insight and unfathomable factors that you never plumb but call intuition. We look for something kindred – our own image enhanced – but also, as Germaine Greer pointed out when she wrote of little girls and horses, 'an other which is responding to [our] control . . . a potent love calling forth a response'.

Here is the nub of it: riding can never be a solitary activity; it's one where in extremis you are thrown back, not on your own resources, but on those of your mount. At the core of all equestrian sports is the bond along which communication between horse and human travels, be it swift and sympathetic or troubled and antagonistic, with one half deaf to the other. It is the great intrigue and the mystery of horses, the same frustration felt between human lovers when you can never be entirely inside your mate's brain, seeing what they are thinking.

The ephemera of horse worship apes that of human crushes: the images of horses – pretty horses, moody horses, magnificent horses – that paper a girl's bedroom, the matching duvet sets, the dolls, the annuals, the stickers and the T-shirts. Give it a few years and that flicked forelock could be replaced with some rock star's quiff and the black, 'painted skin' round that Arabian's eyes will have become a smear of make-up on some androgynous actor.

It's in the romantic shorthand of pony books for, as the academic Alison Haymonds says, 'The girl is the central character with the pony filling an ambiguous role, one that is closer to the traditional heroine who is often both the victim and the object of desire . . . [W]hen the girl in the story sets her eyes on the pony for the first time, her reaction is immediate and possessive, "The pony must be mine."'

Jinny Manders falls for Shantih the instant she dances into the circus ring: 'Jinny sat entranced, hardly breathing, and then her breath burst out of her in a throbbing gasp. She loved the chestnut mare. As if all their long day's travelling had only been for this. As if she had come all the way from Stopton only for this. To see this sudden gift of perfection.' The Pie is Velvet's prince. Christina Russell risks everything to save the strawberry roan Sweetbriar from the kennels in Flambards. In Joanna Cannan's Another Pony for Jean, the heroine goes to school prepared to deal with separation from her beloved horse: 'I put a few oats in my overcoat pockets in case of meeting ponies, and I stuffed a little hay into the pocket of my gym tunic so that I could smell it during dull lessons and be reminded of Cavalier.'

As a child I loved reading these romances and I had pash after pash on different ponies, both fictional and real. My imaginary horses were each a facet of the all-embracing love of Every Horse that I was trying to experience. Some of the real horses I loved, like Petita, were as remote from me as Shantih, but eventually I rode well enough to take my chances with the horses I'd fixed on and to wrestle, like all those caught up in a romance, with the realities of the relationship. A 1983 study published by the University of Pennsylvania Press, in a book on the relationship between humans and animals, showed that a rider typically passed through a cycle of emotions when finding a new horse. It began at a high pitch with the thrill and the novelty of it all, plunged when they realized that perhaps they would not, after all, win at the Horse of the Year Show or Burghley or Olympia, and then finally balanced out into a workaday relationship of affectionate familiarity – comically like a marriage.

I followed this pattern with Red or Honey or Jasper, with all the unknowing predictability of a schoolgirl running through new heart-throbs, which is, of course, exactly what I was. The riding-school system and my ever extending limbs gave me the chance to be positively free with my favours. There was always a new horse to ride that was a little more challenging than the last, until finally I was allowed to ride Pegasus, the glamorous working livery on whom I jumped a little cross-country course and whose gawky greyness I'd recognized in the Pferdberg.

Enough has been written about ponies as proxies for boyfriends – 'ponies come between toys and boys' the saying goes, as harmless as pre-pubescent mashes on beardless boy pop stars. 'They reckon an interest in horses delays girls getting involved with boys by four years,' someone informed me, as if it were proven science. Bettelheim theorized that horse love kept girls from awareness of their own libidos – a safe holding bay until they were mature enough to cope with the real love object, the human male – but not all love is a simple sublimation of sexual desire. With a horse, a girl can have a preliminary equine sentimental education, where big emotions can be suffered and enjoyed, but it doesn't end when we grow up and find human lovers.

Sven Forsling is a Swedish psychologist and social worker who stayed on in 1960s California to work for a year as apprentice to a harness-racing trainer after completing a Fulbright scholarship at Berkeley. He had a love of horses, having grown up with an uncle who was a racehorse trainer, and was working on the idea that horses could play a role in the rehabilitation of young offenders. After returning to Sweden, he worked with the teenagers written off by the Stockholm welfare system as vårsting or 'the worst ones' – truanting girls who came from shitty homes which they escaped via drugs or with boyfriends in gangs. In coeducational institutions, these girls tended to efface themselves, sinking into self-loathing and hopelessness, being exploited and physically abused by the boys.

Forsling got permission to set up a new children's home for these girls that would lift them out of inner-city Stockholm and into a new world: it would be a reform school with its own racing stable. Frossarbo was an old, remote farm north of Uppsala with eleven horses, most of which would be trained as racing trotters. Some, but not all, of the girls already had posters of horses on their bedroom walls, but most had never had the chance to even get close to one. The girls took lessons towards a certificate in horse management and looked after their own horse, which they would also drive round the practice track. Their time at Frossarbo was divided into a series of choices, rather than restrictions. They chose a horse, they chose to come off drugs, they chose to stay on after two months, to stay clean.

In 2003, Forsling wrote about the Frossarbo years in a self-published book called *The Girl and the Horse*. Nearly fifty girls passed through the school between 1987 and 1999, and there were hardly any runaways, even though they were serial escapologists. Only seven of the *vårstinger* dead losses failed the first horse-care test the first time they took it. Every year, Frossarbo organized a trip abroad with the horses to compete, to Hungary or France or Austria, and once the girls travelled to Norwich, to race against the descendants of the 'trotting fraternity' that Munnings found in The Bush in Costessey. No drinking was allowed on these trips, nor drug-taking. The girls were bound by the old *Black Beauty* morality at Frossarbo: it was imperative that the horses were cared for. In order to do that, the girls must care for themselves first and return to their horse after a weekend at home, leaving their boyfriends behind.

One girl had picked her horse unsentimentally because it was fast and she said she'd never had a conversation with it. Eight chose horses like the Pferdberg, who seemed sympathetic and kind.

'I liked Lillen's eyes,' one wrote, 'they seemed so understanding. He was never afraid of me. He put up with me.'

'It felt safe with his eyes,' another commented, after years of being observed by teachers and social workers.

But twenty-five of them wanted something more challenging than sympathy. They struck up an affinity with horses that reminded them of themselves and needed special care. 'He had no tail, nobody wanted him. Then I took him.' Or 'He was a shit, he was cocky and unruly.'

'I knew that nasty horses weren't really nasty,' said one graduate of the school who could have been talking about her sisters at Frossarbo. 'They were misunderstood horses. I could see myself in her . . . I knew that she would understand me.'

The girls snuck out of the boarding house at night and slipped into the horses' stables to talk and to cry. One took a letter her boyfriend had written to dump her, and when she read it to her horse, he pulled it out of her hands. The horses were a living presence that never misled the girls with words.

'Pysen and I could be alone together and there was no need to talk,' said one. 'I didn't need to hang out with the other girls if I didn't want to . . . Pysen made it possible for me to be myself . . . he listened to me . . . He helped me to see myself . . . I always had somebody for me and we had each other.' At an age where friendships are complicated, in a home where a dozen difficult girls were cooped up together, the horses remained a steady, warm constant, something beyond fights and parents who thumped you or didn't care what happened to you.

They were also mirrors that offered an instant reflection back to the girls. One girl came back from a home weekend jiggered on crack; her horse jibbed and threw his head up when she tried to fit his headcollar. The girls realized that if they treated the horse abrasively, it would respond in kind – and of course, the same was true in interactions with humans, although the lesson is easier to learn when it comes from a Pysen or a Grabben, and not a warden in a secure unit.

One girl told Forsling that when she went to the field and called to her horse, and he neighed back and came to her, the thrill she felt was like taking crack for the first time. 'It is a friendship that's not built in the usual way,' she said, 'it's built on the unusual.'

Another girl who was sent away from Frossarbo after taking drugs said she was physically racked with jealousy when she saw 'her' horse, Grabben, with another girl. After that she gave up her addiction and came back to reclaim him. Forsling found that the girls' greatest fear was that their horse would love someone other than themselves. 'I didn't give a damn about anything else,' said Grabben's girl, who became desperate to be back at the farm after her weekend trips home, in case the horse had become distressed by her absence.

A third girl swore, 'In my boyfriend's gang, they stand by each other to the death. This is how strong the bond between real mates can be. I want my horse to have that same strong feeling for me, to follow me to death itself.'

Not one girl swapped her horse for another in the whole twelve years, though they had the chance. Their pride was so fierce that when fights broke out between the girls they included each other's horses in the insults – if one girl was 'shit' then so was her horse. One girl told Forsling, 'When the social workers in my home town say that I cannot build my whole life on a horse, I answer: I am not building my whole life on a horse, the horse is my whole life.'

When Forsling managed to track down thirty-six of the girls of Frossarbo years later, when they were women and often mothers themselves, two had relapsed and a further three were in support programmes, but thirty-one of the vårstinger were clean and managing well in life. All of them still thought daily of Frossarbo. One said she wished she were back there, another continued to 'talk' to her horse, while a third remained anxious that she had had to leave her horse behind so abruptly and he might not have understood. It wasn't that the horses had been useful proxies for boyfriends, or 'transitional objects' for girls transferring to adulthood, or, as Forsling scornfully put it, 'something cute'. 'It was much more than that,' he said, 'it's this dynamic, this power – a therapeutic possibility which is extraordinary.' And love, quite simply.

'It is hard to trust in another human being when I know what kind of a person I am. Scotten was a horse. I could trust him. I also think that Scotten longed for me,' one of the women wrote to Forsling, years on. 'That is what is so amazing. It is like a miracle. Scotten knew me and, even so, he wanted me! It's difficult to understand. I think of it often. Once I woke up crying. In my dream I had seen Scotten in a meadow thick with green grass. He saw me and neighed and then started running towards me. Then I woke up and I cried.'

Ambition

I want everything. When you jump a difficult fence and
you feel the crowd holding its breath and the gasp when you're
safely over, that's what I want. Riding against the clock, going
faster than you dare and yet being dead accurate. Knowing
every split second counts, risking it but not too much, nothing
existing in the whole world but the challenge of the jumps and
the applause . . . and it's the people. They're so different to
ordinary, dull, everyday people. They're chancers. They don't
care about anything except how their horse is jumping. Don't
care about being respectable or polite or what they look like.
They live in a different world and I'm going to be part of
it. Nothing is going to stop me. You'll see.

Nicola Webster in *Jump for the Moon* (1985) by Patricia Leitch

Adolescent impatience, intolerance and restlessness in Costessey
meant I could hardly stand to lay the table in the evening when
laying the table meant unimaginable tedium, repression, the same
unchanging forks and knives. I felt both overgrown and stuck like
Alice in the White Rabbit's cottage with one foot up the chimney and
an arm out of the window. I loved the horses at Cringleford but the
long roadwork through the set route of half-timbered semis and
tedious suburban gardens – each conifer and net-covered pond
committed to heart – bored me now that I could go roaming with
Tav. Our instructors didn't often take us out over the cross-country

fences in the field behind the riding stables, and the jumps in the indoor school were never higher than two feet. When I had a few private lessons for a birthday, I was surprised to find Cricket, who was woolly in February, turn out to be an able jumper and lively ride when removed from the clubby, dragging train of ponies.

I had an inkling that some kind of quantum leap was required beyond the rank and file of my usual group lessons, and felt the faint itch of ambition. In my imaginary horse world I was still jumping big fences and winning the National in a spatter of mud and spruce fronds; in real life I was confident. I hadn't fallen off a horse in all the years I'd been at Cringleford. I'd ridden Pegasus, I'd had horses bolt with me, I'd jumped little courses at riding-school shows and made a string of my own pink-and-white clear-round rosettes. There was no reason why I could not reach a little further. If not, why did I bother? Wanting to ride meant wanting to ride well, on good horses, horses that were a little more spirited than the familiar characters at Cringleford.

So I left the riding school down the loke without really thinking about it, looking firmly forward. My new riding place was a modern, purpose-built equestrian centre on a farm a few miles west of Ringland. To me, accustomed to battered Cringleford, it was as trim as the Royal Mews and had the professional polish of some three-day-eventer's working yard. There were neat-edged woodchip paths set between post- and rail-fenced fields, and the yard with its row of smart loose boxes had a clean-swept concrete base. The indoor school was the size of a dressage ring and completely enclosed by corrugated-metal walls, so that it was like being inside a rectangular silo, or a shipping container. There was a gallery running the length of one side where my mother sat while my small jumping class of four or five took place.

I rode Murphy, Kylie and Wispa. Murphy, the grey, was half clipped out, with blue-tinted skin under the bristle and white fur above the waterline. He walked with his head high, his mane under my nose, while the shoulders that dropped under my hands seemed to me alarmingly narrow after a decade of broad-at-beam ponies. Under those shoulders his legs snatched up at each stride, with a bounce to them, leaving the ground eagerly. Kylie was narrow too, a chestnut mare with a white stripe and a fussy anxiety. Where the ponies had either needed booting to rumble towards a fence, or would charge it with a heaviness in their mouths, Murphy and Kylie were all quivering lightness. When you sat on them, it was hard to gauge their reaction to the pressure of the bit; although they were well trained, they were not only less earthbound, and but also finely adjustable. You could ride a curve smoothly with them by using only your legs, and their mouths were soft gloves, instead of fists that grasped on the bit. The reins were like the steering threads on a paper-light biplane, which, if you over-steered, might plunge into a stall.

The instructor was ex-army, a stubby young man who stalked about the ring with his chest out and liked to backchat with the girls. He would never tell you to put your shoulders back if he could tell you to stick your tits out instead. He drilled us through combinations every week, one fence, one stride, second fence, two strides and the last.

'Straight down the middle, legs, LEGS! You were lucky. Get her moving forward, get her collected.'

He exuded disapproval, but not true strictness; he was good if you fell off, which I had now begun to do. 'You all right? Back on you go,' he'd say and leg me on when I'd dusted off the dirt. My mother brought things to read and bent her head over the pages so she didn't have to watch me bounce and roll.

If the circles and serpentines of flatwork are geometry, then combinations are algebra: you have to balance the equation as you negotiate the fences and the distances between them, which are more important than the obstacles themselves. Scud too far over the first fence and you must take a shorter stride to hit the second sweetly. There is a perfect, most elegant way to write the equation, but you can get the same end result with a degree of flexibility to your sub-expressions; overshoot the cross-poles and you can sneak a half-stride in just before the rails and hup. You can also come mathematically unstuck in more drastic ways, with a horse drifting right or left in confusion, idleness, or simple objection to your calculations.

With a horse that thinks the sum is best tackled at speed, like Murphy, your approach would be a flurry of 'LEGS!' on and slipping your hands one at a time up the reins to shorten them as Murphy's neck appeared in the centre of your focus. His back would hollow instead of rounding like a ball, while his hooves gathered together in a bunch as the fence loomed, too close now to be avoided or for your distance from it to be renegotiated. You felt his hind hooves get right up to his front heels before he scrambled up and over; you pitched up, seat in the air, daylight under you, throwing your hands forward to spare his mouth. Then once he was down you had milliseconds to collect him, his head waggling, blood up, chin on chest, before he launched himself for the second as though his legs could undertake his constrained head. You hop over and, in a fluke, you take it perfectly. At this point his eagerness catches him out because there's only one stride to the third and he's through the top bar before he or you can think about it.

The chestnut mare Kylie and I found a rapport after she'd larned me a half-dozen times by dropping me on the floor.

'You have to get her just right, or she'll stop,' the instructor told me. 'Don't grab her mouth. You won't get away with it.'

When it was our turn we'd strike out, gunning for that perfect jumping canter, that see-saw of impulsion and collection that makes the strides measurable by eye and turns transitions into a perfect bascule over the poles. Kylie went in as if she were jointed with springs. I struggled to judge the distance and the reins, checking her speed, watching her ears, and knowing that if I got too heavy a hand on her mouth, at the last minute Kylie would abruptly stop as though she'd hit an invisible forcefield instead of the parallel bars, and on I would go, coughed up her neck or, worse, shrugged violently over her shoulder and into the fence. I remember once looking up from between the striped bars at Kylie's foreshortened, disdainful muzzle as if up out of a grave, the reins still in my hand.

Riding Kylie was like a delicate negotiation with a foreign businesswoman; you'd be feeling your way without the language, but if you made one slip in etiquette she stonewalled, and there you were, baffled once more and wondering what you had done to offend. You could not trust that she would pull on forward, like Murphy, and take the fence somehow in whatever ungainly fashion. She was not sluggish like the big palomino, Wispa, nor did she swerve in a slow, inevitable curve off the track and round a wing, like a riding-school pony, head down at an angle, jaw working on the bit. She simply stopped. The greatest satisfaction, the praise from the instructor, came as you cantered in, stride, stride, and felt the reins pliant, a slight slackness, not taut, for a split second before she lifted off, and your focus slowed to the reins and the ripple in them, down to the bar of Kylie's mouth, the thin pink gum over bone as she gathered herself and jumped.

I was given Kylie to ride often and eventually I could go a whole lesson without her stopping – which earned me high words from my teacher, who said there weren't many riders who could do that with her. I began to think of myself as having that paradigmatic riderly attribute: good hands, the hands that held birds' eggs in them without crushing them, intelligent hands. Lady Diana Shedden and Lady Viola Apsley, the authors of the 1930s hunting manual, To Whom the Goddess, said there was nothing magical about the gifting of 'hands'; it was instead the sign of 'sympathy between horse and rider'. There were eight attributes to a good rider, they wrote. Understanding, harmony and anticipation were expressed through the hands. Confidence, grip, balance, correct use of aids and resolution went with the seat a rider held on their horse. This new, fine-tuned riding, coming as it did after years of ponies and Tav's immutable moods, was intellectually gratifying.

But something else was happening imperceptibly, like a slow seeping of water turning gradually saline or a rising dryness in the mouth. As 'anticipation' increased, so 'confidence' and 'resolution' flickered. I didn't notice. I went on jumping and falling.

In the end, it wasn't Murphy or Kylie with their thin energy, but long, unbending Wispa. As we cantered into the combination – 'Legs, LEGS!' – Wispa chugged down a gear, I squeezed weakly, and he dodged to the right, suddenly agile. Still riding insubstantially towards the fence, I was hurled forward off his left shoulder and round, like a swag of laundry, back-first into the rotten yellow wing, which broke at the base. My neck whipped back against the defensive curl of my spine, and I fell heavily on the feet of the wing, staring at the soft, jagged teeth of the snapped-off wood and wondering in a spacey kind of shock at the emptiness of my lungs. The instructor, normally brusque, was solicitous; I could see the anxiety in his eyes, telling me to get my breath back. Was I all right? Don't worry about the fence, it was rotten anyway. Not a problem. Anything broken? My back was barely bruised, just smarting as if from a smack. I got up with dirt all over my palms, shaking a little, embarrassed to have done the damage, and he legged me back onto Wispa.

I don't remember that Wispa seemed any less solid, or that I shook uncontrollably, or told my mother that was that in the car on the way home, or even that she put her foot down and refused to watch me ride any more. All I know is that a short time later it was agreed that I would stop lessons and just ride Tav at the weekends instead, as there wasn't much point in training like that when I had GCSEs and no horse but Tav to take to shows.

'The nervous system has sometimes a curious complex reaction,' wrote the authors of To Whom the Goddess, 'and after a shock, entailing mental or physical strain of any kind, it is better to meet the reaction before it has time to settle in permanently and tend to spoil the rider's nerve.' Instead I pushed away the thought and retreated to Tav's round, chestnut safety.

Fear

The fright of falling is ten times worse than the fright in falling.

To Whom the Goddess (1932) by Lady Diana Shedden
and Lady Viola Apsley

For the horse, the world is full of primaeval monsters,
of which man is often the worst . . . The horseman
cannot hope to master his horse's fear until he is quite
certain he has mastered his own.

Horse and Man: Aphorisms and Paradoxes (1937) by Alessandro Alvisi

The Pferdberg and I were ambling at the back of the column of horses in the *reithalle* – he pleased to be out of his box and to oblige by pottering about the ring, me savouring his good mood and the equable waggling of his long, white ears. Earlier I'd mortified myself when Ynes asked us all to perform a *volte*. As the rest of the ride peeled away from the track in unison, circling and rejoining it like a flock of birds wheeling and alighting on a branch, I had ridden the Pferdberg clean across the ring in two opposing half-circles and changed rein. Then, realizing we were both alone and pointing in the wrong direction, I had to steer him in a quick, ragged loop. Ynes raised her eyebrows and the Pferdberg flicked an ear as he dropped into file – *na endlich, junge Dame*, finally, young lady, what was that about?

We were walking down the long side of the *reithalle* when suddenly

228

one of the cobby bays further up the ride erupted out of line, baulked at the wall and went rapidly backwards across the school. He went so fast that his hind legs began to run under him, his quarters bunching, his head high, the bulk of his body tipped backwards. 'Push him on!' called out Ynes as his rider leaned as far forward as she could, but it was too late, and the bay half reared in a ragged levade, overbalanced and came down, his rider's leg caught for a second under him before she wriggled free, and then he rolled back to get up, pushing with his hindlegs, kneeling on his forelegs, and froze. His reins were snagged under his knees, forcing his nose into the dirt while his quarters were high in the air – he looked like a circus pony compelled to kneel. His rider got unsteadily to her feet and brushed at her jodhpurs, staring at the bay, while Ynes crouched and called to him softly, willing him to be quiet as she edged closer.

'A knife! Someone get a knife!' the call went up, and the man who'd been watching in the gallery broke the stillness and raced out. Ynes reached the bay in his horrible kowtow and began to work at the buckles on his bridle, trilling to him. The bay's ears flickered back and forth but he did not struggle. We had stopped when the bay bolted and now stood in a row, riders and horses watching without moving. The Pferdberg's head was raised, his reins hanging loose, his ears brought to bear. The air of the reithalle was thick with suspended panic like an inert gas, the bay at the eye of it, motionless in his bizarre obeisance, his rider standing by helplessly and Ynes trying to hold the centre calm.

A girl ran back in, a knife in her outstretched hand, and then the reins were loose. The bay went over onto his side with a grunt and lay there with his legs curled under him and his ribs leaping. Ynes stroked him and talked to him. Then, gently, with the two women encouraging him, he got up and stood there, shaky and disoriented, as they pulled off his saddle and patted him, gabbling to one another in relief. The bay seemed a little stunned; whatever had sent him back across the ring was forgotten. His rider led him out to the track to see whether any damage was done and to ease the muscles of his back. He stretched his neck out and blew as an all-clear.

Everyone began to breathe and talk and pat their chests, dispersing the panic gas, but when I looked down at the Pferdberg's neck and found it a foot from my face, at eye level, I realised the miasma had settled in me. He stared at the bay, whose coat was caked on one side with bright-yellow sand. The Pferdberg was now very animated, and when the command came to walk on, he pranced and joggled. There were five minutes to the end of the lesson and we carried on, but the Pferdberg flexed his neck like a stallion and made little surges of speed, while I grabbed at the reins with hands that felt as though they'd been disconnected from my body and felt panic whip my innards like raw eggs in a bowl. At the end of the lesson I slipped out of the saddle – as always, it was like dropping off a small bank – and leaned into the white gelding, willing him to be solid. He looked round for a tidbit.

'She did well,' my riding instructor at Costessey used to tell my mother when she came to collect me after a hack or a lesson, when I had fallen off Tino or Mikalo or Ponto. 'She rolled!'

And I did – seven times in three years, the requisite amount to 'make a rider': one crossed them off like days on an advent calendar, or BAGA gymnastics awards. Mikalo, a chunky skewbald with a chestnut head and a broad white blaze, screwed up his quarters and bucked like a goat as we cantered hectically along the top of the Stubble Field, and I hit the ground in a roll like a parachutist. I slipped over Tino's shoulder, bounced off my jodhpured backside and was on my feet before he'd gone three strides without me. Neither embarrassment nor fear are part of these memories; it's as though my mental filing system discarded any attached emotions in favour of recording the mechanics of each tumble, or perhaps what stubble looked like close up, or how it felt when you landed square on a patch of upright stalks (sharp). Fear was not a possibility; riding was imperative.

It wasn't that I was The Boy Who Went Forth Looking for Fear in the

Grimm Brothers' tale; I was as familiar with the emotion and its diverse forms as any child. There was the fear that sank and then rose up again from the pit of my stomach when I realized that I was lost in the supermarket and ran from aisle to aisle, searching for my mother and the shopping trolley. There was a later fear of heights, acquired from my brother, that made your head and your calves feel queerly light and airy, as though you might be blown off the top of the balustrade at Norwich Castle. There was also a fear of some of the girls at school, something so animal and low in the mix that I couldn't articulate or acknowledge it, but which I sensed rise like hackles on a dog. But there was no fear of horses and no fear of falling.

Everyone falls off. Falling off is part of riding. It is frequently unavoidable; it happens to experts. It happened to Pat Smythe over and over again. You get back on and off you go once more until the next time, or until you break something. I had used to understand this, but now that I was a grown-up, it seemed unreasonable to me. When did I change so drastically? Who was the funny little creature in a swimming costume who sat on the enormous Dusky, her dimpled bare legs pinched by the leathers and an old, outsize velvet hunt cap on the back of her head, with a bold grin? Or the three-year-old who demanded that the lady leading her round the ring on a Shetland let her 'go over the jumps' she'd spotted piled in one corner? Why did it take more courage now to walk in a circle on a gentle horse than that girl had needed to picture herself soaring over a double oxer? How could she have been so impervious and how had she not realized how much there was to fear?

The nineteenth-century haute école rider, Emilie Loisset, was impaled on the horn of her saddle when her horse bolted and fell onto her, and she died in agony days later. Mrs Hayes tells the story of the fifteen-year-old daughter of 'a well-known nobleman' whose stirrup was incorrectly fixed, and who tumbled off and was dragged to her death. 'I heard that rider, saddle, and pony were all buried on the same day,' she wrote. Shortly before Ladies on Horseback was published, Mrs Power

O'Donoghue was pitched onto the pommel of her side-saddle by a bucking horse. She passed out and fell from him into a tree. Under doctors' orders, she sold all her horses and did not ride again, though she lived another sixty years. Viola Apsley was confined to a bath chair when she co-wrote *To Whom The Goddess* in the 1930s. Out hunting, she had fallen and broken her spine when her horse caught a hoof in a rabbit hole. The warm, detailed accounts in that book of coming home on a tired, glory-filled horse after a day in the field to toast and bran mash are pure nostalgia, as she would never again get back on a horse.

In my weekly *Horse and Hound* I got news of catastrophic accidents: a little girl kicked in the head and killed when bringing her pony in from the field. A dressage rider in a coma. Another three-day eventer crushed in a 'rotational fall' when his horse caught its knees on an unyielding obstacle and somersaulted violently onto him. A jockey trampled underfoot by the entire field. A government drugs advisor announced that 'equasy' – or 'Equine Addiction Syndrome' – was as dangerous as MDMA and killed as many people each year. Between 1988 and 1992 equestrianism was the third most dangerous sport in the UK after swimming and motor sports, claiming sixty-two lives. Paramedics are most likely to be called to the scene of road accidents and then to incidents involving horses. In an American study of 2007, horse riding accounted for more traumatic brain injuries than any other sport.

When I thought now of riding in Berlin, the terrors furled out in front of me like furiously growing branches, or like dye spreading rapidly up a series of capillaries. If we were trotting, Zofe could start at nothing, jerk left and I might fall off, or she could jerk left and bolt into the horse in front, which would kick and shatter my kneecap, or she could jerk left, bolt, dodge the horse in front and career round the *reithalle*, then overbalance at a corner and come down, smashing my leg, or she might jerk left, bolt, dodge the horse in front, career round the *reithalle* and, instead of taking the corner, leap the barrier at the doorway, twist and slip on the concrete and fall on me and burst my innards like a stamped-on crisp packet. On the U-bahn I dwelled morbidly on the unpredictability of horses and of life.

It is right to be afraid of horses and of riding them, but it is also dangerous. Horses are connoisseurs of fear; it's the element they move in. Thousands of years of fear gave them long legs that struck out from powerful shoulders and quarters, and drew their eyes to the side of their heads so they could see almost 360 degrees of horizon, in case it should heave and take shape as a predator. They choose flight over fight and use every clue they can pick up through eyes, ears, nose, skin, to prepare to flee.

In July 2009, Swedish researchers gathered a group of twenty-seven horses and their handlers, all but two of whom were women. They built a small course of traffic cones and markers thirty metres long along which the horses were to be led or ridden four times. The handlers were told that at the fourth leg an assistant would snap open an umbrella in front of the horse. The heart rates of both humans and horses were to be measured.

Anticipating the flash of the umbrella, the handlers' pulses beat faster, but the assistant kept the umbrella furled. When the researchers compared the pulse readings of humans and horses, they found that the horses' hearts had also speeded up. What telepathy! What ESP! This instant transmission of emotions was better than any leg aid or kimblewick bit. The old Norfolk horseman Jack Juby remembered legging up a nerve-struck rider onto a quiet, reliable horse just before a big showjumping class. The horse had only gone a few paces before 'old Crusader lifted his tail and the shit just flew out of him'. 'The excitement goes through the horse . . . the leading rein . . . [it] is like electric going straight through to the horse,' Juby said. 'Once the confidence has gone, you are in trouble.' Perhaps the Pferdberg and Zofe and Gräfin the Sea Monster had been calibrating my internal atmospheric pressure against their own and adjusting accordingly.

The night before my next lesson, I found out that my father was ill and would require an operation. I cancelled and resolved not to ride until he was out of hospital, telling myself that the last thing my mother needed was both of us in hospital at opposite ends of Europe. Yet I was relieved. A few months went by and my father was given the all-clear, but I did not book another lesson. I tried not to think of the Pferdberg, or of riding, though it nagged at me, and when I did think of it, or picked up the phone to ring the riding club, I felt a small but strong pre-emptive fear drumming in my gut. Recognizing it, I would let a few more weeks go by.

Nearly a decade earlier, after I had graduated and grubbed around for a while doing work experience, I moved to London for my first job and began a gypsyish life of living in friends' spare rooms. Six months along, four of us had found a flat to share for a year on the top floor of a block of mansion flats near Regent's Park. My parents had helped me move, schlepped my books and clothes, given their verdict on the flat, eaten lunch and driven off by the time Lizzie, Guy and Ian parked outside with a hired van full of their own furniture and suitcases. As they unloaded the van in the street below, I had my window flung wide open to catch the last of the mid-September sun and the breeze from Regent's Park, a little sweeter for being seven floors up, and was shaking out my clothes from rucksacks and hanging them in a great, French-polished wardrobe that took up half the room.

In the compression of a second, I heard a shriek of rubber on tarmac, of metal smacked, hammered and crumpled and an inhuman scream, as though all the air had been violently squeezed from a set of lungs. I didn't want to look out of the window. I pulled out another T-shirt automatically, wasting seconds before I thought to grab an old orange blanket and run from the flat. I didn't think any more till I had reached the lobby of the flats and was out of the front doors, seeing people with their hands to their faces, and Ian lying between the van and a car, cradled by Lizzie, and Guy hopping and running up and down the pavement. I reached Lizzie at Ian's head, and somehow there was an ambulance already there, a helicopter coming. Ian was talking and telling jokes, although shock had leached his face of blood and there was sweat on his forehead.

I glanced down at his body once and saw the blood soaking into the denim on his thighs like damp sand. Below them it was Passchendaele. His shinbone was cracked open and exposed, cuttlefish-bone white, his trousers tattered, his skin peeled. He had been standing at the back of the parked van when a car ploughed square into it, crushing him between the two vehicles as one absorbed the speed of the other. I dropped my head to focus on his face, stroking his hair as Lizzie did. After a queasy, spacey stretch of a few minutes, the paramedics took over, and flew Lizzie and Ian off east to the Royal London in Whitechapel in a helicopter. With a sick bag on my lap I rode in the ambulance to St Mary's in Paddington with Guy, who had been smacked in the back of the knee by the car and flipped onto the pavement, shortly before it clipped Lizzie's hip and was finally halted by Ian's legs, the loaded van and the cars parked in front of it.

A month later Ian came back to our flat from the hospital in a wheelchair, minus one leg, the other reinforced with steel. We all lived in that flat for another year together, absorbing a shock delivered like that from a bolt gun. I still slept in the room overlooking the road. Long after the blood had been washed away and the yellow police information sign had been taken down, I'd dream about horses early in the morning, and roll over muggily to nudge aside the curtain and peer out of my window. Below on the road, a dozen or more bay horses of the Royal Artillery jogged three abreast, two horses flanking each soldier and his mount, coats russet, tack black and highly polished. The clatter of their shoes on the tarmac filtered through my sleep.

The fractals of fear that had surfaced and begun to twine when I last rode Gräfin, and that had made inroads into my nervous system after the incident with the bay in the reithalle, were as familiar to me as an old parasite. They belonged to the months after Ian's accident when they'd crept up my limbs and left them tingling whenever I walked down a pavement, sure that I could feel a car about to ramp up off the road and knock me down, or when I was caught on a crossing with an impatient driver making his engine growl, or when there were people on the bus who came too close to Guy's broken knee in its stiff casing.

Once you know that the worst thing may happen at any time, you have two choices. To embrace your odds and to calculate how slim they are, or to feel like any deluded gambler that you can control these odds – that there's a method to roulette, and that your willpower can communicate itself to fate and stop a careening car. The former discards fear, barely even considering it, while the latter allows it to guide every move. If you can picture every shade and variation of eventuality that can drop into your life, you can take minute steps to save yourself, or so I thought, watching for cars that didn't exist and thinking of falls that would never happen.

Why, I wondered to myself, was fear such a bad thing? Fear keeps us safe. Fear is a product of imagination. Viola Apsley and Diana Shedden wrote in To Whom the Goddess, 'There are undoubtedly people born without nerves who are afraid of nothing and do not know what fear is. They are lucky, but somehow people without imagination of any kind lose a great deal of the adventure in living.' Lizzie and I joked that we got such an adrenaline rush from crossing the road that we did not need to go parachuting. While the fantasy disasters in which Zofe and I crashed to our doom were simply imaginary, they could have real consequences if I transmitted that adrenaline to a horse. My imaginary horses had been benevolent beings and I never fell off one – an altogether better use of my imagination than the lurid reithalle catastrophes I was now summoning up. An overactive imagination throws limitations around you as it goes rampaging off to the wilder pastures of morbidity, and you can wear a groove in your brain as you pace out thoughts of disaster.

Neuroscientists have discovered that memory is key to both generating and mastering fear. Denis Paré of Rutgers University trained rats to associate a certain sound with a painful electric shock. He then repeatedly played them the sound without shocking them, and discovered that the rats soon adjusted their memories to the pain-free scenario. They ceased to be agitated when they heard the same noise. However, if the neuroscientists blocked a cluster of brain cells called intercalated neurons, the rats never lost their initial fear, even when repeatedly exposed to the sound without the shock. His team concluded that the intercalated neurons provided an alternative pathway for our thoughts, leading to what was termed 'fear extinction'. If the intercalated cells fire, you can remember a scenario in which your fear is not overwhelming. If they do not fire, your thoughts run a gauntlet of your darkest emotions: post-traumatic stress disorder. A team at New York University followed up his research to show that human memory can also be tampered with, in order to process an experience so that it remains free of association with bad memories.

The researchers taught a study group of people to associate a coloured card with an electric shock. A portion of the group was then reintroduced within six hours to the coloured card, but this time without the shock and pain. This quick and positive exposure to the phobia trigger influenced the manner in which their brains stored the experience. They did not react negatively when shown the coloured card again, even a year later. Those who were not given the experience of the shock-free coloured card in the first six hours after the test had already formed the memory of fear, and experienced it again when shown the card twelve months on.

Here neuroscience only catches up to what horsemen and women have always known. When I fell as a girl, I was always checked for damage and then legged back on straight away 'before you lose your nerve', they always said. Horse people have an almost superstitious fear that if a faller isn't immediately thrown back into the saddle, they will never get on a horse again. It took a few seconds to hit the ground and thirty seconds or a minute at most to be back on Mikalo, threading the reins back through my fingers and cantering again, his neck rising and falling before me, as if the stubble pricks on my palms weren't even there. How many minutes after the crash was I in the road with Ian before they took him away in the helicopter? What were the falls and the crash to the banks of good memories that could have fed my intercalated neurons: of cantering up Ringland Hills on Tav, of the time when Pegasus and I went clear over the tiny cross-country jumps at Cringleford and leaped boldly off a bank, of my first swinging canter on the Pferdberg, even of turning and halting Zofe when she bucked and charged. I should have liked to have my old fearlessness back once more, in all its innocence, and the best way to do that was to get back on again.

Mrs Hayes and Mrs Power O'Donoghue talked about 'confidential horses', and although they used the word to mean trustworthy, I liked its new connotation; if even your pulse is readable to a horse, you are already confiding in him and he knows your mood better than you do yourself. Fear is more acutely intimate for being shared. The rest is a matter of his discretion and wisdom and generosity; he must assume that he knows better than you despite your racing pulse, that there are no boggarts in the corner of the riding school, and that scraps of plastic will not attack him, so he will not throw you, nor bolt, nor shy, even if you inadvertently tell him to do so. The Pferdberg was a confidential horse, but I decided that I would make one further concession to my old desire to control fate and leave the riding club behind. The accident with the bay could have happened anywhere, but I had to accept that neither my nerves nor my German were equal to the group lessons. I needed something more familiar, to reinforce old, good memories. Meanwhile, I could think of much better uses for my imagination than conjuring up disastrous and fictional riding accidents. Instead I'd daydream of winning the lottery and whisking the big grey away to an Olympic livery yard in Brandenburg, where he would have a paddock and friends to graze with.

After a desultory half-hour lunging lesson in the reithalle on the big white rosinback they used for vaulting, I went to poke a carrot through the bars of the Pferdberg's stable and to say goodbye, and, in a stirring display of cupboard love, he followed me as I walked around his box and away.

Pursuit

It is almost as if the Chase were a sort of dope.

To Whom the Goddess (1932) by Lady Diana Shedden
and Lady Viola Apsley

I spent one afternoon with Hope, a lady in her eighties who had
hunted in Norfolk since the end of the last war, although she was
not 'local'. She first rode out to hounds aged four with the Pytchley
in Northamptonshire, one of the fast, grassland-and-hedgerow
hunts beloved by Mrs Hayes. Her parents would drive her to the meet
in a pony and trap, unhitch the pony and saddle it, attach a leading
rein and hand the end of it to the then Duke of Wellington, some
eighty years older than Hope. And off the pair would go. After the
hunt, muddy and exhilarated, they would return to the duke's house
for tea.

She had wide-open blue eyes surrounded by dark, tired skin, a
crest of grey hair and coral-painted lips. Her spine ran in a diagonal
from her right shoulder to her left hip, and she needed two sticks or
her small blue car to get about. She had a false shoulder, an artificial
hip, a knee long since swollen into a gall by osteomyelitis. Most of
her injuries had been sustained while horse riding. She plucked at
what I'd taken for a knitting bag and explained, 'I have to carry this
bag as it has all my breathers in it, emergency bits, puffers and . . .
Thing for heart that has to go under your tongue and guns you shoot
yourself with – that's to stop the pain if the pain gets too much.'

She had hunted fox, hare with a harrier pack that would transport five and a half couple of hounds in a single Morris Minor, and carted stag with the Norwich pack that Munnings joined before the war. Munnings painted Sybil Harker – 'Beautiful painting, that,' remarked Hope – who became Master of the Norwich Staghounds and who always rode side-saddle to hunt, right into her nineties. When Sybil died, her daughters gave Paula Sykes her old numnah, and Paula bought her bowler for a friend's side-saddle rig.

The stags were half tame, more hunt employee than prey, and were kept in a paddock at the kennels. Hope remembered one of them above all: 'I'm sure whenever I see deer in the fields here they must be his children and grandchildren.' When he was tired of being chased, he would either run into a river or find his way back to the red-painted cart, ready to be taken home. One day, in full flight near Wymondham, he ran into an open cottage door and got stuck in the hallway, his antlers gouged into the plaster. The hunt staff had to chip him out and pay for the walls to be replastered. 'It wasn't a very nice cottage before the stag did that,' said Hope, 'but it was much improved afterwards.'

We spent a long teatime poring over the book where I'd found a few clues about Mary Breese: Vic Brown's *The Foxhunters of Norfolk from 1534 to the Present Day*. It was an exhaustively detailed compendium of hound pedigrees – 'Lucifer, Luther, Luton, Lucky, Lustre, Luxury' – and accounts of meets – 'The first fox jumped out of kale north of Leys Farm and ran eastward for Scarning but turned left-handed parallel to the railway and was killed at Watery Lane Farm.' Hope recognized faces of MFHs and foot followers. There was one photograph of an old dame in a bowler hat hunched over a dark pony whose coat was curly with sweat, her toothless smile almost lost under her Punch-like nose. 'Oh yes, that's Mrs Howden! She was in her nineties when she stopped.' Vic Brown noted that Mrs Howden was notorious for being so dedicated to the chase that she didn't bother to dismount to pee. She liked to tell the MFH that when she had hunted her last he could chop her up and lob the bits into the copper to boil up as 'gravy' for the hounds.

I turned a page or two and our eyes fell on a slightly blurred shot of a teenage girl in a 1950s riding jacket with immense shoulders, an angular waist and a full skirt, with baggy dark-fawn jodhs underneath. She was a little toothy under her velvet hunt cap (which just sat on her head with no elastic), with an expression that could be nerves or self-consciousness or exhilaration. She had one white-gloved hand on the neck of her horse, who, although only partially in the picture, can be seen to be geed up with adrenaline: his ears are pricked, his head is high and his snaffle has pulled an inch out the corner of his mouth. All horses love to hunt.

The caption said that the girl was seventeen and had been attending a meet at Raynham Hall in 1954: 'Tragically she died in Tittleshall Church Wood later that day after a fall.'

'Did you know her?' I asked Hope.

'No.' She frowned, then smiled. 'But what a lovely way to go.' And then she said, more boastful than wistful, 'With this left leg completely chewed up I can't even ride astride any more because it just goes out at the hip, but I would still ride if I could get a side-saddle made on the off-side, you know.' She sat up as straight as she could, against her slanted spine, and her eyes gleamed. 'Last fox I saw, not quite the last, but it was in London, coming back from one of the hospitals I'd been to. It was dark and suddenly in my headlights a fox loped across, and I'm afraid I got out and holloaed at it!'

Safety

I do not think that the nerve of the modern children is any too good, how can one expect it, brought up as they are amongst all the horrors of civilization. The 'daring' child who used to be common enough, is seldom met nowadays.

The Young Rider (1928) by Golden Gorse

A dead fox lay sprawled on the hard shoulder of the A47 like an empty glove puppet. Every hundred yards or so there was the corpse of a freshly mashed hedgehog, its exposed insides the cheery red of supermarket mince; some were dry grey patties with patches of prickles attached. There were pheasants too, or at least fans of wing feathers that lifted and waved forlornly as the midweek traffic zoomed past; a rabbit lying, white belly up, on the roadside, four paws akimbo as if waiting for a tickle; and even a chestnut stoat, chin extended as though it had crawled up onto the verge, stretched out with a sigh and died. There should be an I-Spy of roadkill, I reflected. Fifty points for the large grey mound of badger I saw in the Cotswolds on the way to see Paddy Bury, one hundred for the deer you saw slipping in silhouette form across a road sign, 150 for a New Forest pony eviscerated by a speeding tourist.

The first time I travelled on the Norwich southern bypass I was on horseback. I was still at Cringleford and the girls taking our string out hacking had led us onto the broad strip of bright-orange sand where the tarmac would soon be laid four lanes wide across the countryside west and south of Norwich. We had cantered along it in file, defiantly stamping a trail of hoof prints in our wake. Perhaps they knew that the road would be partly responsible for the end of the riding school. It slashed straight through our hacking territory, up by the spinney of beech trees on top of Fir Hill by Intwood Carr, where they'd send us careering one at a time round the little circuit with the tiny rustic fence. The beech copse looked diminished by the dual carriageway, like an ornamental garden clump rather than a flight of woodland.

Just beyond the beeches I passed a field with a blue metal horse trailer – the old-fashioned two-horse type with a pinched, blunt nose at the bow and a square stern – parked up and, side-on to the stream of traffic, a sign with 'Keswick Riding Stables' and a phone number printed in large white letters. We'd always referred to Keswick as our rivals, but they had survived when Cringleford had faltered and closed down in 1997, after its annual rates rose vertiginously from £780 to £9,980, knocking the business out from under Paula. The horses and ponies were dispersed to good homes with people who had loved them at the school, and thirty-four years of children's riding lessons drew to a neat close. One in six riding schools nationwide fell to the new Uniform Business Rate.

In the last twenty years it has looked as though, after decades of growth, riding schools were a more endangered species than the deer, hedgehogs or foxes. The Association of British Riding Schools reported that the number of member schools in the UK had fallen from 3,016 in 1992 to 1,900 in 2004, despite an overall increase in the number of riders. At one point, one licensed riding school was shuttered every week. Others were pinched by the side effects of Foot and Mouth. Some had difficulty finding qualified staff who would work for low salaries, as the great rush of girl grooms willing to work for poverty wages tailed off.

Now I was heading towards Yarmouth and one of only six riding centres in the county that were approved by the British Horse Society. Most of these were large equestrian centres like the place where I'd jumped Kylie and Murphy, but Willow Farm had appealed to me. Its name echoed both the Willowbrook Riding Academy in Norman Thelwell's books, where the pupils leaped road railings and pole-vaulted onto their horses, and Willow Cottage, where Tav had once led the classes riderless. According to the website it had been in the same ownership for forty years, so I felt it was the closest I could find to Cringleford.

A turn off the A47 led me to a series of smaller roads and finally to Ormesby St Margaret, where a screen of elegant, silver willows, as high and narrow as poplars, appeared on my right at the edge of the Yarmouth Road. I turned into the drive and hopped out to open the gate, returning to the car and driving carefully through, before immediately closing the gate in case a pony bolted out and was dashed to strawberry jam on the road. There wasn't much traffic on the Yarmouth Road, but what there was went wickedly fast.

Behind the willow wall was a large outdoor school with wooden-planked sides, and beyond it fields subdivided with flickering white electrical tape. Someone was picking their way across one of the fields past some small cross-country jumps with a wheelbarrow for dung, pursued by a curious chestnut-roan pony. I parked by the entrance to a yard with walls of scrambled flint and thin red bricks, next to a large white hand-painted sign that read:

ALL ANIMALS, RIDERS,
SPECTATORS & VEHICLES
AT OWN RISK

There was a dark, creosoted garden shed in the car park, decorated with a row of tin plaques reading:

Safety

Outside, a rug was drying on a garden bench, and a white board with details of rallies, hunter trials and 'own-a-pony' days ('weather permitting, the cross-country course will be used') was propped up against the door, which also carried a sign: 'Horses kick and bite.' I poked my head into the shed, which was papered with photos of various vintages: ponies and girls with velvet caps in black and white; old white-bordered shots with curled corners; misty Polaroids; girls in colour with modern fluorescent tabards over their riding clothes. A green plastic collecting tin for the ILPH hung over a narrow occasional table with an old handbell sitting on it. There was a cold cup of tea on a floral tin tray and an open, battered ledger with lists of horses, riders and lesson times in biro. A couple of horseshoes were propped against the photos and a three-drawer filing cabinet stood in the far corner.

Someone called and I emerged from the shed to see Jane Russell waving to me from a second, larger shed by the gate.

'Susanna Forrest?' she asked.

Jane was in her fifties, with black-plum hair under a modern skullcap with an anachronistic, faded brown-velvet cover. She wore a body warmer over jodphurs and ankle boots. Looking me shrewdly up and down, she asked how much riding I'd done, before calling over her granddaughter, a teenage girl with bright blonde streaks in her hair, to say, 'Tack up Harry,' then to me, 'I wanted to check you first, because we've got a plodder in the yard that we normally put new people on, but I think you'll be fine with Harry. Did you bring a hat? No? If you go back into that shed and look through the filing cabinet you should find something that fits. We've got all sizes here. Then come up to the yard and get Harry. I'll be waiting in the school.'

I went through each drawer of the cabinet, sorting the plain skullcaps like melons, trying to avoid the child-size ones. It seemed that my skull was long but narrow, and every hat I tried pinched at the forehead and gaped at the sides. Eventually I found one that sat squarely on the head, hugging just enough all round to be secure without digging in. Feeling self-conscious and somehow bald, I left the shed and walked through the archway into the main yard, where there was another noticeboard. Pinned to it were photographs of the ponies and a list, checked by the council's vet at an annual inspection, of the twelve ponies and horses: Copper, Pippa, Hadleigh, Splash . . . Three horse rugs were drying on metal arms that swung out from the wall like signposts.

The stables were a fine old farmyard, its floor running in sloping planes down to central drains. The flint walls of the loose boxes were painted a fresh, clean white above and a tarry black below the tidemark. The tiled roofs were low. Where a clay tile was missing, it had been replaced with a clear plastic one, crimped in the same shape to let more light through to the ponies, some of whom, curious, poked their heads out over the black half-doors. Another large white sign was attached to the wall:

ALL CLIENTS
RIDE & HANDLE
THESE HORSES
AT OWN RISK

The last line was painted in red block capitals; all it lacked was a skull and crossbones.

Jane's granddaughter called to me from one of the boxes, where she was waiting with Harry, a Welsh section D cob of about 15.2hh, whose blazed face was turned to the empty manger that ran along the back wall of his stable. His coat, which was thickening for the coming winter, was the bright chestnut of Tav and he had the same small, foxy ears poking through his long mane, which faded to strawberry blond at the tips. He did not look so pleased to be working and nipped at Jane's granddaughter, but he stepped out of his stable and down into the yard willingly.

She held the stirrup for me and I climbed on, trying to dismiss the slight vertigo produced by the view of the sloping yard from Harry's back as I adjusted the stirrup leathers and the cob pulled to be off. We walked out through the archway and across the small car park to where Jane stood holding open the gate of the school. Underfoot were peculiar rough black scraps, which I took for bark chips.

'No, they're old aeroplane tyres,' said Jane.

Soft enough for a fall. I walked on round the edge of the school, getting the feel of Harry, who stepped out generously. Jane took up position at the centre of the ring and began to teach.

'Now, Harry might be a riding-school horse but that doesn't mean you should ride him like one. He gets out and goes to one-day events and things like that, so let's see you ride him like you mean it. Let's do some transitions.'

For half an hour Harry and I worked. From stand to walk and walk to trot and back again. From standing to trot, and from a brisk trot to a square halt. Sometimes I got my aids right; sometimes Harry cleverly anticipated me and stopped before I could squeeze my reins.

Jane knew it and admonished me. 'He's got a long back. You need to gather him up,' she said, after I ended one canter baggy-kneed and a little scared. 'Now, tell me what you're going to do if he canters on the wrong leg and then let's try again.' She gave no quarter, but she also gave technical explanations and quizzed me – 'Which hoof hits the ground first in canter?' 'Were you on the right diagonal there?'

I was the only child in the classroom and my complete attention was engaged rather than squandered on thoughts of petrifying falls. There was no need to flap my legs on Harry, who went forward beautifully, though he left me to make my own mistakes too. Between the teacher and the cob, I was brusquely put through my paces and well taught.

The little rise of panic I'd felt when he first broke into canter seemed easy enough to subdue as I watched Harry's red ears, feeling reassured by Jane's presence and the steady flow of advice and information.

'Back in the day,' she said at one point, 'I used to make the kids bring their money for a lesson in half-crown pieces, and then I'd put the coins between their knees and the saddle and if they lost them they'd have to find them at the end of the lesson, or else give me another one. We don't grip all the time like that now, because if you're gripping like that to stay on, then you've got no extra. Bring your calves back, they're too far forward.'

Finally she had me cross my stirrups in front of the pommel, and I bumped round for a circuit or two, feeling as though my seat bones were transformed into giant knuckles and puffing like a schoolgirl who's disappointed the gym mistress in a half-mile run.

As I walked Harry to cool him, she gave me an assessment.

'You only really got him going once, cantering down K-E-H on the long side, and you know when that was, because his neck curved and you were going properly forwards. That was because it was coming from behind. Don't worry about getting his head in till you've engaged his back.' I flopped off and patted Harry, who stretched his neck. 'Yes, if I were teaching you,' went on Jane, 'I'd have you riding twice a week. You've got a nice seat but you're very, very, very unfit.'

After Harry had been put away and I'd found the airy tackroom, stowed the saddle on a bracket and put the bridle on a hook that was hoisted up to the ceiling, I joined Jane for a cup of tea in the shed by the gate. The brick walls inside were whitewashed like the stables, and against them stood an old kitchen dresser the height of the room. Two mismatched old tables were jammed together in the centre, surrounded by a jumble of chairs from assorted dining suites. There was a real, articulated fetlock joint for teaching working students and a first-aid kit in a plastic briefcase. I went for a pee in the little WC behind a sliding door, and found that the toilet seat was covered in Thelwell-esque cartoons. A blobby poster-paint master-piece of two girls riding ponies was fixed to the wall, with a typed caption taped to at the bottom: 'Sometimes I ride Hadleigh he won't go fast and sometimes I ride Sam he won't stop.' My tea was waiting for me.

'I was born here,' explained Jane. 'It's a family farm and it's still working. My father used to supply all the milk in the area and he used to deliver it by horse and cart. They would be up at 3 a.m. to do the first milking, then deliver it, then the second milking in the afternoon and then in bed at eight o'clock at night.' She laughed. 'We had Suffolk Punches and Percherons,' which she pronounced 'Persians', 'and there were always ponies too. There used to be two full-time men to look after them, and a stallion came round once a year to serve the mares so we had two foals a year. They were always coming on. I was brought up with them – I've got a picture of me at eighteen months on a pony.'

Were you, I asked, in the Pony Club?

'Not in the early days, no. Once I got to around ten, eleven, then I got friendly with other kids in the area with ponies, and we'd gang up and hire a lorry from the local contractor and go off to shows. But when I was fourteen or fifteen I suddenly thought, I don't want horses any more, I'll go for the two-legged variety.' She grinned. 'But that only lasted two or three years and then I came back to horses again.'

Her parents packed her off to college in Yarmouth to learn shorthand and touch-typing, but in her spare time she was giving riding lessons to family and friends, some of whom used to pay her in boxes of chocolates, which she sold for cash. She broke in and brought on her father's ponies: 'I got quite nifty with the naughty ones.' After a year of Pitman's exams and typing to music, she realized she didn't want to work for Barclays Bank or do anything but be with horses, and as more and more people wanted lessons, she found herself gradually setting up a riding school.

'I got my teaching qualifications, stages 1, 2 and 3 with the BHS, and then the full Assistant Instructor, which in those days you had to do all in one day, the written and everything. I needed some more suitable horses for the riding school, and I remember buying a cob off Paula Sykes by the name of Zambi. Oh, and I hated that horse!' she roared. 'You could sit about six people on her she was so long, but she was probably the start of running the riding school properly.'

'You know Paula?' I asked.

'Oh yes. We used to have a riding-school challenge cup between lots of schools in Norfolk, and Cringleford used to take part. Salhouse, Keswick, Willow Cottage – about ten altogether. We were ever so competitive. There was jumping, and gymkhana, and showing classes, and riding for the disabled. Paula and me, we were friends, but on competition day! Ooh! We wanted to win!' She slapped the table with her hand. 'The turnout had to be absolutely perfect. The kids weren't allowed to set foot on the ground in case they got their boots muddy – they had to be lifted onto the ponies. The whole thing dispersed after ten years because there wasn't enough interest from the other riding schools but I've still got the trophy at home. I'd love to show it to Paula but she isn't going to get it because we were the last ones that won it and I'm keeping it!'

In 1961, a group of horse societies, including the RSPCA, the BHS and the Walbanckes of the Horse Rescue Fund of Norfolk, sent out a team led by a Colonel Boultbee to survey 1,200 riding establishments in the UK. Thirty per cent of these stables contained horses that were starved, injured and exhausted, while the people who ran them had no idea of how to keep a good stable. In one case, a fifteen-year-old schoolgirl was keeping a small herd of unbroken two-year-old ponies in a tiny field, feeding them potatoes from her father's fish-and-chip shop and promising lessons to local kids.

Viscount Massereene and Ferrard stood up in the Lords to ask the house to strengthen the 1939 Riding Establishments Act, which had never been properly enforced, explaining that 'Before the war, the majority of people who rode horses came from the farming fraternity and the so-called leisured classes – rather a misnomer, I must say.' Naturally. He went on, 'Since they were country people, with a country background, one of the many things they were taught was horse management and the art of horsemanship . . . Today, things have changed. We no longer have our cavalry regiments, our yeomanry regiments and the excellent courses in horse management that the British Army used to teach us.'

The Act was updated. 'That sorted a lot of people out,' commented Jane, eyebrows raised, arms folded. Willow Farm was licence number one in Norfolk. The Act was tightened up again in 1970 and since then a steady flow of new legislation has arrived to enforce more safety requirements.

'Now it's very tight. The inspector has to attend some sort of teaching every year, and they're checking all the saddles, the bridles, everything. They're here for three or four hours, checking the horses' feet, their eyes, their hearts, even their backs. They'll come back to check on an injured horse if it's bad enough.'

Eighty per cent of her pupils are children, so she keeps twelve ponies, Harry and a bay warmblood called Remeny, although at one stage there were forty horses and ponies. Now the stables are manageable on a slim staff if the ponies live out for most of the year. Jane is the only full-time staff member at Willow Farm, although there are some freelance and part-time instructors who also come in to teach, as well as some other helpers.

I asked whether children helped out in the stables and she shook her head. 'You can't do that any more. You have to be thirteen to have a paper round, so if the teenagers want to help in the yard they have to get a work permit, right?'

Teenage workers require insurance too. One livery stable faced a settlement of £2.1 million after a girl collecting her own pony from a field was kicked in the head and left brain-damaged. Jane tries to get everyone to join the Pony Club so that they're covered for any mishaps that happen on the premises.

'We're a Pony Club Centre, which is basically to encourage kids who haven't got their own pony to take part and to do the achievement badges. The beauty of it is that every child is fully insured, so on own-a-pony day, if I send them all out en masse to the fields with a wheelbarrow to pick up dung and one of them falls over, I'm covered if they're Pony Club members.'

A series of compensation claims set some awkward legal precedents in the noughties. In 2003 the House of Lords ruled that the owners of a horse that had escaped from its field, bolted onto a motorway and into the path of a car were liable, even if they had taken all reasonable precautions to keep it penned. Some of the high-profile lawsuits that followed on the heels of this case were successful, and insurance soared. In 2004 the *Daily Telegraph* reported that one riding school had seen its insurance premiums rise from £787 to £4,669 in just four years. Only two firms would underwrite equestrian establishments and they made no profit. Lesson costs rose, excluding poorer children, who could, of course, not 'work for rides' as that would be illegal. In 2007, expert witnesses were charging over £100 an hour to root out evidence of 'negligence' by instructors when, as one harassed riding-school owner told the *Guardian* in 2004, 'The only way you can guarantee not falling off is not to get on in the first place.'

Jane Phillips, a solicitor who had acted for the Pony Club's insurers, urged a new culture of caution: 'Remember, being able to demonstrate effective risk management and evidence of record-keeping are the keys to any defence' – hence Jane Russell's protective panoply of signs. You couldn't say you hadn't been warned. New riders should sign waivers, the solicitor advised, disclosing the extent of their earlier experience; as it was, some teachers gave up old cavalry exercises such as riding without stirrups. Premiums have not been hoicked significantly for a few years now. At the time of writing, moves were afoot to amend the Animals Act of 1971, so that non-negligent owners and carers could not be sued when horses act like horses. Fortified, riding schools were reported in early 2009 to be doing good business, despite the recession.

'We're very, very satisfied with our insurers,' said Jane. 'They come round every three years to check where you keep your tack, check where you have your lessons, where you keep your hats. Last time they came I showed them the tiny indoor school we have, so if I've got two or three children up to six years old, that's where they start off. And that's all nice and safe, and then they progress onto the outdoor manège, and then there might be a few more children, a class of six, maximum eight. And the insurance people were nodding along, good, good,' she mimed them, with knitted brow, 'and I should have kept my mouth shut because, then, I said, then they progress. They might go out on to the fields and do one or two of those little cross-country jumps.' She paused and drew back. 'They were horrified. Horrified.'

She threw her hands up. 'Well, how the ... I was about to put a swear word in there ... How are you going to teach a child if you're always going to have it in a confined space? A child or an adult? How are they going to get that feeling of a horse doing a bit of a runner under them, and coping with it?' She shook her head with exasperation. 'And how are they going to be allowed to go on a hack if they haven't first of all experienced a horse really going forward?'

I pictured pallid children and comatose ponies, circling the small, windowless school endlessly for years and never getting out of a trot.

There are a thousand acres of Willow Farm to ride on, but Jane doesn't like to take groups out hacking further than that because they might not turn out to be good riders.

'You're lucky if you get a small canter. We used to go down to the beach and everything, but now your riders have to be at such a high standard because we don't ride there regularly and when the horses hit the beach they explode. My God, it's like taking them hunting. The roads are awful these days too.'

A few months before I went to Willow Farm, a four-wheel drive dragging a trailer ripped past a horse that was being ridden on a road near Mattishall on the other side of Norwich, gashing the horse open from one end to the other. Through the window I saw the cars on the Yarmouth Road flashing by at intervals and a truck that rattled the fetlock joint on the dresser.

'When I was a kid my mum used to say, "Off you go out and play" – and this was when I was seven or eight years old, you know. – "I'll see you lunchtime."' Jane laughed. 'And I'd go off on my pony –

there was good hacking in those days – in an old hat with the elastic under my chin unless it got uncomfortable and then I took it off completely!' Her laughter rose. 'You know, bareback around the field. I used to play Roy Rogers with my dog and God knows what. We all came up here to the farm and if a pony was naughty it was "Who's going to get on that pony?"! Oh, and then the bridle breaks so you've got a bit of string to tie it up with.' She wheezed with laughter. 'But, by God, we were brought up hard and we learned to cope. These kids now, they get one fall and they think that's the end of the world. We fell off all the time, all the time! But you try explaining that to the parents today and they're just so over-protective. I think it's just how things have evolved. I don't think it's so much with riding, it's with everything. Kids are a bit wimpy now.'

Before I left, I watched her give a lesson. The children were zipped into back protectors and crowned with crash caps. In 1999, Roberta Bradby, an eight-year-old Pony Club member from Suffolk, was so horrified by the deaths of leading eventers that she invented a kind of life-preserver for horse riders, which would inflate like an airbag when they were pitched out of the saddle. There are now several air jackets on the market, some offered in child-size editions. As the children trotted round, I wondered how long it would be before they were attached to their saddles by a ripcord.

'I don't care if you trot or canter over this little jump as long as you get over it first time,' Jane shouted as the three girls and the boy circled. The first of them headed out, uncertainly, with Jane growling encouragement, 'LEG LEG LEG! CAN-TER, CAN-TER! You can't go over a jump in walk.' The pony stepped over the poles fastidiously, his rider blushing scarlet.

She was overseeing the children's untacking efforts when I went to my car, breaking off to say goodbye and to point out the chestnut pony with the strange frosting of white hair who stood in the field by the school.

'You see that old boy with the blue rug on? He still has his moments of dumping people. That pony is thirty-seven years old!' Copper pricked his ears and went back to the grass. 'I suggest you upgrade your riding school when you get back to Germany,' Jane suggested. I nodded and then she added, 'Give my love to Paula!'

Growing Up

'Speaking as someone who has had a pony for nearly a year, I
think a person should have other interests in her life than just
ponies and riding. No one could love their pony more than I love
Cascade, but I don't want to grow up a long-faced horsey woman
with no other string to her bow.'

Tamzin in *The Summer of the Great Secret* (1948) by Monica Edwards

'**D**o boys and ponies mix?' asked the headline on the letters page
of *Horse and Pony* just after my twelfth birthday. Rachel of East
Sussex wanted to know 'how many readers will go off ponies and
turn their attentions to boys in the future. I hope I won't.' The
magazine had just published a short story about a pony who had
been forsaken by his girl when she got a boyfriend, and who had
had to be rescued by a fresh little girl. Joanne of Burton-upon-Trent
raged,

I felt I just had to let off steam. The problem in your short story 'Sandi's
Pony' happens all too often in real life. When I hear my friends, also pony
owners, chatting about boys and the discos they are going to that evening,
I wonder how they have enough time to attend to their ponies ... I am
often asked why I can't go out with boys and still love horses. I reply,
'There's not enough time for mucking out and make-up!' Anyway, four-
legged beauties are far more faithful than boys!

Feelings ran high. An anonymous reader had the last word that week, though, and withered the loyalists with scorn.

I keep reading complaints about people growing out of horses and abandoning them for boys, discos etc. In most cases this is a load of rubbish. I have my own horse. All her needs are seen to and I ride her for at least an hour a day. On top of this I go out nearly every night, have fun and listen to pop music, which seems a crime in your magazine . . . It makes me laugh when people write, 'I'm 102 per cent pony-mad' (what bores).

Bores? Bores? Well, to be called a bore was nothing new. I was familiar with that, although I was becoming more self-conscious about boring others. Enthusiasm had to be kept in check and monitored now, in favour of blasé adolescent mooching. I had given up actually galloping on my imaginary horses after the first year at the private school when we were all transferred to the main building, which had no playground. We spent breaks sitting on our desks, bitching and playing vicious card games.

I'd entered a new culture where academic achievement was paramount. Its mores were absorbed and reinforced by us girls, who pegged our self-esteem to A's and B's like investors dicing with commodity prices, watching over our neighbour's shoulders to read whether their own stocks had risen or fallen: if she got 74 per cent, was 69 per cent respectable, or should I get depressed? All this fear and pride in competition had to be carefully covered up with self-deprecation: 'I'm sure I only got an A because I was lucky with the vocabulary,' we told each other. When I rode Tav into the ring at the Aylsham Show, keeping with him as he cleared the first fence and then disdained, three times, to leap the second, I cantered him out again, laughing because it didn't matter as much as my end-of-term exams.

For a while the Ground a Fire saga had remained useful, as he and his dynasty were pressed to excel effortlessly and gallop out my most outlandish ambitions, safe from the crimp of fumbled maths questions and too-concise essays. However, as I reached my mid-teens the Ground a Fire daydreams would wash up and beach themselves on an increasingly massy rock of reality. They seemed aimless, all endless galloping. What do you do after winning the Derby? Freeze-frame and replay the most exciting bit? My own plots were thin compared to Patricia Leitch's ever evolving tales of Finmory. Unnourished, the chestnut stallion passed from three dimensions to two, flattened like metal beaten to foil, and then, with a last flicker, all that was left was embarrassingly bad doggerel. The desert, the stud farm, the ranch and the racecourse were gone in a scrunch of paper, flat and unexplorable once more.

Burying the lot in my wardrobe, I gave up writing stories about horses and then stories altogether, unless I was obliged to do so for coursework. I packed up my Sindy and Barbie horses higgledy-piggledy into a big round raffia basket like a shambolic Scythian kurgan and hefted the whole lot up into the attic to join Dobbin, who stood, his chin chewed open by the dog, miraculously unmolested by moths, strapped into an improvised rug I'd made from an old cot blanket.

My new friends were a bobbery pack. None of us dressed the same out of school – Sarah F in her tie-dye skirts; Sarah G who looked like a Titian; Em with her wild long hair; me in drooping black men's jumpers from Marks & Sparks and Lycra minis; Sara in nice blouses with upturned collars; and Mel in bright-yellow leggings and a geometric-print dress – but we shared a sense of humour pillaged from Python and the Goons, as well as the conviction that we would never be governed by the petty, shifting politics that drove all the other girls in and out of friendships. In this we failed, although our circle, which doubled as a life-raft, held up reasonably well in the swells and storms of life in a school of several hundred ceaselessly stroppy teenage girls.

None of them was interested in horses. One day I took them all out to trek round the Railway Line with Tav, but Em turned out to be allergic to him, and the rest of us got so dusty trudging alongside whoever was riding that we didn't have the taste for it after that. I redoubled my pursuit of real horse racing instead, going through the morning paper with a highlighter pen and settling down in the living room after riding Tav on a Saturday morning to watch the races on the telly with my newly washed hair wrung up in a towel. I picked winners for the pattern races by their pedigrees and charted the winning family tree to ten generations on taped-together sheets of graph paper, which I pasted up in my bedroom.

At school there were evening meetings with parents present, to talk about GCSE options, and trips to the attic over the headmistress's study where the careers officer, presiding over a little library of pamphlets and books, asked what I wanted to be when I was grown up – a moment that had apparently leaped closer while I hadn't been paying attention. I held out stubbornly for the racing business, even if I knew I was now too tall to be a jockey, and Mrs Lane, with her grey bun and peer-over glasses, humoured me and did not suggest, as my parents had done, becoming a barrister. Would I, she queried, be able to find some work experience?

My mother mustered her old Newmarket knowledge and wrote to the British Bloodstock Association to ask whether I could tag along for a day. Gawky in my new navy trouser suit (purchased from a specialist shop for taller women) with my hair drawn back from my face and tied ineptly, I turned up at the square Georgian building on Newmarket High Street, opposite the vet's yard where Mum had worked, and hung around awkwardly in a corner of the office. My two chinless hosts, unsure what to do with me, let me biro new entries into their copies of Weatherby's Stud Book and took me to the BBA's equine swimming pool, where I watched a man in a camel coat slip the attendant some cash and take his greyhounds for a swim. The men from the BBA loaded me up with leather-bound stud books full of glossy photographs of shining, deep-girthed stallions in brass-buckled headcollars, run to portly maturity in their early retirement, like City Boys who had made their mint by thirty.

When they stood under the elegant, white-columned portico and waved me off in my mother's car, I was confident that both sides were quite sure that I was not the right stuff for the racing business. I felt inadequately 'horsy' for once – a daydreaming amateur with a little book learning and no useful family connections. I went on buying the *Racing Post* on the way to school and consigned a job with horses to the unthinkable territory of 'if I fail my A levels'. I saw a fraction further beyond the borders of the horse world and thought of lands that might lie there, where university might offer a better escape. Some days I didn't buy the *Racing Post* at all. I got the *New Musical Express* or the *Melody Maker* instead.

I still read pony books, but found little to carry me over into teenagehood and gradually shelved them for one last time, not even to raid them as comfort reading. The plots of most of them seemed as circular as my daydreams, with heroes who tended to freeze at fourteen or fifteen: Jill Crewe went off to learn to be a secretary instead of a woman MFH; Alec Ramsay never seemed to actually grow up; and Jinny stopped at book twelve, Shantih safely hers, a balance struck between real life with the plastic people and the world of the Red Horse and the Finmory moors. Only K. M. Peyton's Ruth Hollis seemed to bridge the gap and try to negotiate both hormones and horses. She started her period on a day of the Pickworth horse trial, fainted and had to spend the day tucked up in the horsebox while a team-mate rode her horse, Toadhill Flax. After a date with the truculent Patrick Pennington, Ruth had a revelation in a passage that threw that old love of horses into a rather revealing and embarrassing light:

Now, the moment he had gone, she felt an agony of longing for him to be there again. It was so sharp that she had to stop in the middle of the drive, unable to face her parents with this empty, demented feeling draining all of the sense out of her. She stood and looked up at the sky through the pear trees, lifting her face and feeling the coolness of the breeze that came off the river. It occurred to her, quite inappropriately, that once these strange feelings had been to do with ponies and winning something very special, the times when she had looked at the sky and been filled with inexplicable longings. It was the only thing she had to compare this present ache with.

I felt more comfortable with Jilly Cooper's *Riders*, where the loves of the protagonists were less acutely drawn and the horses were like old characters from pony-book days – Sailor, dying for Jake, or loyal Macaulay attacking the cruel Rupert Campbell-Black.

Boyfriends remained on one of those non-horsy horizons till I left school, but I did go to discos and to clubs, and speculated about boys with my hugger-mugger gang of friends. As my riding world shrank to leisurely hacking with Tav – he was the only being to whom I ever sang the indie songs I bought – there were new thrills in the grottiest Norwich nightclub, or at one of the eight universities I had to list on my much-Tippexed UCAS form. I left riding off those forms in favour of Amnesty International membership, as I thought it more relevant. I was worried about reverse snobbery now, having had my poshness dubbined into me on every day I walked to school in uniform, when the kids from the city state schools came to spit on me when I went down into the subway at the top of St Stephen's or, once, memorably, punched me in the head.

Later, at university, I told people that I liked horses, still somehow surprised that my new friends didn't know this. I hadn't brought any horse pictures with me – I had giant Manic Street Preachers posters or Martin Kippenberger artworks instead – but on arrival it turned out that there were plenty of people posher than me. I dabbled with clove cigarettes and wore an unravelling, second-hand astrakhan coat with gaping sleeves up which the damp, bitter fen winds blew. The countryside outside Cambridge dwindled to a narrow, blurred strip of RAF blue at the edges of my student existence of digs, bars, lecture halls and college dining rooms. There were supposedly muntjacs in the college gardens, but they were never glimpsed. One night as I walked home in my ridiculous coat from some tipsy dinner party, I paused by the railings of the causeway and looked down into a conduit that flowed up from the river to see a pike motionless in the water.

If one cycled far enough out, there were flat, arable fields bounded by motorways, and, allegedly, riding stables, but after a Swedish girl told me of her outing with the riding club and how she liked to whip horses and make them sweat, I decided that the college horsy crowd was not mine. London was more interesting than the countryside, and it seemed easier to go there by train than to flog out into the fields in an attempt to escape the motorways and the tourists. I was too fascinated by my new friends, too worried I would miss something, and, of course, there were finally boyfriends. Horses were familiar, horses were home and Mum and Dad. I could ride Tav when I was back in Costessey, although after my second year he changed homes and, knowing he was well cared for, I found I didn't miss him so much after all.

He'd gone to a new place deeper in the countryside, to a couple who needed an extra pony for their children and who knew how to look after old horses. He had a good few years with the two little boys, giving pony rides at the village fair and being groomed by mobs of children at a time. He shared his field with a few bullocks and some sheep who kept the grass short enough for his old molars to chew. No one knew, still, how old he was. When the family lost the mother suddenly and tragically, the stock had to be given up and the grass grew too long. Tav seemed to deteriorate and the decision was taken to put him down. He was buried on the farm. My mother phoned me to deliver the news, her voice rising at the corners in the 'All right?' she'd used when I was a child and at the snivelling end of a storm of tears, but I took it as calmly as I'd taken Dusky's earlier death. I didn't think too hard about what happened to their chestnut forms, just of what good, long lives they'd led.

Four years at university were enough to cure me of the notion that horses had a permanent place in my life. I couldn't integrate them into my new adult existence. Horsy jobs did not appeal as much as the ones I now pursued, jobs that would never pay for me to keep my own horse in London, which was where I was headed, along with most of my friends, and I consigned horses to childhood. By the 1990s, horses had in any case become something that one was expected to outstrip and leave behind with adulthood unless you were irredeemably horsy. The salad days of riding lessons were not intended to be an investment for a well-rounded adult, but instead an ephemeral thing to be treasured as a memory. I had used to feel frustration when my mother, or someone else's mother, looked at me wistfully and commented that I would 'grow out of it', but now I had to agree. One in five British people is under sixteen, yet nearly a quarter of British riders are children. Somewhere lies the unseen Rubicon where pony-mad girls make the transfer to horse-mad adults and I lost interest before I even reached its bank.

My jodhpurs remained in my cupboard at home in Norfolk, facing the ten-generation pedigrees for Celtic Swing and Lammtara whose Sellotape had gone yellow and brittle. I pulled down all the old posters and binned them, taking gobs of paint off the walls along with the Blu-Tack. The model horses pranced in dust on the shelves. A plastic pencil case unzipped to reveal a clutch of rosettes: a pale-green one for the minimus on Honey in 1990, red for first in the handy pony with Cricket, a double blue-and-white one for the team gymkhana on Joe, third in the Arab Horse Society Utility Pony with Tav, that time he'd nearly peed on the judge's feet. I'd pencilled the now forgotten details on the peeling cardboard backs. A clear round on Red, '2ft 3in showjumping course against forty others, four faults in jump-off'.

In London, I stroked the noses of the Household Cavalry horses on sentry duty in the Mall and thought weakly of paying fifty quid an hour to ride in Hyde Park, before dismissing lessons as too expensive while frittering my meagre wages on cheap clothes and expensive make-up. The old qualities I'd thrived on with horses were no longer required of me – too much passion and you'd scare off any twenty-something man, and there was nothing about my office-bound life that demanded physical bravery and exhilaration.

I wanted a get-out clause of scepticism, something to hold in reserve against total commitment of body or heart, which is how I became the person who, in later years, couldn't fly to Sydney and find escape by prancing about in a pony outfit with Shyanne, or lose myself in a trance for Epona like Devon. All that was left was a tendency to get weepy when I heard the Grand National theme. After the accident I accepted the noise of the Royal Artillery horses trotting smartly under my bedroom window as a comfort, and a sound of childhood.

The March of the
Pink Hooves

One Christmas I asked for a My Little Pony and ended up with a
real one. Little did my family know I couldn't be arsed to actually
ride it, but our groundsman looked after it. It was white, and my
mum dyed its mane and tail shocking pink, which did look cool.
She also tried to stick wings on it but it didn't work.

Dominique, email to author

The corridors behind the main arena at Olympia in December
2006 were busy – girls of all ages were milling around,
galloping down the carpet, peeking up through the gangways and
into the main arena. The five-year-olds were almost too excited to
speak, some carrying stuffed-toy horses as big as themselves, their
mothers reining them in, while the ten-year-olds tried to give off an
air of nonchalance when famous showjumpers walked by in blouson
team jackets with their names printed on the back. The teenagers,
with flat-ironed hair and eyeliner, slouched by, flicking their fringes
and eating pizza and candyfloss. I barely saw a dad. Twenty-foot-high
posters of Sweden's hot young showjumping star, Malin Baryard,
modelling H&M frocks, were pinned to the back of the staging. A
clown brandishing a yellow balloon the size of a spacehopper waited
at one of the gangways, down which washed the sound of cheering
from the arena where the matinée show was on and the Mountain
and Moorland Pony finalists were going through their paces.

Lonsdale's Royal International Horse Show left the Olympia Halls in Kensington after the Second World War, transferring first to the huge, open-air arena at White City, and thence to the Birmingham NEC. For a while there were no major horse shows at Olympia. In 1972 the BBC commentator Raymond Brooks-Ward proposed a new international horse show for London, and the Olympia International Show Jumping Championships was born at the height of the sport's popularity. Olympia was as 1970s as the tinsel on the horses' bridles, Noddy Holder and Cadbury's Selection Boxes.

In the spirit of Lonsdale's original show, there was a variety of serious classes, Grands Prix, speed competitions and the puissance or high jump. Then there were the pantomime spectacles: fancy-dress showjumping, with Harvey Smith guyed up as Barbara Woodhouse; Jim'll Fix It winners taking on their heroes over the jumps; the Shetland Grand National; the cast of Hi-de-Hi doing dog training; camel racing with Stirling Moss and Prince Charles. Every year it held a regular slot in the BBC's Christmas schedule, beside the Only Fools and Horses repeats and the black-and-white classics. When I was little, viewing figures peaked at 11 or 12 million. To me Christmas wasn't Christmas without Olympia, just as at least a few summer days had to be spent indoors, glued to the sight of Nick Skelton's bold, white-faced Apollo plunging down the Hickstead bank, while autumn meant Ginny Leng and the bullish Priceless bounding over timber at the Burghley horse trials.

Down at the arena floor, finally really there at the heart of it all, I looked up around the tiers of seating and saw pink. That year, 2006, Olympia was presided over by Haven, the breast cancer charity, but it wasn't just that there was a sea of pink ribbons out there – everyone was wearing pink: pink T-shirts, pink jumpers, pink scarves, pink jackets, pink rabbit ears on pink headbands, all set off nicely against the green plastic seats. There can't have been more than 8,000 people there, a crowd equivalent to that at a League Two football match.

Overhead, where Lonsdale's standard lampshades had once floated, was an immense swag of raspberry-pink-and-white-striped curtain gathered at the top of the roof like a tent. Corporate hospitality boxes crowned with more raspberry-and-white awnings framed the top layer of the arena, where the loggias for visiting statesmen had been ranged in 1910. The hall seemed small, almost cosy, and the front rows of the audience sat right up at the edge of the arena. Between show-jumping classes and displays by the Metropolitan Mounted Police, I wandered into the Olympia Shopping Village, where the promenades lined with palm trees had charmed the Edwardian visitors, to sniff leather and stick my nose in hoof-oil cans.

I quickly became lost in the souk, distracted by the kind of horsyana that, as a pony-mad eight-year-old, I would have rolled in daily if anyone had let me. At a saddlery stand, I browsed bridles hung in bunches, the leather dark and stiff, ready to tell anyone who might ask that I was shopping for my own horse, a 17hh thorough-bred et cetera. There were nylon headcollars in all colours, the straps an inch wide, and nosebands – grackles, cavessons, flash, drop – and fresh-from-the-factory purple currycombs with plastic flash still on their handles. You could buy browbands wrapped with two thick velvet ribbons in contrasting colours, threaded with something sparkly and framed with stubby velour rosettes like bosses that sat at each ear, or plunge your hands into tubs of different-sized studs. I tried and failed to open a tin of hoof oil, but remembered the scent of it, part creosote and part nail varnish, then squeezed a pile of soft, thick sheepskin numnahs that were stacked high on trestles.

In a cardboard display box I found new grooming products born of the pluperfection of the American show ring: sheath cleaner for swabbing out the foreskins of male horses, colour-enhancing shampoos whose lists of ingredients put Aveda to shame; 'sparkle wax' and 'highlighter gloss'. The labelling boasted, like quality Afro-Caribbean hair products, that they contained 'no mineral oils'.

'Them rugs are well nice.'

I turned to see the object of the teenage girl's admiration: loud pink fleece horse blankets with a repeating print of cartoon ponies in paler pink capering across them. Another girl walked past swishing a pink whip against her jeans. A Parisian journalist in the 1840s had complained of lady circus riders or *écuyères* who rode with pink whips and golden stirrups, but the merchandise at Olympia seemed to go beyond dainty affectation. You could get everything here in pink, and every shade of pink too: pale-pink headcollars, bright-pink dandy brushes, bubblegum-pink jodhpurs, purple-pink riding fleeces, pink silks for crash caps, pink grooming boxes, pink hoof picks, pink cowboy hats with plastic sparkly tiaras on the front and silver sequins round the brim, pink fluorescent road-safety belts. Pink, pink, pink.

Shortly after the show, I read a piece by the journalist Peggy Orenstein in the New York Times about the 'princess mania' phenomenon gripping the world's little girls. She traced the pinkification of girls' toys to mid-1980s marketing. It's nigh on impossible to get anything for girls that isn't pink nowadays, she said, and as I recalled gazing at the saddlery shops at Olympia I realized that soon it was going to be impossible to get anything for horses that wasn't pink.

Orenstein tested out a few rationales, wondering whether 'maybe princesses are in fact a sign of progress, an indication that girls can embrace their predilection for pink without compromising strength or ambition; that at long last they can "have it all".' At Olympia, girls were certainly having it all. Girls ruled, crowned with sparkly pink cowboy hats. What would The Times correspondent of 1910 have made of it all? 'If it be true "that a good rider on a good horse is as much above himself and others as the world can make him",' he had written, 'then the ladies and the children whose progress we have been watching ... may indeed flatter themselves on holding an exalted position in the world of the sport.' But what about swallowing the sport whole in a roseate, glittery tidal wave?

In the alleys between the stalls, the girls wandered intently in groups. There were men working on some of the stalls, but none browsing them. A few little boys raced around too, looking bored, trying to make their own entertainment. The In the Saddle stall advertised riding holidays and showed a video of a grey-haired woman galloping bareheaded over savannah. They also had an enormous saddle on a stand, and people hoisted little girls up onto it, where they grasped the pommel and had that look I recognized from old photos of myself on Dusky – a look of exhilaration that tried nonetheless to maintain the gravity of the occasion.

An energetic young man handed me a flyer for a self-published series of children's books, Hairy Ponies and Friends. I admired the lively, herky-jerky illustrations. 'I did those,' he told me. 'We didn't want it to be just pink and fluffy, but for boys too.' I wished him luck for bucking the trend; there was a crowd of girls gathered round him, which I suppose proved that non-pink horses were still enough to reel them in. No boys, though.

Another stall doing brisk business was Sugar Cubes, where I picked up a catalogue and flipped through the pages of smiling girls posing in pink T-shirts with pony designs, pink scarves, hats, gloves, bags, nighties, 'snuggle sacks' and duvet covers: 'We have a new pony camouflage collection so you can stay in fashion and still have your ponies . . . We've also introduced a jacket, keeping it simple, dark and flattering with luxurious touches like the pink piping and silver satin lining . . . Putting a smile on any pony girl's face.' Little girls were concerned about wearing 'flattering' black? When they were riding their ponies?

The camouflage was made of repeated black, grey and pink elongated pony shapes. There were trinkets for bracelets too: £3.99 for the chain, pony charms £2.50, pink presentation box £3.99. I remembered looking wistfully at adverts for horsy jewellery when I was ten or so, but it was always impossibly expensive: exquisite horse-head brooches in cloudy gold, or finely braided and twisted locks of real horse tail set on a pendant. Sugar Cubes was all key rings and danglies for mobile phones and handbags. There was a pink hay net full of soft toy horses suspended from the roof.

A little girl dressed in pink had rooted herself next to the display and was trying to go into meltdown, but her Sloaney mother was having none of it. 'Yes, darling, we've got this one already. You do not need any more horses.' The girl's bottom lip quivered and I thought a tantrum was about to burst on us, but then she was distracted by another stall. As I turned to a complimentary copy of *Pony Magazine* ('New year, new you – new year's rezzies to make, not break', 'Welsh Ponies – they're the only greys in the village!') I heard her starting up again. 'I want one . . .'

A lady in her fifties, standing next to me, drank in the scene. 'You get such nice things for horses now,' she said, dreamily and to no one in particular. 'When I was little there was only one thing.'

I trailed into the last section of the fair, tired and dazzled by merchandise, with pink impacted on my retinas. A man wearing a Happy Christmas rosette sorted buckets of smaller rosettes with novelty slogans, singing 'Jingle Bells' as he did so and flanked by pre-teen girls who sifted through the barrels like bran tubs, choosing then discarding ribbons. It was a little quieter at this end of the hall and I got the sense that things were winding down in anticipation of the evening show.

I took in one last stand, Pony World, which was offering those cheap plastic model horses that are flocked in some godforsaken factory in the Far East and which I've seen on sale everywhere from the Grand Canyon to Vietnam. The doll riders had bulgy foreheads that looked familiar.

The girl next to me examined them and sniffed: 'They're Barbie.'

'No, they're not Barbies,' said the man on the stall.

'That's a Barbie,' chipped in another girl.

'No, it's not,' said the man. He sounded exasperated – it must have been a long week.

*

In 1981, Bonnie Zacherle, a designer at Hasbro who'd dreamed of owning a horse as a child, produced sketches of small-scale horse toys – realistic horses, in true colours such as piebald and Appaloosa – for children, although the vice-president of R&D said it would never do, because girls only wanted to play at housework. After another stage of development, Bonnie's little dream horses had become squeezable vinyl tchotchkes with falls of synthetic hair. Marketing suggested pink and purple coats. US patent #D269986 was granted in 1983, with Zacherle listed as co-creator, and a Stepford horse, cut to fit the market-researched desires of girls everywhere, was born: My Little Pony.

When I visited Olympia in 2006, we were three years into the toy's relaunch and Hasbro claimed 40 million of the things had hit the US marketplace. In less than two years, HarperCollins had sold 5 million copies of the tie-in books in 'an eye-popping palette of girl-friendly pinks and purples', with titles such as *Pony Popstar* and *Butterfly Hunt*. The film, *My Little Pony: A Very Minty Christmas*, went straight to the top of the US *Billboard* DVD charts in December 2005.

My Little Pony Mommies, as the girls are dubbed, can buy their ponies such treats as the Crystal Bride outfit with veil and pink bowed shoes, a lilac scooter with matching safety helmet, nappies, handbags and a Frilly Frock Boutique. Hasbro calls MLP a 'total lifestyle experience for little girls', so the Mommies can press their parents to buy them all kinds of bric-a-brac: a Cookie bake set, a Sno Cone Machine, board games, stickers, popsicle holders in the shape of ponies (which spin the lolly to make it easier to lick), a pink bike with pink streamers on the handles, nail polish sets, a seventeen-ounce 'stadium cup' for soft drinks, tableware, lip balm, jewellery boxes, charm bracelets, chequebook covers, party packs, backpacks, a 'friendship camera', music CDs, a role-playing game and the Cutie Mark Tattoo Book, sunglasses, perfumed body spray . . .

Collectors call them 'pink crack'; a friend of mine admitted to stealing them from other girls. Back in my pre-Tav days, I had my brown Sindy horses, my palomino Barbie Dallas and my beautiful, fine-sculpted Breyers, but I still wanted My Little Ponies. When my parents refused to buy them as gifts, I saved pocket money for trips to Kerrison's toy shop and brought home my vacuum-packed booty. Once it was broken out of its plastic cocoon, the complimentary comb had been waved about and the purchase ticked off, I was at a loss. I did not know how to play with my My Little Ponies. They couldn't jump, race, or whinny like wild stallions on the rocky outcrop of the mantelpiece; I had no rider dolls small enough to fit them and they barely looked like horses. Someone gave me a pomander in the shape of a My Little Pony parked on its star-dappled haunches, full of sickly-scented powder that made me itch. I kept them separately from both my Breyers and my Sindy horses, in case of contamination. It was too late, though – Barbie's Mattel and Sindy's Pedigree began producing palomino horses with pink side-saddles, bridles made out of flowers and purple heart-shaped stickers to apply to their rumps.

The slow creep of segregation between girls' and boys' toys, which Orenstein identified as beginning in the early 1980s, has accelerated in the last ten years, fed by toys like My Little Pony. Now the girls' aisles of toy stores are gulleys of lurid pink. Robots, pirates, footballs and adventure are for boys, while girls are sold dolls and kitchen sets and friendship and fairies, and they cradle MLP 'babies' (not 'foals') with retroussé snouts and kiss-curls. Horses used to be an alternative to pink and princesses and playing mother; now horses are pink princesses with Lullabye Nurseries™ and sparkly handbags.

In the same period, alarms have been raised at the sexualization of girls' toys: the high heels for toddlers, the Bratz dolls in their miniskirts. Even pony toys have been affected: in 2009, Playmates' Toys launched the willowy, sloe-eyed 'Struts', 'a collection of four fashion forward horses, all with a unique sense of style', which could be purchased with a selection of hairpieces, earrings and a mirror compact, rah-rah skirts, a catwalk set and boots sold separately – all for the little girl who had outgrown My Little Ponies. My Little Ponies themselves have morphed, becoming leggier, their rumps tit-tupped higher, causing the feminist magazine Bitch to cry, 'Just take off the pony's tail and add hands to the front legs, and what you have is a human doll that could be used in a stop-animation paedophilic porn flick.'

But what about the pink and the spangles at Olympia on the real ponies and the real little girls? The shopping village was broadcasting loud and clear: horses are now the exclusive territory of girls; girls are glorying in them and in girliness too. Were ponies being sucked into the homogenous, mass-market girl culture of Bratz and Disney princesses? Or, is the girlification counterbalanced by the fact that the girls who bought pink whips at Olympia were still riding strong, muddy ponies and risking life and limb over showjumps while harbouring the ambition to canter in the spotlight in the ring at Kensington? Was the pink wash simply a tribal assertion of a post-feminist pony culture?

Perhaps, but there is another, more worrying phenomenon at play. The rise of pinkification in the mainstream has taken place at the same time that most equestrian sports have vanished from the screen in the corner of the living room. Olympia was buzzing in 2006 because, for the first time in fifteen years, the BBC had shown the puissance in real time. The Horse of the Year Show almost didn't happen in 1997 and it was off the TV schedules by the time the twenty-first century rolled in. In 1992 the Royal International Horse Show could no longer afford the NEC and had to be moved south to Hickstead in Sussex. The BBC long ago dropped live coverage of any major showjumping event and I doubt that the average man or woman in the street could name our last Olympic medallists. It has been suggested that equestrian sports should be removed from the Olympics altogether.

In fact, the screening of the Olympia puissance marked the first time in eight years that the BBC had allowed any equestrian sport into the mainstream schedule – it would clock up about 1 million viewers – and according to an aggrieved lady I met up in the press balcony, 'It's only because Zara Phillips won the Sports Personality of the Year thing; they wouldn't be here otherwise.' Phillips won thanks to a grass-roots campaign by horsy internet message boards, much to the disgust of many other sports fans, who wanted a working-class hero. It is decades since there's been a showjumper with a public profile as high as Pat Smythe's. Real horses and real sporting idols are vanishing from the mainstream and no other sport where women compete against men on equal terms has risen up to fill that gap. Women players at Wimbledon earn less than the men; British sportswomen who win equestrian medals are all but invisible. Team GBR topped the medal table at the 2010 World Equestrian Games, but not a single British newspaper sent a sports correspondent to Kentucky.

Periodically, equestrian sports find themselves awkwardly shuffled into 'celebrity' territory, as showjumpers appear as trainers of C-listers on reality TV shows, or when a pop star turns up at a horsy event. Katie Price, already a keen horsewoman, invested in some superb dressage horses and announced her intention to train for the 2012 Olympics. Her decision was greeted with mockery and colour spreads in the press, and by quiet realpolitik in the equestrian world, whose commentators suggested that the added attention would be 'good for the sport'. She and Tony Terry, the wife of the former England football captain, rode dressage displays in jackets with sequinned lapels. The BBC did not add dressage to its schedules. Outside of the racing world, the best-known riders in the country are a princess, an actor (Martin Clunes), a WAG and a glamour girl: it is as though Cheryl Cole were our most famous footballer because she played Saturday League.

From time to time, equestrian sportswomen attempt to catapult themselves into the same celebrity-obsessed orbit, with lamentable results. In 1999 a think-tank sponsored by Sport England – the governing body responsible for divvying up lottery and Treasury funding – said that women showjumpers should sex up their image in order to give the media, and therefore the sponsors, just what they wanted. A British Olympic three-day eventer posed for a tabloid naked but for silver paint and a saddle, and it didn't appear to raise the profile of her sport one centimetre. Nine years later, two showjumpers pulled cheesecake poses in boots, fake tan and knickers before the Barclays Wealth British Masters Invitational showjumping competition, with the unfortunate consequence that Barclay's Wealth withdrew their sponsorship – giving Sport England something to chew on.

I had thought that horses gave girls a corner of the world where they were freed from the burden of being 'girls', where they could be ambitious and brave and strong, and take risks. It seemed that even if they were all those things – and all those things wrapped in pink and sparkles – the world outside was no longer interested unless the sparkles were on a bikini, the showjumps were pink and the photos appeared in Now magazine with a smiling glamour model pictured alongside. There were no more heroines like Pat Smythe, sleeping in a cattle truck and covering up her black eyes with powder.

When I pottered back out to the stands at Olympia, the arena had been crammed full of giant fences for the Links of London Grand Prix, with powdered 'snow' sprinkled round the base of the wings like icing sugar, as if to make them look innocuous. I wasn't fooled. I walked down to the seat I'd booked at the edge of the ring and tucked myself behind the sponsor's adverts to size up the jumps. I'm just under six foot, with long arms, but I reckon that if I'd stood in front of one of the parallel bars and tried to reach across to the far pole, I wouldn't have been able to touch it. They were high, broad, deep: oxers, wall, spreads, triples, combinations; the course was 410 metres of twists, turns and redoubles, a distance that had to be covered in seventy-one seconds or less to avoid time penalties. The striped poles were tree trunks fetched up as pick-up sticks.

The curtains at the far end of the ring opened and the first rider, the Austrian Julia Kayser, entered. With a note of mild exasperation in his voice, the commentator announced, 'Some of the very best showjumping you'll see this year. It always is.' The audience went on chatting as the rider – who wasn't British, after all – cantered round the ring. As she passed me, biding her time till the bell went, something clicked in my head.

In a ringside seat, tucked behind the advertising panels for H&M, you can be close enough to hear the rhythmic, fluttering snort that horses make to mark every stride. You can see the way their fine-skinned coats wrinkle for a split second on their necks or their quarters; you can hear their joints click as they land after a fence and sometimes a quiet 'oof' noise of effort that comes from their chests. I got close enough to feel the disturbance in the air as they passed, their lower lips wobbling with concentration.

I admired Eugénie Angot of France and her mare Cigale du Taillis, who had a funny, balletic canter almost like skipping. Cigale caught one pole on the fence immediately in front of me, which trembled in its cup but didn't fall, and then turned to the last, a flimsy upright of three poles suspended in space. Cigale cleared the upright and there was a wash of applause.

We all rode the course with the young rider of the moment, Ellen Whitaker, her long blonde hair flying behind her, while all the girls who'd cadged her autograph in the shopping village held their breath. As her stallion Locarno cleared each fence – and he had a beautiful jump, a real bird's soar of the kind that gives you the optical illusion that for a second he's hanging suspended over the fence – I could feel the tension behind me. We only breathed out when all four hooves were safe on the sawdust and the poles still standing.

Ellen was heading down the opposite side of the arena through a tricky combination when Locarno tossed his head and then a flash went off. Distracted, the stallion clipped the fence, the pole resounded with a deep twang that vibrated along its length and then jumped out of its cup. The crowd groaned as one and the commentator admonished them not to use flash photography.

The audience started to cheer Tim Stockdale over each fence but were shushed by the commentators. When he jumped the first British clear, they exploded. I was enjoying myself too, I didn't care who won, but I clenched my knuckles every time a horse took off and lifted slightly out of my seat along with the rider. I could hear the sawdust being kicked up and settling back down. Every time a horse jumped away from me, their aluminium shoes caught the floodlights – showing 'a clean pair of heels'.

John Whitaker got the biggest cheers; he'd never won the competition before, but he managed a faultless round. Markus Beerbaum, who had two faults and a refusal, opted to retire. He tried to jump one fence on the way out in order to get his horse's mind back on the job, but there were two officials in black tie standing in front of it, who, seeing a snorting horse bearing down on them, scooted out of the way. Beerbohm brought his horse up just in time. 'Come on, Markus, give us some sport!' shouted the showjumper Geoff Billington, who'd joined the commentator.

But this wasn't the puissance and it didn't seem fair that there were no terrestrial TV cameras there when the jump-off was so electrifying and the crowd so intoxicated by the moment. It would be shown only on specialist equestrian channels. As Stockdale turned to the last, I felt the magnitude of the audience's focus bubbling up to a squeal, then quelling itself so as not to distract him. In this final round, something shifted and I got the sense that the spectators were throwing themselves behind all the riders, not just the Brits: Beat Mändli's horse jumped so far to the right of one fence that he missed the wing by a few centimetres, and we all flinched together, picturing the horse coming crashing down, tangled in the wood.

Eugénie Angot and Cigale went round like a collie dog, skimming the fences, turning in mid-air and slicing off the corners: she whacked two fat seconds off Stockdale's time. After that it was all over

– the others went careering over the fences, trying to erode her lead, but the knife edge between speed and accuracy was too narrow. Paparazzi had had enough of the crowds and kicked down the last jump. The Italian rider Bonomelli was slower than Stockdale, and for all the cries of 'Go on, John!' Whitaker finished his circuit to a roar of disappointment: one down. Angot had it by a mile. The tension broke into a shower of applause; this was world-class showjumping and we were sitting only a few feet away from it.

A strip of red carpet was rolled out like a tongue into the centre of the ring and the winner and runners-up rode in. The Duchess of Cornwall trundled up the carpet to meet them and the heroic music faded, to be replaced by the 'Marseillaise'; Cigale looked round at everyone, then tried to rub her nose on her leg. As Camilla and two attendants approached bearing trophies, she sidled demurely. The spotlight whizzed after Eugénie and the mare as they galloped their lap of honour and chased full pelt out of the arena, through the red curtain.

All that remained was the traditional Olympia finale, with Santa Claus on a blinged-up horse-drawn sleigh followed by a troop of children waving in Victorian nighties and mob caps. We sang 'the Olympia Carol' – 'The First Noel' – drowned out by a lady on the PA who was belting it out as if it were 'The Star-Spangled Banner'. Snow fell on Santa. I stuffed the programme into my goodie bag and thought about trains. People were already leaving as the commentator went on thanking everyone for 'the best showjumping ever in London. You'll never see anything finer in the world.'

Lost Boys

'You know it's funny about those contests,' he went on seriously.
'For years I tried to win a horse that way. But it was always
women who won those contests.'

'Housewives,' Alec added, as serious as Steve. 'I don't
understand it either.'

The Black Stallion's Challenge (1964)
by Walter Farley

Professor Harald Euler teaches psychology at the University of
Kassel, favouring evolutionary theories. Eighteen years ago he
was working on various ideas about the differences between the
sexes, when a colleague who taught gymnastics to girls happened to
remark that whenever the vaulting horse was used, the girls would
begin to pretend that it was a real horse. His curiosity piqued, he
went on to complete a short study of *Pferdevernarrtheit* or 'horse
infatuation' in girls, which has proved, he told me, the most popular
work he's done. He's had three or four hundred requests for
interviews in Europe and many calls from anxious parents. He says,
'They have heard this dumb statement from Sigmund Freud where
he conjectured that women like horseback riding because it models
sexual intercourse. It's bullshit. The girls really love the horse but it's
not a sexual love, not at all, far from it.'

I telephoned Euler and we talked a little about his conclusions –
that horses boosted a girl's status, that they felt safe on them, that

they liked to care for them as mothers do babies and that they are easy to talk to.

'You could say that the horse is the last doll a girl has,' he said. 'It's the last, most grandiose acquisition to your own personal zoo – until that phase is over. The prime motivation for the little girls is to take care of the horse. Very many of them say they love to brush the horse and to take the manure out and all these kind of things. It's like caring for babies. When you ask women how do they like to change diapers, very many mothers say, "Well, it doesn't smell bad – it's kind of neutral." They don't dislike the task at all, whereas men if they care for babies say, "Oh, that stinks. I do this strictly to get it all done."'

What about horse shows, I asked, and the ambition that girls show? I had been reading internet riding forums and had come across many tales of nasty little females spiking their rivals' hopes, or beating ponies over fences.

'For girls, when they think of competition it's a beauty competition,' Euler reassured me. 'The little girls think it would be nice if they can show off their horse, make their horse really pretty and so on, but they don't think in terms of winning the showjumping. A few of them, of course, get into that and then they stay with horseback riding, otherwise we wouldn't have that many female participants in the top category.'

This seemed somewhat simple – after all, there were plenty of us girls who had dreamed of red rosettes and yet not made it to a professional horse-riding career, just as many boys dreamed of playing in the Premiership but as grown-ups were reduced to playing five-a-side before the pub on a Sunday. Surely this didn't mean that we girls had had no desire to win?

He sidestepped sceptically around my tentative, social anthropologist's proposition that girls had adopted horses with such enthusiasm, not just because they were like great, pettable dolls, but also because they offered a channel for all those princely virtues otherwise forbidden to them: physical bravery, risk taking, courage.

Role models such as Pat Smythe must have galvanized those post-war girls as a heroine, not as the person with the shiniest horses with the neatest manes. When one of the girls at Frossarbo drove a horse alone round the racetrack for the first time, she cried out, in Sven Forsling's hearing, 'Yes! I am divine!'

'What we observe with sport in general but with other things too is that very often a new activity is first taken over by men, and after a while women emulate it,' Euler went on. 'For example, soccer, or parachuting, or even drinking coffee. I think that even if the feminist movement had not been there, women would have gotten into these activities all by themselves.'

The Pazyryk grave's priestess and the Sarmatian girl-warrior came to mind with their amulets and riding boots, and the Mongolian girls of today who race against their brothers in twenty-kilometre races, and the Ancient British women like the lady in the Yorkshire grave, and Boadicea and Cartimandua driving chariots into battle. Who could definitively say that the first human to ride a horse was not female?

'Horses worked for boys up until the end of the nineteenth century,' explained Professor Euler, and on that I could agree – it seemed that everything I'd discovered about the emergence of the pony-mad girl confirmed this – but then he went on, 'getting into the world for boys means hunting, patrolling and roaming around – that's what our male ancestors did. They are better at spatial cognition and maps.' He gave some more examples of recent evolutionary psychology experiments to show the difference between the sexes, adding: 'This all shows that men always have been individuals that tended to go out farther away to see what is out there, to check this out, to bridge distances. That's why men always have had an inclination for mobility appliances.'

I thought about Ethel Tweedie riding her pony across volcanic rock in Iceland, and Isabella Bird, and all the huntresses, Mary Breese, 'Old Sarum', Nannie Power O'Donoghue and Mrs Hayes, and I bit my tongue. Meanwhile, as the horse was no longer the optimum mobility appliance, Professor Euler stated, men and boys had moved on to machines powered by the internal combustion engine. 'If you look at old paintings where men get depicted with or on their horse, they show the same pride about the horse as they do these times with their cars. Women don't. There were some exceptions, but for women the horse and carriage was never something that they identified with, took the same pride in, paid lots of money for and used as a means of intra-sexual competition, like men.'

Farewell the nineteenth-century horse-breakers of Hyde Park, like Skittles in her modish pork-pie hat and paletot, who, The Times commented in 1862, inspired well-bred ladies to spend 600 guineas on a matched pair of ponies 'on the condition they should step as high' as beautiful, chic Skittles' horses. Farewell the courtesan Cora Pearl, who managed to spend more than 90,000 francs in three years on thoroughbred English horses on which to be seen in the Bois de Boulogne. Farewell, too, to those fine gentlewomen who made their grooms crank up their horses' heads with bearing reins so that they would draw all eyes as they pranced. I wasn't convinced.

It wasn't that twenty-first-century boys didn't start out liking horses, Professor Euler explained, backtracking. Afterall, 'At the very young age – the four-, five-, six-year-olds – there wasn't much of a difference in interest in horses between boys and girls, although boys have different kinds of interest in horses than girls do. They think in terms of knights and cowboys, but then a gap opens up.' In that gap he saw biological pressures, and I saw social ones; if the boys had few male role models in the horse world, and were told that riding was a girl's sport, surely they would be put off as they grew older and more self-conscious. An Italian friend had told me that riding schools and pony clubs in Italy were, unlike British ones, pretty much split fifty-fifty between boys and girls. If boys' lack of interest in horses was merely a matter of biology and technology, why wasn't Italy like Germany and the UK?

I was finding it hard to follow the switchbacks – men had once liked horses, but circumstances had changed and they no longer did, except when they were young. Were those changes cultural and historical? Yes, said Professor Euler, but underneath them chugged the pure old hunter-gatherer instinct, a theory that I was beginning to find elastic to the point of bagginess and infinitely accommodating of anything you wanted to weave into its framework. I thanked him for his time and we rang off, leaving me to think.

Everything that girls love in horses – their beauty, their power, their speed, their company – might also appeal to any boy. An unpublished British study by Professor Daniel Mills of the University of Lincoln suggested that 'the emotional involvement of male riders in the relationship can be just as great as that of females.' An American study from 1983 indicated that while both men and women saw their horses as family members, men were more likely to see them as 'adults' and not children. Many of the pioneers of the new empathetic 'natural horsemanship' treatment are men, like the horse whisperer Monty Roberts. Long before him, there was Gervase Markham, writing in 1607 that a rider 'shall never approach [the Horse], but the Horse shall with a kind of chearfull or inward neying, show the joy he takes to behold him, and where this mutual love is knit and combined, there the beast must needes prosper, and the man reap reputation and profit'.

Young Lucian Freud used to sneak down to the stables at his boarding school to sleep in the straw with his favourite horses for comfort, and the Labour MP Keir Hardie, working in a coal mine as a boy, raced to the side of his beloved pit pony Donald when there was an accident. I'd read interviews with teenage boys at the Hollesley Bay Colony young offenders' institute who used to work the magnificent Suffolk Punch horses bred on the farm there, grooming and primping them for shows, plaiting their tails and threading wool into their manes with great pride. Sven Forsling told me that after he gave one talk on Frossarbo, he was approached by an old farmer who told him he knew exactly how the girls felt – he had had the same bond with his plough horse.

When Sir Robert Carey rose in the House of Commons to make the case for the Pony Act of 1969, which would endeavour to protect British ponies from continental meat markets, he recalled without inhibition that 'In boyhood, and later, during the First World War and for some years afterwards as a Regular soldier, my life was dominated by horses and ponies. Among all those who shared my life, those upon which, I think, my greatest affection was centred were four blue roan ponies and four strawberry roan ponies in my care.' Carey told his listeners that after an earlier debate on the export of horses to the continent, Winston Churchill, then prime minister, had cornered him to express his concern, saying, 'I understand that the poor darlings are tied up for hours on end, without even a drink.'

One of the oral historian George Ewart Evans's interviewees in *Horse Power and Magic* recalled his father playing with carthorse colts every Sunday on the farm where he worked: 'He handled them and they pushed him about, and they'd play with him. I've seen one or two of them nearly knock him down – swing their neck up against him as if they were playing with another colt. He'd throw his cap and his jacket down and he'd play with them for about half an hour, the sweat streaming off him. He'd play with his horses just like a big kid.'

To these men, horses were not mere flashy modes of transport – a thoroughbred Bentley, say, or an Appaloosa Ferrari; they loved them as much as Euler said his girls adored their riding-school favourites.

I did not, however, remember there being a single boy in any one of the hundreds of riding lessons I took at different riding schools between the ages of five and fifteen, although there were boys in some of my dancing classes. My own brother, I realized guiltily, had withered in the onslaught of my *Pferdevernarrheit*. Boys can be made to feel that a stableyard is no place for a man. George Ewart Evans quotes John Cossey, a Norfolk blacksmith, who told him about an Arab horse stud where all the grooms were girls. The horses had grown so suspicious of men that the smith had tried to dust himself with his wife's talcum powder so that they'd let him close. There are racehorse trainers, often male themselves, who say they prefer stable lasses to lads as 'it's better for the horses'. You hear the equal and opposite prejudice too – women will talk about how a certain horse doesn't like a man near him, or how they wouldn't want a horse after it had been ridden by a man. 'A lady's ride' has come to mean a sensitive, nervous horse, not a reliable one, as it did to Mrs Hayes's contemporaries.

Think of those poor boys running loose at Olympia, stranded in a pink girls' horse world, where nearly every image they were offered was that of girls and women on horseback. Of 33,065 Pony Clubbers in 2009, only 5,409 were male. The last strongholds of male equestrian dominance are falling one by one: the British field all-female polo teams against men, while there are women who have driven teams of eight draught horses, become farriers, charged gun horses in military displays and ridden out the bucks of a bronco. What is left for the boys?

The Thirty-Mile-
an-Hour Pony

The stallion's strides became even greater as he swept
gloriously down the backstretch. His hoofs pounded with a
thunderous rhythm that silenced the voices in the stands.
He was black flame. He was not a horse but a phantom, a flying
black shadow in the eyes of the spectators. And they watched
him finish the race in quiet homage.

The Black Stallion Revolts (1953) by Walter Farley

The front of the giant, cream-coloured lorry read: Julie Magnus
Racehorse Transport HORSES; on the radiator were two unicorns
rampant and the legend 'Kalasadi' in looping script. It was an icy
Easter Monday morning and the car park round the back of the livery
stable wasn't sheltered from the scouring Cambridgeshire wind.
When we took the horses from their shared loose box there was a
delicious, embracing, stable scent of chewed hay, warm horseflesh
under blankets, woodchip, fresh dung and malty grain, but the wind
had blown it to molecules and made short shrift of my nice black
thermal underwear, which might as well have been made of cheese-
cloth for all the heat it retained. My socks were cotton when they
should have been wool, and my wellies as chilly and clammy as if I
were standing in a stream. I reflected that the bacon butty and sweet
tea I had had for breakfast at seven would probably have long since
exited my metabolism in a puff of nugatory body heat.

I hauled myself up into the centrally heated cabin and dropped into the passenger seat onto two raw-hide chew balls and started looking for the seat belt that wasn't there. Julie was in the driver's seat, adjusting the SatNav and getting comfortable amid a nest of old shortbread wrappers, liquorice packets, grey sheepskins, dog hair, horsehair and folders of paperwork – the debris of long-distance driving. Two stuffed-toy dogs were wedged, tails north, down the front of the dashboard, the hard drive was winking away and the monitor that showed Julie what was happening in the back of the vehicle had a grey image on the screen. A mug of newly brewed herbal tea was stowed by her knee – all she needed to take the edge off the weather.

Julie had a round, reddened face and a dark-blonde ponytail crammed under a battered, broad-brimmed leather hat that she only removed to put on a crash cap. She walked with the toes-out, feet-planted stride of a long-time rider and bossed us with patience born of a dependable, unshakeable confidence. She used to be a primary-school headmistress, and you sensed that children and horses would know exactly where they stood with Julie and what they couldn't get away with, too. Despite that, her voice could rise to a girlish peak when she was excited and I couldn't guess her age. She was ticking over like a child on her way to her first gymkhana, impatient to be off; I thought she might be a worse daydreamer than me, though one who gets things done, at least. She handed me a printout for navigation: 'M11 down towards the Colchester road, then we can't miss the turn and the course is off the A12.'

Behind us was a little sitting room where Julie's Doberman, Thor, wrapped in a miniature horse rug, lay in state on a cushioned bench by the window. He climbed over the gearbox, placed one long, elegant black paw with muscular toes squarely onto my lap and leaned into me, poking me with his nose. I abandoned my notebook and wrapped my arms round him. In no time, I too was covered in short black dog hairs.

The jockey was also in the little sitting room, taking up

considerably less space than Thor and wrestling with a back protector whose zips had become jammed. His small, freckled face was gathered and solemn under his sandy hair. Tom was twelve and weighed all of five stone; it was his first race and even though you might have had a job getting him to talk about it, he had been dreaming of it for years.

Julie ran through the list. 'You've got your medical band? Your silks? Your hat? I've got the horses' passports and the entry form. Your boots?'

'Yes,' said Tom, very quietly. 'I can't get this back protector done up.'

I reached round Thor to try to disengage the two halves of the zip, and together Tom and I managed to sort it out. Correctly zipped in, he looked like a particularly worried turtle.

Behind the sitting room was a narrow compartment piled with saddles, bridles, spare rugs and a dampened hay net, and behind that was our cargo: in a rubber-floored pod stood Kalasadi, son of Shahrastani (Derby '86), grandson of Nijinsky (Derby '70), nephew of Kahyasi (Derby '88), winner Noel Murless Champion Hurdle at Cheltenham 1990, rated 114 over fences, a bay with a crooked stripe down his nose like his great-grand-daddy, the legendary Northern Dancer. His breeder, his Highness the Aga Khan, named him for a fifteenth-century Muslim mathematician and thought he'd win the Derby. His bearing was noble, his eyes intelligent – though Julie said he was as camp as Christmas and quite the show-off. But Kalasadi, or Kali, was not running.

Tom's mount shared the pod with Kali. Days of Thunder was forty-three inches high at the withers, had no known pedigree, a hay-rick of a mane and legs that were shorter than my arms. His race name came from the Tom Cruise film, 'because he's little but he's great'. He was going to show the world, or at least the Marks Tey point-to-point in Essex, just how fast a small black pony can go, up against the big boys – the 13.2hh and under ponies, that was.

Julie had paid a work rider at the livery yard to breeze him and keep him on his toes because Tom had school and couldn't ride him, so the little pony was primed to run. Under his mint-green rug his coat had been half clipped out in a kind of all-body crewcut; his legs and top half had an inch or two of soft black fur while his sides were shorn, bristly and sooty grey. Most small native ponies expand behind the girth like a fuzz-covered Barbapapa but Thunder was sleek and streamlined with his go-faster stripes, his muscles hard and his legs clean-chiselled on hooves the size of coffee cups. He just about fitted under Kali's belly.

The engine started with a crunch and a hum that vibrated every fibre. Julie skilfully steered the juggernaut through a gate that we might have crushed like matchsticks, down the muddy drive and swung it out onto the road. We needed to be at Marks Tey in an hour and a half so that Tom could declare and walk the course. The pony races were happening before the main point-to-point card, and the course had been covered in snow the day before, so we'd been delayed till we found out whether the going was safe. If the ground were still frozen, the whole race card would have been scratched, which would've been a bit of a disaster.

'All we want to do is let Thunder run his heart out in a straight line. That's all that's in his head, being a racing pony. If he doesn't like it, then fine,' said Julie as we hit the motorway. 'Last year I wasn't even thinking of pony racing. When I rode out on Kali with Thunder on the lead rein, I told everyone we went at Thunder speed, not Kali speed. Then one day I was out with a friend on her ex-racehorse and we were galloping along in a pack. I checked the speedo and we were going at 30 mph! Thunder had changed his gait; he was keeping up with the thoroughbreds.'

The British Horse Racing Board introduced what's now 'the fastest-growing equine sport' to the UK in 2004, so that children aged between eleven and fifteen could compete on real racecourses with all the paraphernalia of the grown-up sport of kings: silks, weight cloths, TV coverage, bookies, dope tests and an uneven playing field. They hoped to produce a new generation of jump jockeys – the Irish have been running pony races for ever and plenty of champions paid their dues on this amateur circuit before moving on to formal apprenticeships – and also to prevent the great drop-off of boys' interest in horses. Even though there are men at the top of many equestrian sports – dressage, eventing, polo and showjumping – they tend to compete against women. However, women have made limited headway in horse racing proper, where they are in a distinct minority. Perhaps it's for that reason that it remains the last great bastion of interest for boys who like horses. The tough, wiry champion jockey punching home the Derby winner is male.

Professor Euler had told me he'd completed a small study for one of the German national horse authorities about boys and horses. He'd concluded that, in order for boys to stay interested, they had to have lessons apart from girls. He'd gone on, 'The second thing is, don't do this dressage for the boys. How do you call this? On the leash, you go round and make *bella figura*' – I think he meant vaulting – 'That is something you can't get boys interested in. You have to do things that boys want to do. Rrrrracing. Competition.'

At an earlier pony-racing meet, I'd endeavoured to interview two young jockeys who had clearly modelled themselves on that old mumbler Lester Piggott. They faced me as though I were a faux-jovial TV presenter with just the slightest grasp of the real grit of racing. Later I found a video one of them had loaded onto YouTube, of photos of himself aged six, perched, tiny and solemn-faced, on a weighing-in scale at Huntingdon races, or thoughtful under his crash cap as the rising sun silhouetted him on the gallops. In the action shots he rode his ponies like a champion jockey, as soft rock pumped out background inspiration: 'Take your passion, make it happen!' The only smile was caught as he leaned against champion jockey A. P. McCoy's BMW with its personalized number plate. Boys dream of winning the Grand National too.

Julie spoke for Tom, as pugnacious as any jockey's agent: 'Thomas is the youngest in a big family and he wants to be a jockey. Tom's dead serious. He will win the Derby. End of. He'll be riding out for Michael Bell next year, won't you?'

A murmur from the jockey himself, who was putting on his silks: scarlet sleeves and bottle-green-and-white chevrons – the colours Kali bore to victory at Cheltenham, scaled down to Tom size. The motorway spooled by the cab, the lorry negotiating the Bank Holiday traffic in a stately fashion. I asked Julie where she'd found Thunder and Kali.

'Kali did his tendon so he hasn't raced since he was seven. His owners worshipped the ground he walked on and were really careful how they rehomed him. He just turned up in the lorry 'cause I'd said I'd take him on faith. I trusted the owners. And the lorry opened and there he was and the presence was just there. Oh my God, he's amazing.' If Thunder adored Kali, he couldn't love him as much as Julie did.

'And Thunder?'

She frowned. 'Well, Kali was just so institutionalized from being a racehorse. When you turned him out in the field he'd just have a buck and gallop around a bit, then he'd want to come in. So I thought I'd get him a Shetland to keep him company, but then of course as soon as I started looking there wasn't a Shetland to be found. ILPH, Redwings, nothing. Nobody had one.'

Thor looked at me – I'd stopped stroking him – and poked me in the arm with his nose.

Julie went on, warming to her story, 'I was out in the lorry one day and I saw this thing being tortured by some kids by the roadside. I thought it was a dog at first, because it was so tiny. So I jumped out and walked over to tell them off. Then I saw the caravans in the background and I thought, uh-oh, I'm in trouble now – travellers – but all the grown-ups were away nicking things so I was in luck. And when I got closer I realized it wasn't a dog but a pony. He was only about 8hh then. I asked the kids what the hell they were doing and one of them said, "Do you want the effing thing?" It turns out he was causing arguments among the kids and they wanted to get rid of him. They'd stolen him from the meat man in a thunderstorm, hence the name. So I said, right, and I put him in the box, drove him home, chucked him in the stable with Kali and said, "There you are, he's all yours." I thought he might have lice but he didn't – he just hadn't been cleaned properly, but he was really skinny under the mud. And then he grew and grew and grew. There's the course.'

A field and a hedge away, I could see a set of railings, some lorries, tents and caravans, like a circus or a gypsy camp. We turned off the main road and rolled ponderously down a narrow lane, occasionally pulling over onto the chewed tarmac edges to let some minuscule car pass. Then we took a left into the field, flagged on by an official, who tried to direct us into the designated pony-racing parking area.

'We are not going there and getting stuck,' declared Julie, reversing the lorry into a slot on higher ground. We sat there for a minute and watched another horsebox lumber into the pony-racers' enclosure, sink into the mud and spin its wheels. Over in the centre of the course, a tractor could be seen pulling an ice-cream van out of the mire and it was only 11 a.m. It was a good job the pony racing was on first, at one. No one was getting out of the place before midnight without caterpillar tracks.

The car park was by the finish at the narrow end of a course shaped like a porterhouse steak. It sat on the bare crown of a low, flat hill, while the T-bone end lay down the slope out of sight, the course passing in and out of a few small copses. Its only permanent structures were a grey, pebble-dashed ladies' loo and the fence that marked out the circuit, with its green-plastic-coated chicken wire that sagged where years of spectators had leaned on it.

We climbed out into the teeth of the wind and walked our green-faced jockey across the course towards the marquees in search of the stewards. The strip of grass looked too narrow for the forty horses entered in the first point-to-point race proper, and the turf was to Epsom what a Hebridean golf course is to Pebble Beach – chewed and coarse. We picked our way around puddles with a skin of ice still on them, mindful of Tom's thin riding boots and the patches of snow lingering here and there.

In the centre of the course a little Easter fairground was setting up shop for the business of Bank Holiday entertainment. We passed swing boats and a merry-go-round with fire engines and dolphins, and a test-your-strength game with a four-feet-high cut-out of Noddy on top. There was a lucky dip ('Prize every time') with separate sides for boys and girls, and a few stall holders struggling to hang up rows of stuffed-toy horses in plastic bags in the gale, or wheel out racks of puffa jackets and fleeces. Behind them the bookies set up their black boards and counted their floats.

The wind made my eyes and my mouth water, carrying a whiff of the golden chunks of pig rotating on the Hog Roast van's grills, and espresso from a chic little Lavazza coffee tent with a pagoda roof. Clustered around it were customers clutching dinky paper cups.

Following Julie and Tom, who were deep in a discussion of race tactics, I ducked into a grubby white marquee furnished with the rackety contents of some horsy attic. The Essex Farmers and Union Hunt had only been in existence since 1984 but it was an amalgamation of two outfits that were first formalized in 1822. Everything in the tent must have seen decades of service: there were hand-painted, chipped signs reading DOCTOR or LADIES CHANGING; a pile of wooden-handled flags for signalling, rolled up on a trestle table – red for an objection, white for an ambulance, orange for a vet; more trestles with mouldering canvas trunks filled with white-cotton number cloths like a long-forgotten trousseau, the numbers on each one printed in a different script; a stack of grey Tannoy horns like old-fashioned ear trumpets.

A muddy blue carpet had been rolled out underfoot and mud-smeared white tarps screened off the changing areas. On a pristine tablecloth sat the treasure: silver horses on ebony stands, generous chalices with copperplate engravings, trophies beaded with silver grapes and lilies with old polish in the veins – each with a champagne bottle, decanter and punch cups standing beside them.

A few girls and boys were hovering with their parents, clutching paperwork. Despite having only been to a handful of meets over the last six months, I recognized a couple of them as old hands on the circuit. In the car park I'd spotted the customized horsebox of Alex, one of the boys I'd interviewed at another meet, with his white-and-black racing colours painted on the back. At Cottenham a few weeks earlier, his dad had confided good-naturedly in me, 'Well, he'd better win today, it's cost us a fortune to get this far. Better win it all back today.' Alex had gone on to finish fourth on Crosswell Robbie, a fizzy little pony who was blind in one eye and refused to be clipped out, but had been racketing around the pony-racing circuit under different jockeys for years now – in fact, he won the first 13.2hh final in 2004. Alex would be in the same race as Thunder and Tom.

Julie briefed her jockey: 'Keep to the right rail and check the ground there when you're walking the course because you know how he veers off to one side. And you know how to get him to go – just talk to him and tell him to go WHIZZY.'

Just at that point, the organizer, Paula Twinn, burst in out of the wind with her red-blonde curls blown loose around her face, her eyes bright and blue, lugging a box of more paperwork.

'Sorry I'm late; the lorry wouldn't start and I had two point-to-pointers in there as well as the ponies' – Paula's son Edward was riding Cracker in Tom's race. She sat down and began to work her way through the queue. The children must declare for the race and surrender their medical band, which would be chucked in a basket in the stewards' tent for the duration of the race.

As we waited, Julie told me she'd ridden out on racehorses as a teenager and wanted to be a jockey, but her parents thought she was too academic for racing school so that was that. That made two of us, although I had well and truly scuppered my racing career by beanpoling to five feet eleven inches before I even set foot in the British Bloodstock Association for work experience, while Julie had peaked at a little over five feet. I tried to imagine Tav in the field at Marks Tey, bright chestnut in the sleet, leaning hard on his bit and scuffling along in pursuit of the others, with me on board in gold silks with my legs jacked up in short stirrups. Tom, who was saying less and less as post time drew nearer, would just have to ride for Julie and me.

Someone co-opted a passing dad into driving the children down to the start so they could walk the course. Julie and I relinquished Tom and turned back to the food vans, thus missing the droll sight of thirteen muddy children being compacted into a nice clean four-wheel drive.

As we waited for burgers at one of the vans, Julie explained the new intelligence she'd picked up from Paula: 'So it turns out that there's a 12.2hh and under class, and it's combined with the 13.2hh and under race, so even if Thunder doesn't get whizzy and beat the bigger ponies, he's still in with a chance of qualifying for the 12.2hh final.'

She bought a bacon butty for Thor and we retreated back to the lorry to get out of the wind. Thor swallowed the bread roll whole. I asked Julie whether she had had her own pony as a child.

'Well, I used to ride horses for this local dealer, Mr Shelley. Every week I would ride one of them home and call my mum out and ask her if we could buy it and she'd say no. I started with the old racehorses; I wanted a racehorse' – this said with a sudden passion that was different to Julie's usual amiable bluster – 'but she said ex-racehorses were nutty, so I worked all the way down through the horses to the ponies until Princess Di's wedding day. Mum had everyone over because it was a big house in the country and we had a big colour TV. I turned up on the drive with a little 10hh grubby pony. "Mum, he's five hundred quid with the tack." And then she cracked. She knew if she didn't say yes, I'd be off round the village on my bike and any other village to find horses to bring back, so she said, "If I say you can have a horse, will you leave us alone to watch the wedding?" And that's how I got Glimmer. We saw her the next week. I'd been riding her dam for Mr Shelley and she was by a champion palomino. She was wonderful.'

'But you had always wanted a racehorse?' And now Tom did, too.

'Oh yes.'

We sat quietly for a moment, lost in thought. I remembered all those hours I had spent watching Channel 4 Racing as a teenager, or hanging over the paddock rails at Newmarket, Epsom, Longchamp, or Hoppegarten, playing 'take my pick' and wanting that tall steel-grey who didn't stand a chance in the first but was beautiful, or the compact, conker-coloured mare with an Arabian face that was a throwback to some desert stallion of 300 years ago, or the liver chestnut with an old-fashioned Roman nose whose father won the Derby. The idea of having one of those in the field behind your house, to ride down the familiar local roads and have them transfigured by the sauntering, elastic snap of its gait; the knowledge that this was your own personal keepsake of the sport of kings . . .

Tom hove into view through the windscreen, looking even paler and now accompanied by his mother, father and little sister. Julie and I climbed out to greet them.

I'd met Tom's dad earlier at the stables, where we'd chatted about the recently imposed hunting ban and a chestnut mare called Whoopsy that someone wanted to board with the family. He and Tom's mum were sensibly dressed in countryside mufti and were considerably more laid-back about the whole thing than Julie. I think they had been to many gymkhanas and race meets with a lot of nervous children, and were unperturbed by the rangy point-to-pointers that were now swirling in circles between the horseboxes, led by their grooms, or by the requirement that everyone should wade in and adjust a browband or a surcingle if necessary.

The lorry ramp was lowered to reveal Kali, nostrils wide and eyes shining. Did he recognize the scene as a racecourse, or did this just look like any old horsy event to him? What was he remembering, if anything? Julie led him out onto the grass and Tom walked Thunder, who was looking inscrutable, after them. Julie was going to remain with Kali in the car park during the race, joking that if he took off after his friend she'd be as good as waterskiing on the mud. As Thunder was tacked up by Tom and his dad, Kali paced restlessly, alternating between snatching at grass and staring at the big point-to-pointers as they were led in by in their mustard-coloured wool rugs.

A few of the other racing ponies were being prepped too and Paula Twinn appeared, once more leading Cracker, a nice little bay. Julie had picked up enough from the bush telegraph to know that we needed to walk our race pony over to the other side of the car park where the runners were gathering before a tack inspection. Kali and Thunder joined the merry-go-round of fellow competitors, circling to keep the chill off and their muscles busy. The thoroughbred dwarfed them all, mooching around like the old pro he was, Julie stepping out with pride.

Tom's dad played stable lad, walking Thunder behind Kali and Julie, while Alex's dad, in his official safety-inspector capacity, had a brief Q&A with Tom: 'You've got your back protector? It's done up right? And your goggles? Now don't take off too fast, we're here to have fun. And mind the jumps. Keep over on the left.'

Tom answered in monosyllables that were threatening to turn into demi-syllables, and then, prompted by his dad, tried to wipe the worst of the mud off his boots on the long grass. His mum confided in me that he'd been in a state of high excitement and apprehension for weeks. Marks Tey on a freezing Easter Monday could be the first rung of a ladder that led all the way to Epsom Downs on the first Saturday in June.

Tom didn't chat with the other riders who were also standing watching their parents and siblings walk their ponies, but I overheard one girl, whose 'silks' were made of knitted wool and who stood with her back curled like an old jock of thirty years' standing, discussing Thunder with her friends. 'Isn't he cute? Imagine if he passed everything!' Paula called us over to the paddock proper.

The centre of the course had filled up with the weekend point-to-point crowd: county girls in buff-coloured furry hats that blended with their blonde hair; young fathers hanging on to a dog lead and a buggy; stalwarts of the scene with greying hair and weather-beaten cheeks; and dogs, dogs everywhere, including one fat bulldog that had pooled itself on the ground like a jellyfish in an effort to sniff a Labrador's behind. The fairground was starting to see some custom. You could see the point-to-point jockeys striding around in every direction with coats over their riding clothes, swapping gossip and sucking nervily on cigarettes.

The bookies were taking bets on the 13.2hh and under race, with Pat Cash offering 2-1 on Thunder – rating him over Cracker – although the favourite was Jack Andrews on Clonross Jesse, followed by Alex on Crosswell Robbie. Either Pat had some information on our dark horse and the secret of the speedo, or else he had a lively eye for a potential housewives' favourite: Thunder was a good eight inches shorter than anything else in the field, but already there was a buzz as people pointed out 'the little one'.

After Tom's dad legged him up, he handed me the reins and we walked on round the paddock, feeling self-conscious as everyone leaning on the rails cooed, 'Awwww! Look at him!' Tom pulled up his yellow-plastic goggles and retreated into some private, nerve-rattled space. I felt somewhat lost without Julie's patter.

'Are you OK?' I asked Tom, who replied, 'I just need to do something with my goggles.'

He dropped his reins and started fiddling with the strap. Thunder trundled along like a miniature bullock, his hooves pegging into the soft turf, his tufty ears pricked and his nose poking out. The sense of occasion and the racehorse mix that Julie had primed him with started to kick in. He made little rushes into a trot, or leaned into me impatiently, wanting to be out on the turf and running.

The bell rang and the other runners started to file out onto the course where the hunt staff would accompany them down to the start. When Tom had sorted his eyewear and picked up the reins, I relinquished him into their care. I paused for a second to watch Thunder on the course, ears front and his walk springy, with Tom crouched over his neck, then got out of the way of the last ponies to go through and joined Tom's mum on the other side of the paddock rail to walk over to the finish.

We tried to kill time while the runners were out of sight down the hill by wondering what would happen if Thunder was first past the post. 'If he gets through to the next stage, Tom'll have to carry three stone of lead to make up the minimum pony racing weight,' she pointed out. 'I don't think he can lift three stone to get it on the weighing scale.'

'They might have changed the rules by next year,' I offered, 'or Tom might have grown, although then he'd be too big for Thunder. And you'll have to find him a new racing pony—'

We were interrupted by the nasal tones of the Tannoy: 'AND THEY'RE OFF!'

There was a flicker of attention through the crowd, who could only see the ponies at this stage if they had binoculars. We strained to hear the commentary: 'Annnumanumanumanauma ... Crosswell Robbie ... annummunnuannanna ... Days of Thunder dropping back.'

The field came into view in the distance, then vanished into a dip and behind a copse.

'Annnnnumanuma ... Clonross Jesse and Cwrt-Bettys Vocalist, Clonross Jesse and Cwrt-Bettys Vocalist, then Crosswell Robbie, Crosswell Robbie's making a move, back to Cracker, the Dykebeck Wild Bramble coming up on the outside ...'

They were coming up the hill on the inside of the jumps, and the crowd began to shout 'Go arrrrrrrrrrrn!' and 'Come on, Daisy!' In a burst of thudding hooves, two ponies rocketed past, locked neck and neck, with their riders shouting and hustling at them, legs thrashing against their sides, hands scrubbing up and down their necks. They swept by the finish in a splatter of mud and hurled turf. Jack Andrews and Jesse had it by a head from Daisy Taylor on Vocalist, then there was a pause of six lengths and Alex and Crosswell Robbie hurtled by to claim third, Alex hissing at Robbie through his teeth. Then another pause and Wild Bramble scooted by, heading a small knot of runners who were slackening their pace yards before the post, napping towards the car park and their hay nets. This was followed by another pause that stretched for ten or twenty seconds.

'Where's the little 'un?' asked someone near us.

Ten more seconds passed. Suddenly there was a ringing whinny from the car park – Kali.

And here came Thunder and Tom, the black pony bowling along in a leisurely canter, unhurried. Tom's face was frozen and he looked stiff perched up on his stirrups.

'Well, thank goodness for that,' said his mother, who was never the least bit ruffled. We watched as Thunder took a sharp right into the horsebox park, making a beeline for Julie and Kali.

When we reached them, Julie was exclaiming over the pony. 'He hasn't even broken a sweat! He's not puffing either. Why didn't you run, Thunder?'

'We overtook two at the beginning,' piped Tom, 'but after that he lost interest.' Thunder thrust his head into the turf and began to graze, watched by a relieved Kali.

As Tom's little sister walked Thunder to cool off the sweat he'd failed to raise, Julie puzzled over the mind of her racing pony. 'Last weekend when we were galloping together at Thetford, Tom said he'd never been so fast – his eyes were streaming, weren't they, Tom?'

Thunder dragged his handler off around the back of a horsebox. I wondered whether he preferred to race only with his friend the thoroughbred. Or whether he was just, well, a pony. Kali spotted that Thunder was missing and whinnied urgently, and Thunder appeared round the other end of the horsebox as if he'd been playing hide-and-seek. Once Kali and Thunder were loaded back into the lorry, I climbed into the cabin to sit with Thor and defrost while the others headed off to the marquees. Thor wuffed gently, watching his mistress disappear.

A sudden wild flurry of snowflakes blew past horizontally and the clouds parted to let the sun through for a second. I watched children walking back from the winner's enclosure with armfuls of Easter eggs, trophies and fluttering ribbons.

Julie cracked open the door and thrust a royal-blue-and-white rosette and a keyring with a stirrup on it into my hand. 'He came second of the 12.2hh ponies! He's qualified for the final, wherever that is. We're going to the racing school at Newmarket for a course next week so we'll have to ask them what we can do to persuade him to gallop more. Here's the photos.'

She handed me the cardboard frame in cellophane. The course photographers had captured Thunder and Tom mid-gallop, the Shetland's fuzzy forelock blown back, the perfect little racehorse, one fore hoof extended, and Tom relaxed and almost smiling, as if he were going down to the start for the hundredth race of his career.

'You know,' said Julie, 'Thunder's a sensitive soul. If you don't see the point, neither does he. We'll ask them at Newmarket. I'm sure they'll know what to do. Maybe we could put him in the Shetland Grand National instead?'

Eponalia

These thoughts were interrupted by my catching sight of a
statue of the goddess Epona seated in a small shrine centrally
placed, where a pillar supported the roof-beams in the middle of
a stable. The statue had been devotedly garlanded with freshly
picked roses. So in an ecstasy of hope on identifying this
assurance of salvation, I stretched out my forelegs and with all
the strength I could muster, I rose energetically on my hind legs.

The Golden Ass, c.AD 170, by Apuleius, translated by P. G. Walsh

The winter after I left the riding club in Berlin, I became ill, in a
debilitating, long-lasting fashion that ruled out riding, or even
walking very far, so I took to circular rambles around Prenzlauer
Berg, to see whether the hoof prints were still manifesting themselves on the pavements. For a while I found no fresh trails, but I did
find that the street-pony population was more varied than I had
guessed. Painted on a yellow postbox was a stencil of a horse's head,
tendrils of blue mane lying on its neck, while a tiny pink horse no
bigger than a horse-chestnut leaf, with its tail flying behind it,
galloped across a flagstone. Another horse head that had appeared
here and there had a star on its forehead and a fanciful sweep of
forelock like a wizard's horse on a fantasy-novel cover. Then there
were the My Little Ponies, paper cut-outs in lurid colours, pink, sea-
green, purple, holding their nubby fore hooves rampant like the lion
and the unicorn about to box. On the back of a street sign, I spotted

a badly sketched rearing horse whose neck and head had been replaced by a penis, like a herm centaur.

Someone had spray-painted 'Pony*' in purple on the peach-coloured building round the corner from mine. It was soon rollered over by the housekeeper, only to reappear further down the street, crammed into a doorway, minus the asterisk:

Pon

Y

One day I even woke to find the pavements were stamped with the demand, 'PONYS FÜR ALLE!', which turned out to be the slogan of a student disco.

I found the ghosts of real horses too, from the times when Berlin ran on horsepower. A house near the old Jewish orphanage on Teutobergerplatz had a faded sign in neat black serif, reading 'Sattlerei', or saddlery, around which the developers, at pains to maintain authenticity, had carefully painted. In a street preserved by the former East German leader Erich Honecker for his own peculiar and rather un-socialist nostalgia, there was still a sign advertising Nante's hired droschken or hackney cabs, and carriages for weddings. A bay horse's head loomed over the top of the sign; the metal tracks for cartwheels had been stripped out of the hall that ran from street to courtyard, and replaced with tiles. Further afield I found a print of a nineteenth-century map in the Mauerpark flea market. Tracing the Tiergarten with a finger, I realized that every time I took the S-bahn to the Zoologische Garten, I passed over the site of the old hippodrome where Mrs Hayes had watched – and mockingly disapproved of – German ladies riding astride in divided skirts.

On weekends in Kollwitzplatz, two Norwegian Fjord ponies waited, harnessed to a large wagon with a green tarp cover, and gave children cart rides around the neighbourhood. They passed under my window four or five times every Saturday. I'd make my way automatically to the window each time and look down on them as they passed, gold-dun like the Pazyryk horses, their endomorphic torsos divided by a dark eel stripe, their erect manes trimmed so that the black streak down the centre stood longest. Sometimes I wandered over to the market when they were resting, their coats curling with sweat on their chests, and gave them a good scratch behind the ear.

One wintery day, when the sun hadn't penetrated through thick clouds and the whole morning had passed under a grey wash before dimming to gunmetal in the afternoon, I noticed a horse trailer parked outside my flat. As it didn't belong to the Fjords, I assumed the driver must be lost or looking for directions. The road is busy, a main artery into the centre of East Berlin, with two lanes of traffic on either side of a green central strip lined with lime trees whose leaves were limp, but blazed bright yellow in the gloom.

Opposite, sandwiched between a drab, pre-war tenement and a drab, post-war DDR apartment block, was a red-brick church with a flat front, a scalloped Dutch gable and a pitched roof topped by a tower that ended in the green-streaked German version of an onion dome. In the summer its broad balcony was always filled with bright tubs of geraniums, which clashed with the brick. There was a gaping, dark archway in the façade over which someone had hung a single star-shaped lantern. The archway gave onto a small, dingy yard as narrow as a chimney, immediately in front of the church itself. The street façade of the church still bore shrapnel damage and bullet dings from the war, punctured inches deep in the brick. The Red Army had entered Berlin down this *allee* and they fought using the gravestones in the Jewish cemetery opposite as cover.

Later, at teatime, a tint of leaded inky blue began to seep into the sky: it would soon be dark. I checked again and saw, on the path between the limes in the middle of the central strip, two women holding a placid grey mare, who rested one hoof patiently, not even interested in attacking the shrubbery near by. She had a grackle nose-band criss-crossing her muzzle and her saddle was covered with thick sheepskin from cantle to pommel. She dozed, oblivious to the traffic, though it was what passed for rush hour in East Berlin; the soft, ashy roar of the cars was loud in my flat and as I swung open the window, the air tasted grey with exhaust fumes.

At a cue, a man in an orange reflective waistcoat crossed over to the women and the horse, and led them across the road to the church. A crowd of children and parents spilled out of the great black mouth of the archway under the star, all padded in sombre winter clothing, hoods and hats over pale hair, faces muffled in scarves. The horse glowed like a snow creature in a Lowry, pearly in the gloom, as the crowd, indistinguishable in the shadows of the door, let off camera flashes like fireflies that were soon swallowed in the darkness as the horse gained luminosity. They put a little girl on the mare's back and led her away north up the pavement along the road. The people followed, the children's chattering and excitement reaching me three storeys up, as the parents held the children's hands and pointed to the horse, which clopped steadily on and out of my sight. It was Children's Day. St Martin's Day. The saint who rides a white horse.

I missed the Pferdberg. A short time later, I found a fresh crescent of hoof prints 200 yards from the church. Walking back up the hill on the other side of the street, I found another matching crescent, even closer to my home.

On Eponalia, 18 December, I took an apple, a stick of incense and an inch of hair I'd trimmed off. Placing them on a sheet of foil on my balcony, I planted the spillikin of the incense in the apple, like a primitive Christingle. Thinking vaguely of horses, I lit the incense and tried to ignite the hair. A small flame licked around it and petered out, so I tried again. This time it burned slowly like a wick. The incense gave off a thin whiff as though the scent molecules were pinched by the cold night air. Unsure what to do next, I left the apple and the hair on the balcony as we used to leave out onions for Santa's reindeer when I was a child.

Posh

A lot of people in our class just go in for balls and things, and
spend masses of money on new clothes and fashions and all that.
I'm really lucky. I've got a hobby, they don't know what to do
with themselves. I'm not all that keen on clothes and dances and
things; I can't think what I'd do if I didn't ride.

Jemima Goldsmith, aged thirteen, interviewed in The English and
Their Horses (1988) by Libby Purves and Paul Heiney

'Look out for needles,' said Rose Spearing, surveying the grass
keenly as she stepped across Wyck Gardens, incongruous in her
navy jodhpurs in the middle of Brixton, her long dark hair pulled
back in a damp ponytail. 'This place used to be covered with them.'

A train passed by on the line on top of the brick arches, bucketing
commuters to Victoria Station.

'There used to be people down here day and night injecting
heroin into their groins and anywhere. Here's one . . .' She kicked a
hypodermic out of the rain-softened turf with the toe of her riding
boot. 'No needle on it but I'll put it in the sharps bin anyway,' she
said, picking up the empty syringe carefully and carrying it over to
the red metal bin with a one-way lid that was set on a post at the edge
of the grass. 'People keep chucking their takeaway boxes in the bit
where we're going to have the stables, but there are hardly any
needles any more.'

She gestured to the end wall of a row of Victorian terraced houses, where some of the grass was sectioned off behind a metal fence with a large sign on it reading: EBONY HORSE CLUB RIDING CENTRE DEVELOPMENT. There were photographs of children grooming and riding horses, and a young jockey hovering over the outstretched neck of a galloping racehorse. In the centre was an architectural drawing of the stables: loose boxes, a classroom, tack and storage rooms snug against the railway arches, a riding ring and a paddock overlaid with faint circles representing trees.

Even in a perishing, overcast February drizzle, there was light and space and green. If the money were raised and the stables built, people would look down from the balconies of the maisonette flats, stacked in units on the Loughborough housing estate, and see the horses grazing in the paddock below, or venture down to Wyck Gardens and hang over the rails of the outdoor school as the lessons go on. I was there in 2010, when the stables were still just a laminated blueprint awaiting a large cash investment. It was midweek and the streets were almost empty apart from a Waitrose delivery van parked outside the neighbouring row of stolid, gentrified Victorian terraces with brass letterboxes and white columns at the doors. If you walked down Station Road and ducked under the railway arches, you were in Brixton market, where there were trays of stout yams and pyramids of green okra pods, hairdressers' shops with swatches of black curls and tubs of glutinous hair butter, and butchers' stalls where young men, in white hygiene hats and neat black beards, piled calves' feet or hacked at raw, sickly-sweet-smelling halal chicken.

Rose Spearing was living on the Moorlands Estate on the other side of the railway arches when she decided to give the children on the estate something that she had never had – a horsy childhood. She started taking groups from a local youth club for riding lessons in 1996. The Coldharbour Ward in Brixton is one of the most deprived boroughs in the country and at that time there was an average of three shootings a week on Coldharbour Lane, which runs parallel with the railway lines that divide Moorlands from Wyck Gardens.

Four kids taking a half-hour riding lesson at Wormwood Scrubs stables turned into eight children, then twelve, sixteen, twenty-two and twenty-eight. 'We just asked if they wanted to come.' She shrugged. 'They were just open to it, they didn't find it strange. It just come naturally. There wasn't a problem with recruiting; we always had more people than we could take.'

She went on: 'There used to be a stable quite near here with twenty horses and ponies, but it's gone now?' Rose's voice lilted up at the end of each sentence, a South London interrogative tic. 'When I was growing up in West London there were stables everywhere. There were hundreds and hundreds of horses. Little stables tucked away – the children of florists, of the coalman, the grocers, the people who delivered goods by horses: they still had a love of horses in the family. They used to come together for the Harness Horse parade at Easter. There were horse shows in Lambeth and at Peckham Rye. The GLC had a big horse show on Clapham Common in the sixties and seventies, and people hacked from all over London to get there. There were so many horses in Earlsfield that the council built them a riding ring, and there was a riding ring on Tooting Bec Common too. All those stables have gone now,' she repeated. 'It's all housing.'

The last remains of the horsepower that built and fed London have now run underground, like the old rivers the Fleet and the Quaggy, although you can find the last descendants of Beauty and Ginger if you know where to look. There's a man who rides around Clapham on a white horse and an old mews near Hyde Park, where Rose learned to ride when she'd graduated and had the cash. Sam Martin, who hopes to represent Nigeria at the 2012 Olympics, grew up on a Lambeth housing estate and learned to ride at Vauxhall City Farm. There's a riding school tucked behind a row of semis in Lewisham. Rose used to keep her own horse at a small yard in Kennington, less than a mile from where I lived for four years in my twenties without ever realizing there were horses near by. The Pony Club has two branches in the city, at Wormwood Scrubs and Docklands, and there are over seventy riding establishments, from the purpose-built equestrian centre at Lea to the old railway veterinary yard in Bermondsey, where horses are still kept in the Georgian stables where injured draught horses recuperated in the nineteenth century, dosed on whisky and balls of 'medicine'.

The Ebony Horse Club is a new wellhead. There are now forty-six children aged between eight and nineteen in the club with a waiting list of twenty more and several former alumni helping out as they train as youth workers. In 2009, they took sixty children from local primary schools on 'introduction to riding' days and twenty of them went onto the waiting list. When I visited, club members had four after-school riding lessons or more a term at riding schools in Kingston and Lewisham, although they were in the minibus for longer than they were on a horse. If it got its own stables, the Ebony Horse Club would be able to offer 160 lessons a week, although whether that would shorten the waiting list or not was a guess. Riding has become a tradition in Brixton.

Later, in the club's office at Loughborough Community Centre – among blown-up photos of smiling children cuddling horses, stacks of fund-raising applications and a dinky model of the stables set on a miniature Wyck Gardens, dusted with green flocked grass – I talked to one of the children that Rose took on that first riding lesson, Shannel Foster, now twenty-two and a youth worker. She explained, 'In Brixton, riding is a norm. It's a norm for your brother, your sister, your little sister, your little brother to join the waiting list and go to horse club. I've got a nephew who's three now, and at home when he sees a horse he says, "I'm going to go horse riding."'

Ebony has done something that Frossarbo could not: put down roots in a community. Rose handed me a checklist for the children who qualify to ride. The categories included the following: income support, parent ill/disabled, bereaved child, child excluded from school, behaviour problems, physical/mental disability, dyslexia, asylum seeker, looked-after child, other special needs.

'Usually they probably have three or four problems like that,' she said, sitting back, stretching her legs out and propping her jodphur-boot heels on the carpet. 'If it's really urgent and they're having difficulties that might exclude them from school, then we put them quite high at the top of the list.'

'What kind of difficulties?' I asked.

'Growing up in a very violent, difficult place and having a lot of trouble in the education system and being low income. The kids that really excel with us are the ones who are having problems at school. The fact that we're part of the community, and not part of the school system, helps a lot.'

A handful of the children have mothers or fathers who are alcoholics or junkies, but most of the parents are hugely supportive, wanting their kids to 'stay on track' (a popular catchphrase here) and have chances that they didn't. Rose keeps a watchful eye on the girls whose parents she knows aren't looking after them properly, aware that there are men who home in on vulnerable teenagers.

The mother of a boy who has both attention deficit hyperactivity disorder and Tourette's told Rose that the only time she'd seen him concentrate since his birth was when he was on a horse. Sometimes riding teaches them something as simple as sitting still.

'Quite a lot of them just haven't learned to sit and listen; they just wriggle,' said Rose. 'They can learn it over time with horses and then it just naturally transfers to the classroom. Common sense really!' She threw up a hand. 'Children can really calm down a lot through learning this. I think in today's society children are either on the phone or the computer or these electronic games, and we're training them to have very short attention spans. And then, when they can't concentrate at school, we wonder why. You need to be calm and alert on a horse.'

'Do you have more girls than boys?' I wondered, but Rose said it was usually split fifty-fifty between the sexes.

'We've always taken girls and boys equally. It's not a girl thing here.

If they don't know anything outside Brixton, why tell them it's a girl's sport?' she said, bristling. 'With riding elsewhere it's become a self-fulfilling prophecy because you have loads and loads of girls and the boys feel left out.' Then she softened a fraction and added, 'The only thing I have noticed is we have lost a lot of boys to other sports. Football is so all-embracing. We have had very talented boys, one who plays for Crystal Palace football club junior team or something; we lost one to fencing. Quite often there's other things that boys have to do, and girls don't have so much available to them that's interesting.'

Rose plucked at a heap of paperwork, distracted, and bored with talking about the importance of girls and ponies. Ebony has to employ a full-time fund-raiser to keep up with the endless cycle of filling in grant applications and bidding for the cash that would keep the club functioning. I tried asking where they would get the ponies for the riding centre.

'Everyone wants to know about the horses and where we're getting them from,' said Rose, 'but keeping them costs nothing compared to the rest of the club.'

The club had just lost out on a grant from Children in Need and the news was nagging at her. 'People think we're really established, they praise you and say you're doing fantastic work and there should be more of you, but it doesn't really help. You're still struggling along. It's always been a struggle to get money but we probably shot ourselves in the foot,' she smiled, unrepentant, 'because we're always taking on more and more children and doing bigger and bigger things. You have to keep in touch with so many sponsors and in so many different ways. At least that means we're not vulnerable because we're not dependent on just one, but it's tiring, it's really, really tiring.'

Every last penny of the grants must be justified and catalogued. Rose rubbed her eyes. 'I haven't got any salary after June. I just had to say to Letty the fund-raiser, don't panic. This is her third bid she's put in that we haven't won.'

The phone rang and Rose broke off to answer it, handing me three big scrapbooks of clippings on Ebony. One was dedicated to Shannel's brother Nathan, who was shot and killed in central Brixton in 2007, when a seventeen-year-old took him for another boy who'd stolen his neck chain. Nathan was another of the children at that first riding lesson.

'He had real difficulties in school, learning and stuff, and sometimes he used to get suspended from school, for no fault of his own,' Shannel had told me. 'My mum was able to encourage him and he enjoyed horse riding and that was probably why he was so good. Rose always says, when you get on a horse they don't know anything about you and they don't know how naughty you might have been in the playground or the problems you've got at home, you can just clear your head of everything and just concentrate, because you know if you're a pain in the arse of that horse, he's going to give you problems, so you're going to concentrate and you're going to dedicate your hour to that horse.'

At the time that he was murdered, Nathan was working at a charity called Kid's City. Shannel's nephew, Nathan's son, is the three-year-old who wants to ride at Ebony.

I went back to the community centre on Ebony's Annual Championship Day, finding the fluorescent lights a relief from the ceiling of dreich grey skies nailed down over the estate. Earlier there had been a written exam about horse care for all the children (sample questions: 'What is a "puissance" competition?'; 'What kind of bedding is bad for a horse with COPD?'), set by youth worker Ailsa, who was now overseeing the practical test. I sat quietly in a corner as a boy of about twelve struggled to fit a yellow and black nylon headcollar on a life-size, black-plastic horse while Ailsa stood by with her clipboard. The horse was like the one I'd seen in the window of the deserted room on Christinenstrasse in Berlin. It rocked a little on its stiff legs as the boy turned the halter upside down and thrust it at its nose, its heavy plastic mane brushing its neck.

After a minute or two, Ailsa gently took the halter, slipped the noseband on and buckled the headstall. 'Now show me where you stand and how you lead it,' she went on, returning to her notes. The boy took up his station at the near shoulder, perfect, and watched for her nod.

Next in was Chloe, turned out in jodhs, hoodie, pierced nose and a hairnet. Her cheeks flushed as Ailsa asked her how you caught a horse in a field.

'You go up to it, head down, and if it runs away, you step back. Go to this bit,' she said, approaching the dummy's flat black shoulder, 'and then, if it lets you, put the headcollar on.'

'And how tall is that horse?'

Chloe stepped back and looked the horse up and down. 'Fifteen and a half.'

Ailsa stuck a circular piece of paper on its forehead. 'And what's that marking?'

'A star.'

Outside in the lobby, the children were crammed onto benches over the radiators, eating packed lunches and digging in bags of crisps, waiting for the minibuses that would take us to a riding centre in Kent for the last part of the championship. Some of them had their own jodhpurs like Chloe, while others were in tracksuits, rucked up over riding boots loaned by the club. They talked in rapid fire, making it almost impossible for me to keep up with the exchanges, but snatches cleared the din, the 'shut ups', the joshing, and the fact that someone knew someone who had been taken away and sent back to her home country. Rose lectured them on their turnout, saying they'd be marked on this, looking briefly but sternly at the girl who had left her hair hanging down to her waist as she said it.

'I want to see you riding properly,' Rose said, and the crisp packets were stilled. 'You've got to show the horse authority from the beginning, because they'll know if you don't mean it. I expect the best. I know how well you can all do.' Her eyes ran over them all in turn. 'It's like school – if you can't do two plus two, you won't get on to four times five. You'll move on to something more difficult, more faster. That's the same what happens in riding lessons, it's progressive. If you can't all trot together, you won't move on to the hard stuff like jumping.'

Rose held all the strings that drew the club together – the names of the children and their parents, the whereabouts of the waterproof clothing and the riding boots, where each child lived, who had bad nerves, which youth worker had been late and who was having a difficult time at home.

'For seven years I didn't even nip to the loo when there was a lesson on,' she said, 'and then I thought I was being paranoid, so I went, once, and when I got back someone was on the floor. You've got to be there.' She was missing some of her own daughter's half-term to supervise the championship, a phone at her ear, replacing kids that didn't show up with children from the reserve list. The top group were the only competitors but she had invited along some of the younger children to watch as she wanted to keep them interested in the club the following year.

There was counting and a checklist of names, after which we went out to wait outside the corner shop, which was open, despite looking as if it had been battened down for trouble. The estate was one of the most densely populated parts of the country, but it often felt as though there was hardly anyone about. The concrete walkways between flats were empty and every window was defended with net curtains. When the minibuses arrived the children piled in and I took the back seat between the speakers.

We started the slow wind out of the city, south through Dulwich, the estates giving way to 1930s semis crammed up to the edges of clogged roads. The children chattered. One of the youth workers, Aaron, craned round from the passenger seat to quiz Chloe.

'And if they say this horse is difficult, will you get on him?'

Chloe squared up. 'I will get on him.'

The radio pumped out Beyoncé and Rihanna. Two girls sitting side by side, one in a veil, tracksuit and trainers, and the other with a topknot of braids, sang along and danced, wriggling in their seats, giggling as they fluffed the moves. The songs were intercut with public service ads warning teenagers about cannabis, and advice on identifying an abusive boyfriend, then more songs about making it in New York, a deafening, disorienting jumble of messages, affirmations, aspirations and dangers.

Once on the M25, we moved faster at last, free from the sleeping policemen that rattled the negligible suspension of the old minibus, and pulled away from the city past congratulatory signs reading, 'London Low Emissions Zone'. After ten minutes we left the circular for a slip road and climbed up an incline, where a chink of countryside opened up to the left – great flat fields of monoculture.

'Look, it's Emmerdale!' called out a boy who'd been sitting quietly on his own.

We cut off the road and up a steep slope to the Chelsfield stables, where a teenage boy dragged a wheelbarrow out of the way and pulled open the gate for us, waving as we turned into the drive. The children spilled out and clustered round the buses, unsure what to do as we unloaded the bags of boots and rosettes – red, blue, yellow, green and orange, new whips with colourful woven plastic wrap, calendars of horses galloping in meadows, the silver trophy with the purple-marbled base with 'EBONY HORSE CLUB ANNUAL CHAMPIONSHIP awarded since 2004' engraved on it. Ricky Alleyne was the lad galloping the racehorse on the sign at Wyck Gardens – he'd gone on to the British Racing School – and his name was there; Shanice, one of the girls who was competing that day, had had her name on it twice already. Small, with a short, straightened bob poking out from under her crash cap, she was quieter than her twin Shaneka and her boisterous brother, Junior. The others caught sight of the trophy and one of them called out, 'Shanice is gonna win again!' Shanice, not even smiling, looked appalled.

The sun was stark in a chilly blue sky, warming the yard, a big, open, sloping sweep of cracked concrete surrounded by white-painted and flat-roofed boxes set between old red-brick barns. It absorbed the children and their noise into the sound of brooms on wet concrete, horses shifting on their beds and snorting, and water gushing into a bucket. The lower doors of the stables had been opened, with just a bar to hold in the horses. Light streamed in and gleamed on the straw underfoot as the horses basked in the sunshine with their ears pricked, watching the children. A rooster with oily black tail feathers strutted around and a group of hens padded into the hay store, clucking anxiously. People passed to and fro in the yard with wheelbarrows, smiled and passed comment on the sunshine. Two horses, turned out together in a small paddock with sawdust underfoot, lipped at each other's withers as the Ebony children hung over their fence and cooed over them.

Rose, smiling in the sunshine and at ease now in the middle of the children, called out to one of the boys, 'Come and take Mouna to see my horse and give him these two Polos.'

The kids scattered, striking out to stroke noses and explore. I followed a group of them, together with Mouna and the Polos, to a corner of the yard, where the stables ran into a little cul-de-sac, and, like a prize at the end of a maze, Rose's great black horse, Hugo, lowered his head, looking for mints.

The children had to demonstrate that they could tack up a horse and complete a riding show. The judges included a tall, smart young man from the British Equestrian Federation, teachers from the riding centre and Mary-Anne from the Emile Faurie Foundation, an organization that sponsors riding lessons for pupils from inner-city schools. Another patron of the club, Ronke Phillips, an ITN journalist who used to ride as a child, watched from the gallery of the indoor manège with an older lady from the British Horse Society called Janet, whose wispy white hair was caught up in a bun. There were old adverts for saddlers ranged on the walls and a rag-tag collection of dusty chairs on which we perched to watch the first group go through their paces.

Ebony has had mixed support from the horse world. The latest newsletter announced that the Warwickshire Hunt had just raised £1,000 for the club. The Duchess of Cornwall sought the club out and volunteered to become its patron after Nathan's death. The British Horse Society had supported the club in its early days, but the man from the Pony Club came and spent a whole day with the children, watched a lesson and went back to head office, promising to send books that never arrived. Some of the London riding schools did not like the way Ebony operated and I got the impression that the club was considered 'the wrong sort'. The legacy fund for the London 2012 Olympics had just contributed a large sum towards the cost of the stables, but the donations Ebony receives from the public are meagre compared to the millions generated for horse rescue centres and sanctuaries such as Redwings.

I was reminded of my conversation with Sven Forsling, who'd said horses were good for his Frossarbo girls because they were 'high status', but I didn't think the Ebony children realized that. They were cut off from the horse world, despite the trips to the National Stud and the National Horse Racing Museum, and this smattering of official presences. There's not much horse sport on the television for them.

'It's all just so different,' Shannel had said.

Rose had talked of taking the children out of their comfort zone and challenging them. 'You say, "You can do this." A lot of them get bored with being on the same estate, going to the same school every day.'

Poshness is the second great false cliché of horses, after sex. Someone who'd spend fifty quid on a night out in London would cock an eyebrow if I mentioned £50-an-hour riding lessons: 'Bit much, isn't it?' When I'd asked a friend what she'd thought of girls who loved horses, she had snapped back, 'I thought they were probably rich.' Money helps. I wouldn't deny the benefits of a sympathetic, middle-class upbringing in a village. The weekly riding lessons to which my parents ferried me. My own room to paper with posters. The holidays with a ride. Tav so readily lent by friends. The bridle paths, the stubble fields, the woods. Magazine subscriptions and paperback books and hardback annuals and toy horses from America. Riding boots and jodhpurs. The prizes we'd unloaded from the back of the minibus at Chelsfield were things I had been able to walk into a tack shop and buy with my pocket money.

By the age of ten I had also learned that horses were 'posh', although this did not match my own experiences. At primary school, I was singled out as 'posh', although that was equated not with horsiness but with my tendency to elongate the wrong vowels, and the fact that I had a wooden recorder instead of a plastic one. There were girls at school who had horses, but they were not posh. When I moved to a private school at eleven, I could not count one child in my year who owned a horse of her own – the nearest was a girl whose dad was a bookie. The people who worked at the riding schools I attended were not posh. Denise, who owned three horses and hunted on occasion, worked as a seamstress in a wedding-dress factory. In 2006, one in four horse riders in the United Kingdom earned less than £10,000 a year.

There was another girl in Costessey who used to ride Tav for Linda. Linda's daughter, Carol, was out on Tav one day when she came across a teenage girl who said her name was Nikki and that she was from the children's home in New Costessey. She'd ridden before, so Carol and Linda adopted her as a new rider for Tav, as I was leaving soon for university and wouldn't be around to take Tav on our long, meandering hacks at the weekends. Nikki groomed and mucked out Tav one day a week, and together they went out exploring as the old gelding and I had done. My mother once saw them on a roundabout in the centre of Norwich, having chased the Railway Line as far east as it went.

Tav must have given Nikki the same gift he gave me, the long hours alone with his ears twitching and listening, the quick surge of adrenaline when he'd gallop for home with his teeth locked on the bit. When the children's home got too much for Nikki and she ran away, the manager would ring Linda and ask her to check whether Tav had been 'done'. If his feet were picked out and his bed changed, they knew Nikki was all right. Away from the other kids and the social workers, she would sleep in the stable, curled up in the straw by Tav, as the pony dozed and listened for foxes, his round, warm sides rising and falling.

The Ebony Club children competed in two sets, riding in file round the judges in the centre. As they were put through a series of transitions, a great, lumbering grey cob tried to cut across the school. His rider, Junior, Shanice's brother, reined him back. Shaneka had to wrestle with the little grey, Misty, who took fright at the judge's flapping piece of paper and bolted. Everyone panicked for a second before she wrestled him to a standstill, half thrown out of her saddle. One of the teachers went over to help her. Although Shaneka looked as if she were in pain, she sat quietly and took the little pony back out onto the track as he made a show of spooking once more. They trotted together as a ride, circled and changed rein. It was quiet, save for a persistent collared dove cooing away somewhere in the roof. Shaniel, with a yellow jersey and a heavy coil of braids on the nape of her neck, couldn't get Nigel to canter on their first circuit, but with the teachers and Rose calling encouragement, she kicked him smartly onto the right lead and brought him on an arc back to the rear of the ride.

While the second group did their show, I wandered out to the yard where the other children from Ebony were taking turns to tack up a very tolerant pony for the judges. Junior clowned around with the saddle as I watched and made a fuss of not knowing which straps went where. The cockerel, who'd been hand-raised, prowled silkily around my legs like a cat, asking to be stroked. I found Shanice hovering in the yard and coaxed a few words out of her.

'How long have you been riding?'

'Five years.'

'Do you want to do more riding?'

Her voice was infinitely gentle. 'Yeah.'

'Do you want to do a job with horses?'

'Yeah, I want to work with them and train them.'

Someone called her over for her test and she set off, relieved.

Later, when the sun was lowering and it grew colder, a collapsible table was folded out and dusted down outside the indoor school, and the prizes set up on it. We all stood round in a half-circle, stamping our feet and crushing our fingers under our armpits for warmth. Rose took up her place and fished out the notebook with the results. There were purple-and-yellow double-layer rosettes and a copy of *Horse and Pony* from the Emile Faurie Foundation for everyone who'd taken part, followed by the main results.

Girls took the first five places: Chemilla, fifth, Shaniel, fourth, Shaneka, third, Jadine second, and Shanice, looking as if she wanted the earth to swallow her up, won for the third year running by a clear eleven points. The others burst into wild applause and cheering as she went up to take the trophy, her shoulders hunched around her ears.

'First hat trick!' one of the boys yelled. 'I knew it! Shanice did it again! I told you!'

As they lined up to have their photographs taken, with Shanice, smiling tentatively, tucked at the end of the row, clasping an armful of books and the silver trophy, I asked Nashon whether he was going to go on riding. With the purple-and-yellow rosette fluttering on his anorak and a woollen hat pulled low over his forehead, he said, 'I'm going to be a jockey.'

Mouna teased him. 'You're fifteen, fifteen sounds so old.'

I asked her whether she'd be riding here in twelve months. 'Yeah, I'm going to be back next year. I'm going to compete.'

When we returned to Brixton in the minibus that evening it was dark as we drove from street to street, dropping off the children. The parks outside the pools thrown by streetlights were dark and sinister, the walkways overhead between the stacked maisonettes shadowy and deserted. I thought of what Rose had said, about how riding took the Brixton children out of their 'comfort zone' and challenged them. How would that change when the ponies came to Wyck Gardens? They would be able to ride every week and to have a favourite pony like the girls at Frossarbo. They could be in the yard every day after school, taking round buckets of feed and water, and mucking out, perhaps taking their Pony Club tests and going to gymkhanas. Maybe the Lambeth Show would even revive its old riding classes.

I thought of the reassurance of horses, the earthy smell of pony nuts and leather over traffic fumes, of stables by the railway arches with thick straw beds, carrots from Brixton market, Polos from the corner shop and of ponies grazing in a city park.

Kassane

'Oh throw your heart over,' says Lucy, 'and then follow it as
quickly as you can.'

Lucy Glitters in Mr Sponge's Sporting Tour (1853)
by R. S. Surtees

I was riding again, this time in deep countryside to the east of
Berlin. It was the spring of 2010 and I was once again happy to be
on a horse.

'Let your reins longer, you understand?' Marie instructed, as her
horse, Mel, jogged alongside my grey mare, causing her to whirl her
ears back and trot up to the horse in front.

'I would, but she keeps trotting when I don't want her to,' I
answered.

Marie h'mmed. 'Reins longer.'

Kassane shook her head in irritation, flinging up the tips of her
long smoky mane. I let the reins out a notch, and then a notch more,
till she settled and pricked her ears, walking forward with an active,
loose and lithe stride. I could gather up the reins for a while, but then
she would push her nose at them, edging her neck out until they
were comfortable for her.

I rode more easily than I had done for a long time. I'd never ridden
horses so free-going as Sabine Zuckmantel's herd of Arabs and Barbs.
They moved as I'd only known over-excited or scared horses go. At
first it made me want to clutch at my reins before I began to realize

that all this did was to bother Kassane and spoil the ride for both of us. I relaxed into the lightness of her, trusting her.

The lady riding the cream mare, Tequila, kept her reins short. 'All this horse does is pull, pull, pull!' she complained, while a glance at Tequila's rolling blue eye told you her thoughts: All this woman does is pull, pull, pull.

The horse capered backwards, head to her chest, ears pinned in confusion. 'That's right, back now, till we are in the right place,' the woman told her as she reversed rapidly through the ride. 'Good horse.'

Sabine, with her swirl of long brown-grey hair and scarlet cheeks, had waved us off from the yard behind her house, lighting a cigarette as we set out through the fields and into the Havelland. The house was halfway through being done up, bare breeze-block here and there, and oozing foam insulation around the door. In the cloakroom where I left my rucksack hung ten waxed riding coats like old chrysalises for enormous moths. The yard stood between two old barns with brand-new roofs, and in the centre was a wild patch of garden with a long table set up, overlooking the overgrown lawn that sloped down to the fields, where Sabine's ten horses grazed and bickered as a herd. Foundling and Gonda, the head mare, were left behind, but too busy ripping up the long grass to even watch us as we led the horses out through the fluttering-tape electric fences and, on the other side of a hillock, checked girths and mounted.

Two friends had sent me to Sabine's hof outside Berlin for wanderreiten – you could inadequately translate the word as pony trekking, although it suggests more the spirit of rambling or roving. All year round Sabine organized rides that lasted between three hours and six weeks. There were excursions to the old Schorfheide nature park to watch the Przewalski horses, or to the Rhine and the Camargue, rides with stops for champagne and truffles, or to light a bonfire on Midsummer Night. In the winter there were the 'foul weather rides' when the waxed coats were shaken out and martinis were served afterwards to burn a little warmth back into freezing toes. Once a year she retrod Marion Countess Dönhoff's seven-week-long escape on horseback from her family's estates in east Prussia in 1945 to Hamburg as the Red Army closed in.

I could only afford the basic Saturday rides, which were meant to take three hours, but with a forty-minute train ride from Berlin into east Germany, unhurried grooming on either side, and a snack of bread, cheese and salami at the picnic table afterwards, I would be gone from my flat from 9 a.m. till 7 p.m. I returned, sunburned and stoned on horses, to my uncomprehending friends and sat in city bars, distracted and smiling, my eyes far away and my legs lumpy with hot cleg bites.

There were eight of us on the late May ride: a father and his two young daughters, the woman on Tequila and her husband on the big grey, Oued, myself and Matthias, who came up from Berlin every weekend to ride the little chestnut, Honorine, who was never bothered by anything much. Another rider had told me that one day when Sabine was taking a group cantering through a Polish forest, a tree was felled onto the path in front of them. All the horses had skittered and spooked in horror, apart from Honorine, who pulled up gently with a quizzical 'Blow me' expression on her face. Now Honorine and Matthias plodded at the back of the train in a happy daze.

'It is the best way to see the countryside,' Matthias had told me. 'From a horse.'

Kassane's coat was white, flecked here and there, her long mane, her tail and the soft fur in her ears dove grey. The North African Barb was brought to Spain by the Moors, and it gave the Andalusian and later the Lipizzaner its 'ram's head', a long, intelligent, expressive face with a slightly convex, blunt nose. In Kassane, combined with Arabian blood, the Barb face was elongated and slender with barely a dish, sweetly handsome, and ending in an expressive, pinched upper lip, which she'd used to gently feel over my pockets after I'd caught her in the field by offering a carrot. Her build melded both sides of her pedigree, the flamboyant Arab curves tempered by straight Barb substance, her tail set low, not high and kinked. I thought she had the quizzical beauty of a Houyhnhnm, like Edwin Landseer's grey mare in The Arab Tent.

Some of Sabine's horses wore Western saddles, but most had Australian stock saddles, with deep seats and a cantle higher than your coccyx. At the front, on either side of the pommel, were two fins holding your thighs in place. The stirrups were boxy metal, open, and the leathers thin, while the girth was thick sheepskin over a stout saddle pad. Two quirts of leather trailed on either side of the back of the saddle, for tying bundles of clothes or sleeping rolls, although I used them as a fly whisk if Kassane skipped a step to try to bite a cleg off her chest. Since reading about the wife of the distinguished Royal Academician who had been recommended the stock saddle by Captain Hayes for hunting astride in Devon, I had been curious to know what they looked like and why the captain would have recommended them to a lady. Now I saw how secure and comfortable the saddle was, and how easy to sit straight in, even for hours at a time.

The morning of my first ride at Sabine's yard, I'd woken up from a dream in which I'd been riding Gräfin last in a four-horse quadrille in the reithalle. We rode down the centre line in file. The lead horse peeled left, the second horse right, the horse in front of me left. As I tried to curl right to follow my partner, Gräfin napped left, impossibly strong, me tugging at her head, all decorum and collection lost. Then she broke into a canter, trying to catch up with the other two horses, me looking frantically ahead to see how I could cut across the school and rejoin the ride without too much more disruption, while seeing the pair of horses weaving elegantly around one another in the centre, and Gräfin tugging and cantering stronger and stronger. I pushed her on and let her canter, so I gave her her head, and on we went, faster and faster round the ring, and my fear lifted and was gone. Then I woke up.

On that day, the countryside had still been struggling into a partial spring, stunted by months of thick snow that had blocked some of the lanes – 'So deep,' indicated Suzanne, who'd led the ride, gesturing a hand at Gonda's shoulder. Many of the trees had been bare, the black branches of some strung with great bolls of green mistletoe. The silver birches in the woodland had been breaking into green, while the fingers of the horse-chestnut leaves had been pinched and tented, close together. The vast, undulating fields of oilseed rape had been blue-green then. Now in late May Kassane and I skirted crops dazzling yellow with blossom, and the trees were in full fig, the leaves a richer green than that first neon spring colour. On one hollow grey tree trunk, with its canopy rotted and its branches borne away, I saw three huge fungi like coolie hats.

I could have been in Norfolk in this landscape of flat, drained water-meadows, with great deep dykes crossing through them, and the occasional gently rolling hill or valley almost too shallow to register. The sky was blue and huge, smeared with a few white clouds. We rode on long, sandy tracks like the Railway Line between fields, couched by banks thick with powdery cow parsley and wild grasses bulked out by fertilizer from the fields. We toed carefully down the edges of sown crops, on a narrow strip of bare earth with wheat whispering on either side, or crossed ploughed, unsown land, the horses picking their feet up and rushing forward against the suck of the heavy soil. Here and there were wooden watchtowers, little square huts perched on stilts with crudely nailed ladders leading up to them. I asked what they were, and Marie told me, 'They're for hunters of wildschwein. They go up into one of those and wait, and shoot from there.'

As we passed one of the ditches, some ten feet deep, two brown geese shot up and Kassane leaped sideways. I went with her, reins still slack, and as the geese scudded away, honking, she settled back behind the dun, Etincelle, as if nothing had happened. In the same way that a flock of birds moved as a whole, with a few outliers looping out but always coming back to the mass, so living in a herd seemed to set limits on what Sabine's horses did. They stuck together. If enough of them held steady, it calmed the others. Tequila's rider would not canter on 'this horse which pulls so', so she and the man on Oued turned back along a short cut, to meet the rest of us later. Although the two horses were always in sight and we were separated from them for a matter of minutes, Marie's black gelding Mel called out to them as though they had been lost for months.

Sabine's regular riders were fascinated by the politics between the horses, which they followed like a slow-unfurling soap opera. If Sabine took the lead mare, 'die Chefin' – the boss lady – Gonda, and Kassane, who was the newest and lowest in the herd, to the Camargue, how would they get on? Etincelle as Gonda's dam was dubbed the 'queen mother' and must not be allowed to challenge her daughter for the lead at a canter. There was an optimal sequence of horses for the ride, taking into account the complexities of the pecking order.

Two beautiful Trakehners came rushing up to their paddock fence to watch our string as it went past, their small heads gored with wide, flared nostrils that they lifted up for the scent of the *wanderreiten* horses, who turned their heads briefly and walked on, uninterested. We filed into a cool, pine plantation where the track was lined with a wall of sawn and stacked logs packed tightly as a jigsaw, and where the insects descended to plague the horses.

One of the little girls rode ahead of me in silence on Etincelle, whom I'd ridden the month before. I watched the mare's black tail – spiky at the top like a Przewalski's – swishing at flies. Behind me came the younger of the sisters on the chestnut, Daisy, and she peppered me with questions in German. Which saddle did I prefer? How long had I ridden? Who was better, Etincelle or Kassane? Kassane was fast, wasn't she? She had been riding for four years, herself, although her father, riding behind on the cocoa-coloured warmblood, Murka, reminded her that it was nearly five. I tried to ask her about the Pony Club as there was a branch in Berlin, but collapsed into a lack of vocabulary, leaning back, brushed by branches and trying not to ping them back at her.

'I kept Daisy back OK, didn't I? She wasn't up Kassane's bum?'

I turned in my saddle and saw her, all ponytail, braces and back protector. 'No, no, *kein Problem*.'

As we emerged once more out of the plantation, the landscape spooled on and on. I hadn't the slightest idea where Marie was leading us. We passed through a pair of bland, rusticated villages, with neat, box-like farmhouses with peeling paint and crumbling barns, and square-towered stone churches, some topped with small onion domes. We barely set hoof on tarmac the whole day, but turned down what might have been old carrier's roads, with paving of irregularly shaped, round flagstones underneath, and trotted on till we were clear and back to the fields.

As we walked along one meadow, following Indian-file through dense, high grass, Marie pointed down and to the left of Mel. As each rider passed the spot they exclaimed. When Kassane and I reached it, I looked down to see a red fawn as small as a housecat, curled up and trembling in a nest of grass. The mare picked her way delicately past it, and five minutes later we startled a red doe, who went bounding away from us.

Every now and then Marie would fling up an arm and give the command to trot. We would jog on, the horses keen, me rising against the long stirrups on the stock saddle. Then 'Ho . . .' She put her hand up again and we all slowed to a walk, turning in our saddles to see Honorine, fifty yards back, her ears pricked, and Matthias with his hands on the rein buckle and a smile on his face as the little mare caught up with us. She always took her own sweet way.

'Honorine and Matthias know each other,' Suzanne had explained on my first ride. 'Way back.'

We had taken a few canters, to which I sat down, unsure whether to sit deep and rock or to stand in my stirrups, Kassane with her ears pricked. We were on a shaded lane homewards, the horses keener, when Marie pulled off to a field's edge and indicated a track that ran round a copse.

'Another canter? OK?' the call went back along the ride.

'OK!'

'OK!'

Mel danced, tossing his thick forelock, and then Marie sat deep, pushing him on, and they took off, Etincelle quick and low behind them, her rider's ponytail flying. I squeezed Kassane's flanks with my calves, though she barely needed it. She leaped and, without pulling, each stride seizing at the earth, grew swifter and swifter and lighter under me. I thought briefly of rabbit holes and falling, then pushed the thought away and stood up in my stirrups, knees against the fins, body streamlined over her neck as she reached her head out. I felt the lightness transmitted to my limbs too, not the queasy shift of vertigo I'd felt when Zofe spooked or the Pferdberg pranced, but a fluid, airy headiness, without space to think of horrors. A line of Wilfrid Scawen Blunt's from an old anthology flashed up – 'my horse a thing of wings, myself a god' – and was scattered behind us, leaving me all blank exhilaration as Kassane flew. As the mare ran on, her speed stripped away fear and thought, the fantastic falls and accidents, the gripes of adulthood and the memories of childhood, leaving behind an intoxication as pure and sweet as cold spring water.

Afterword

I returned to the Ebony Horse Club in February 2011 to find foundations had been laid for the stables in Wyck Gardens: Rose and her team had reached their fund-raising target and building was under way. The club was enjoying a brief respite from money worries, although they were braced for worse to come, as council funding cuts had eliminated all the local youth workers' jobs and were threatening many other youth organizations. Gang violence was already rising on the estate.

To support Ebony's excellent work, please visit their website: http://www.ebonyhorseclub.org.uk/

Tom and Thunder came third in their next race, despite nearly being brought down in the closing straight, but sadly missed the local pony-racing finals as Tom broke his arm playing rugby. He and Thunder later qualified for the East Anglian Endurance Team for the National Finals at Ludlow, only to be unable to compete as Kalisadi died suddenly. Thunder overcame his own illness to bond with a three-day eventer by the name of O'Leary, appearing in Horse and Hound in April 2011.

The staff at Redwings have coaxed Norris into accepting a headcollar and being led. He also allows them to handle his feet and legs. He will probably remain at the sanctuary for the rest of his life.

More about Redwings' work can be found here: http://www.redwings.org.uk/

Chance led me to an article entitled 'International Pony' by journalist Maria Motter on the Berlin graffiti hoofprints. The artist behind the hoof trails, 'Rosinante', said that the street art had been a response to the 2006 Football World Cup in Berlin: 'As an adult you're allowed to be football crazy, but the passion that many girls have [for horses] when they are little, vanishes or has to vanish. That's why we wanted to start a counter-movement.'

Q. 'Did you ever own a pony? If not, what schemes did you come
up with to persuade your parents to buy one?'
A. 'I blackmailed my dad when I knew he was having an affair,
but he just confessed to Mum and divorced her.'

Response to author's survey (2004)

Author's Note

Ignorance is bliss, but often, as Anna Sewell put it in *Black Beauty*, 'the worst thing in the world, next to wickedness'. I've written here about feeding horses I came across on walks, but I would not do this again, having been schooled in the evils of the practice by the commenters at Horse & Hound Online. Never feed a horse unless you have the permission of its owner; you may be breaking a vet-recommended diet or feeding it something altogether harmful.

Select Bibliography

PBS documentary 'Ice Mummies: Siberian Ice Maiden', aired on NOVA, 24 November 1998.

Apuleius, trans. P. G. Walsh, *The Golden Ass*, Oxford University Press, 1999.

Argus, Arabella, *Dick, the Memoirs of a Little Poney: Supposed to be Written by Himself; and published for the instruction and amusement of little masters and mistresses*, J. Walker, 1799.

Athill, Diana, *Yesterday Morning*, Granta Books, 2002.

Bagley, H. L., *The Beast Seekers*, Pendulum Books, 1968.

Bagnold, Enid, *National Velvet*, William Heinemann Ltd, 1935.

Bale, Bernard (ed.), *25 Years of Olympia Show Jumping*, Johnny Mans Publishing Ltd, 1997.

Belben, Rosalind, *Our Horses in Egypt*, Chatto & Windus, 2007.

Bellamy, Joyce, *Hyde Park for Horsemanship*, J. A. Allen, 1975.

Bettelheim, Bruno, *The Uses of Enchantment*, Thames & Hudson, 1976.

Blewitt, Audrey, *Ponies and Children*, Country Life Ltd, second edition, 1934.

Bright, Deborah, 'Horse Crazy', in *Horse Tales: American Images and Icons*, Katonah Museum of Art, 2001.

British Horse Society, *Mounted Games and Gymkhanas*, 1948.

Brooke, Geoffrey and Searight, Pamela, *Horsemen All: For Parents of the Rising Generation and Young Aspiring Horsemen*, Charles Scribner's Sons, 1938.

Brown, Vic, *The Foxhunters of Norfolk: 1534 to the Present Day*, J. J. G. Publishing, 2006.

Budiansky, Stephen, *The Nature of Horses: Their Evolution, Intelligence and Behaviour*, Weidenfeld & Nicolson, 1997.

Buxton, Meriel, *Ladies of the Chase*, The Sportsman's Press, 1987.

Buxton, Meriel, *The Pony Club, Dream and Reality*, The Sportsman's Press, 1994.

341

Select Bibliography

Campbell, Judith, *Royalty on Horseback*, Sidgwick and Jackson, 1974.

Cannan, Joanna, *A Pony for Jean*, John Lane, Bodley Head, 1936

Carr, Raymond, *English Fox Hunting: A History*, Weidenfeld Paperbacks, 1986.

Chenevix Trench, Charles, *A History of Horsemanship*, Longman, 1970.

Chitty, Susan, *Anna Sewell: The Woman Who Wrote Black Beauty*, Hodder & Stoughton, 1971.

Cleaver, Hylton, *They've Won Their Spurs*, Robert Hale Ltd, 1956.

Cone, Carl B., *Hounds in the Morning: Sundry Sports of Merry England*, University Press of Kentucky, 1981.

Cumming, Primrose, *Silver Snaffles*, Blackie, 1937.

Cunningham, Hugh, *Children and Childhood in Western Society since 1500*, Pearson Education, second edition, 2005.

Davis-Kimball, Jeannine, *Warrior Women: An Archaeologist's Search for History's Hidden Heroines*, Warner Books, 2002.

Dent, Anthony, *The Horse Through Fifty Centuries of Civilization*, Phaidon, 1974.

Dent, Anthony and Machin-Goodall, Daphne, *The Foals of Epona: A History of British Ponies from the Bronze Age to Yesterday*, Galley Press, 1962.

Dickens, Monica, *Cobbler's Dream*, Michael Joseph Ltd, 1963.

Dickens, Monica, *Talking of Horses . . .*, Heinemann, 1973.

Downes, Alison and Childs, Alan, *My Life with Horses: The Story of Jack Juby MBE, Master of the Heavy Horse*, Halsgrove, 2006.

Elwin, Verrier, *Myths of Middle India*, Oxford University Press, 1950.

Ewart Evans, George, *Horse Power and Magic*, Faber & Faber, 1979.

Fachiri, Antonio P., *Pamela and her Pony 'Flash'*, Arthur Baker Ltd, 1936.

Fairweather, Janet (trans.), *Liber Eliensis*, Boydell Press, 2005.

Farley, Walter, *The Black Stallion*, Random House, 1941.

Faudel-Phillips, Major H., *The Child's Guide to Horse Knowledge*, Vinton & Company Ltd, 1927.

Ferguson, Ruby, *Jill's Gymkhana*, Hodder & Stoughton, 1949.

Forsling, Sven, *The Girl and the Horse: Images from a Reform School*, translated by Siv Tunnicliffe, Book Art Productions, 2003.

Freud, Anna, *Normality and Pathology in Childhood*, International Universities Press, 1965.

Fuchs, Thomas, 'The Memory of the Body', PDF on University of Heidelberg website.

Gavin, Adrienne E., *Dark Horse: A Life of Anna Sewell*, Sutton Publishing Ltd, 2004.

Golden Gorse [aka Muriel Wace], *The Young Rider: Pointers for Children, for Parents and Grown Ups*, sixth edition, Country Life, London, 1942, first published 1928.

Golden Gorse [aka Muriel Wace], *Moorland Mousie*, Country Life, 1929.

Gordon, W. J. *The Horse-World of London*, The Religious Tract Society, 1893.

Grimshaw, Anne, *The Horse: A Bibliography of British Books 1851–1976, with a Narrative Commentary on the Role of the Horse in British Social History as Revealed by Contemporary Literature*, Library Association, 1982.

Hale, Sarah Josepha, *Woman's Record or Sketches of All Distinguished Women from the Beginning till AD 1850*, Harper, 1853.

Harris, Marvin, *Good to Eat: Riddles of Food and Culture*, Allen & Unwin, 1986.

Harris, Paul, *The Work of the Imagination*, Blackwell Publishing, 2000.

Havelock Ellis, Henry, *Psychology of Sex*, William Heinemann, 1933.

Hayes, Mrs Alice, *The Horsewoman: A Practical Guide to Side Saddle Riding*, Hurst & Blackett Ltd, 1892.

Haymonds, Alison, 'Pony Books', in Peter Hunt and Sheila G. Bannister Ray, *International Companion Encyclopaedia of Children's Literature*, Routledge, 2004.

Haymonds, Alison, 'Rides of Passage: Female Heroes in Pony Stories', in Dudley Jones and Tony Watkins, *A Necessary Fantasy?: The Heroic Figure in Children's Popular Culture*, Garland Publications, 2000.

Herodotus, *The Histories*, translated by Aubrey de Sélincourt, revised by John Marincola, Penguin, 2003.

Holbrook Pierson, Melissa, *Dark Horses and Black Beauties*, Granta Books, 2001.

Holme, Thea, *Prinny's Daughter: A Biography of Princess Charlotte of Wales*, Hamish Hamilton, 1976.

Horse and Pony magazine.

Impecuniosus, *Unasked Advice: A Series of Articles on Horses and Hunting reprinted from The Field*, Horace Cox, 1872.

Im Zeichen des goldenen Greifen. Königsgräber der Skythen, exhibition catalogue, Martin Gröpius Bau, 2007.

343

Karr, Elizabeth, The American Horsewoman, Houghton, Mifflin & Company, 1884.

Kean, Hilda, Animal Rights: Political and Social Change in Britain since 1800, Reaktion Books, 1998.

Kelekna, Pita, The Horse in Human History, Cambridge University Press, 2009.

Krafft-Ebing, Richard von, Abberrations of Sexual Life: The Psychopathia Sexualis, Panther, 1951.

Leitch, Patricia, Dream of Fair Horses, Collins, 1975.

Leitch, Patricia, For Love of a Horse, Armada, 1976.

Leitch, Patricia, Night of the Red Horse, Armada, 1978.

Leitch, Patricia, Chestnut Gold, Armada, 1984.

Leitch, Patricia, Jump for the Moon, Armada, 1985.

Lockley, Olga E., Nannie Lambert Power O'Donoghue: A Biography, self-published, [n.d.].

Masters, R. E. L., Forbidden Sexual Behaviour and Morality, The Julian Press, 1962.

Miletski, Hani, Understanding Bestiality and Zoophilia, East-West Publishing LLC, 2002.

Mills, Daniel and McDonnell, Sue (eds), The Domestic Horse: The Evolution, Development and Management of its Behaviour, Cambridge University Press, 2005.

Mitchell, Elyne, Silver Brumbies of the South, Hutchinson, 1965.

Munnings, Sir Alfred, An Artist's Life, London Museum Press, 1950.

Murray, Amanda, All the King's Horses: Royalty and their Equestrian Passions from 1066 to the Present Day, Robson Books, 2006.

Newsum, Gillian, Women and Horses, The Sportsman's Press, 1988.

O'Hara, Mary, My Friend Flicka, Lippincott, 1941.

O'Hara, Mary, Thunderhead, Lippincott, 1943.

O'Hara, Mary, Green Grass of Wyoming, Lippincott, 1946.

Opie, Iona and Opie, Peter, Children's Games in Street and Playground, Oxford University Press, 1969.

Padel, Ruth, 'Saddled with Ginger: Women, Men and Horses', Encounter, 55, 1980.

Peyton, K. M., Flambards, Oxford University Press, 1967.

Peyton, K. M., Fly-by-Night, Oxford University Press, 1968.

Peyton, K. M., The Team, Fidra Books, 2008 (first published OUP, 1975).

Pickeral, Tamsin, The Horse: 30,000 Years of the Horse in Art, Merrell, 2006.

Polosmak, Natalya, 'A mummy unearthed from the pastures of heaven', National Geographic, October 1994.

The Pony Club Yearbook 2010, The Pony Club, 2010.

Power O'Donoghue, Mrs, Ladies on Horseback: Learning, Park-riding and Hunting, W. H. Allen, 1881.

Power O'Donoghue, Mrs, The Common Sense of Riding for Ladies with Hints on the Stable, W. Thacker and Co., 1887.

Pullein-Thompson, Josephine, Six Ponies, Wm Collins Sons & Co. Ltd, 1948.

Pullein-Thompson, Josephine, Pullein-Thompson, Diana and Pullein-Thompson, Christine, It Began with Picotee, A & C Black, 1946.

Pullein-Thompson, Josephine, Pullein-Thompson, Diana and Pullein-Thompson, Christine, Fair Girls and Grey Horses: Memories of a Country Childhood, Allison & Busby, 1997.

Purves, Libby and Heiney, Paul, The English and Their Horses, The Bodley Head, 1988.

Rousseau, Jean Jacques, Emile, translated by Barbara Foxley, Dent, 1933.

Rubinson, Karen S. (ed.), Are All Warriors Male?, Alta Mira Press, 2008.

Rushen, Joyce, She Heard Their Cry: The Life of Ada Cole, ACMS Publishing, [n.d.].

Salmonson, Jessica Amanda, The Encyclopedia of Amazons, Anchor Books, 1992.

Sebba, Anne, Enid Bagnold: A Biography, Taplinger Publishing Company, 1987.

Sewell, Anna, Wells, Ellen B. and Grimshaw, Anne, The Annotated Black Beauty, J. A. Allen, 1989.

Shedden, Lady Diana and Apsley, Lady Viola, To Whom the Goddess, Hutchinson & Co., 1932.

Smythe, Pat, Jump for Joy, Cassell & Co. Ltd, 1954.

Smythe, Pat, One Jump Ahead, Cassell & Co. Ltd, 1956.

Smythe, Pat, Jumping Round the World, Cassell & Co. Ltd, 1962.

Smythe, Pat, Flanagan My Friend, Cassell & Co. Ltd, 1963.

Smythe, Pat, Bred to Jump, Cassell & Co. Ltd, 1965.

Smythe, Pat, Leaping Life's Fences, The Sportsman's Press, 1992.

Spufford, Francis, The Child that Books Built, Faber & Faber, 2002.

Stephenson Brown, Theo., *In the Riding School: Chats with Esmerelda*, Lothrop Co., 1890 (with thanks to the transcriber, Elizabeth Durack).

Taylor, Marjory, *Imaginary Companions and the Children who Create Them*, Oxford University Press, 1999.

Treverton Jones, Tamsin, *Becoming Paddy*, Windmill Print and Graphics, 2008.

Trollope, Anthony, *Hunting Sketches*, Chapman and Hall, 1865.

Vaux, Baron de, *Ecuyers et Ecuyères: Histoire des Cirques*, J. Rothschild, 1893.

Vieille Moustache, *The Barb and the Bridle, a handbook of equitation for ladies and manual of instructions in the science of riding, from the preparatory suppling exercises on foot, to the form in which a lady should ride to hounds*, reprinted from *The Queen* newspaper, 1874.

Webster, Richard, *Why Freud Was Wrong: Sin, Science and Psychoanalysis*, HarperCollins, 1995.

Welcome, John, *The Sporting World of R. S. Surtees*, Oxford University Press, 1982.

Wilcox, Rebecca, *The Human Pony: A Guide for Owners, Trainers and Admirers*, Greenery Press Inc., 2008.

Williams, Dorian, *Clear Round: The Story of Show Jumping*, Hodder & Stoughton, 1957.

Williams, Michael, *Show Jumping in Britain*, Ian Allan, 1964.

WEBSITES

Tom Barley's Costessey webpage: http://webspace.webring.com/people/pt/tombarley/cossey.html

http://www.epona.net/

http://www.janebadgerbooks.co.uk/ (essential for all pony book queries and purchases)

Times Online archives.

Archive.org.

Acknowledgements

Without my mother, Rosemary, my father, Robin, and my brother Matthew there would be no book.

I was welcomed without question by Nicola Markwell, Sarah Hallsworth and Adam Joslin at Redwings Horse Sanctuary, Jackie Crook at the Horse Rescue Fund, Rose Spearing and her team at the Ebony Horse Club, Julie Magnus and Tom, Jane Russell at Willow Farm and the Olympia Press Office. Paula Twinn and Rebecca Morgan were my guides to the world of pony racing, and Zoe Horne at the Northern Racing College was extremely helpful. Ponygirl Shyanne talked generously and without reservation, as did Devon, Maid of Epona. Sven Forsling and Harald Euler took time to explain their theories to me and gave me plenty of food for thought. Hope put some fire in my belly. Paula Sykes, Paddy Bury, Monica Koechlin-Smythe and Lucy Koechlin were delightful hosts and great interviewees on the subject of Pat Smythe. Jane Badger helped put me in touch with Patricia Leitch, who was a true inspiration and set the golden horses dancing.

Much thanks to Richenda Gillespie, Deborah Moggach, Helen Walsh, Sarah Morgan, Kate Copstick, Mary Woolner, Dominique Rigby, the crew at Tackroom Gossip and everyone else who responded to my survey in 2004 and made me feel less alone by telling me about their imaginary horses. Stephen Alexander set me straight on *Equus Eroticus*, and The Other Pony Club operated their bush telegraph to great effect. Andrew Curry threw me the odd archaeological crumb that proved worth its weight in Scythian gold. Tanya Ott introduced me to Sabine Zuckmantel and her wonderful horses. Paul Rutledge shared the curious story of Miss Howard of Colkirk. Kirstie Pritchard at Mason Williams supplied My Little Pony facts, and Clare Roberts at the Pony Club sent me a very useful yearbook. Susan Lewis at the

Acknowledgements

HorseTrust responded swiftly to an enquiry about Ann Lindo and provided a crucial part of the jigsaw.

Judith Murray has been everything an agent should be – equal parts den mother and lawyer. Angus MacKinnon managed deft editorial judgment and warm encouragement in the face of mulish pessimism. Atlantic Books took a punt and backed me to the hilt, with Sarah Norman leading the team. Celia Levett reined in my runaway clauses. Rowan Pelling gave me a job because I'd read *Black Beauty* and later set me on the trail of hoof prints. Annie Blinkhorn wouldn't let me give up. Karen Krizanovich provided my daily horse email and Dr Dorothea Schleehauf kept the show on the road. The Riseborough family and the Perrotts lent me Tav, and Mrs Margot Whiting filled me in on his mysterious early days. Ailana Kamelmacher and Robin Duttson provided a spare room, an ear and sustenance.

I learned a lot about being a writer from Michael Scott Moore. Ian Lilley, Lizzie Pomeroy, Guy Robinson and I shared fear and friendship. Cheryl kept me company at Costessey Infants and Junior School and was a true friend.

The staff at the Staatsbibliothek Berlin, the British Library, Cambridge University Library and the Norfolk Record Office never raised an eyebrow, whether I was ordering the Princess Tina Pony Annual or bestiality textbooks.

Thanks also to all the Berliners, Cambridgers and Londoners not singled out by name who put up with long, rambling digressions on pony play, Proto Indo-European, Mactavish and side-saddle.

Index

Index

Index

Index

Index

Index

Index

Index

Index